NEW ORLEANS HOLIDAY

Books by

ELEANOR EARLY

AND THIS IS BOSTON!
AND THIS IS WASHINGTON!
AND THIS IS CAPE COD!
BEHOLD THE WHITE MOUNTAINS
PORTS OF THE SUN
ADIRONDACK TALES
LANDS OF DELIGHT
A NEW ENGLAND SAMPLER
AN ISLAND PATCHWORK
SHE KNEW WHAT HE WANTED
NEW ORLEANS HOLIDAY

"Poets have loved New Orleans, artists and dreamers, and people like you and me . . ." From a gallery in the Vieux Carré, the Cathedral of St. Louis, framed in iron lace work.

New Orleans
Holiday

ELEANOR EARLY

DRAWINGS BY
JOHN O'HARA COSGRAVE II

RINEHART & COMPANY, INCORPORATED

NEW YORK · TORONTO

Grateful acknowledgment is made to Little, Brown & Company, for their permission to reprint four lines from "The Single Hound" from *The Poems of Emily Dickinson,* edited by Martha Dickinson Bianchi and Alfred Leete Hampson; also to Charles Scribner's Sons, for permission to quote from *The Inn of Tranquility* by John Galsworthy.

To acknowledge the invaluable aid of

BILL COKER

who inspired this book by his
enthusiasm and his stories of
New Orleans,
her people and her customs.

Contents

NEW ORLEANS HOLIDAY

SHE TELLS HER BEADS AND WEARS AZALEAS IN HER HAIR

There are some cities that resemble women in one way or another, which is not an idea of my own but something I picked up from that poem about "Paris is a woman's town with flowers in her hair." New Orleans in some ways resembles Paris, although not as much as you might suppose. There are streets in the Vieux Carré that are more like streets in the West Indies than streets in Paris, and many courtyards in the French Quarter that are not French at all, but Spanish . . . but before we get into this, let me quote a verse that is about Boston (I think) but it might as well be about New Orleans:

> I like a city that is worn and old,
> Where stones are hollowed by the press of feet,
> Where gables sag and open doorways hold
> A store of legends, where a narrow street
> Will twist and turn before me leisurely,
> And windows stare at me like tired eyes.
>   I know these cities and I love them well
>   Because they seem to me
> Like old men who grow more feeble yet more wise
>   With nothing much to do but much to tell.

As a matter of fact, they seem to me more like old ladies than old men, but that would spoil the meter.

When I was very young I wrote a book about Boston that began like this: "Boston is a nice old lady. If you don't know her well, you might think her prosy and a little dull, because Dame Boston—dear old soul—doesn't always put her best foot forward . . ." and on I went, about lavender and old lace, and dignity and ageless grace. Younger cities, I said, might be gayer and more modern. But Boston for all her old-fashioned ways was the fairest of them all.

The truth is I hadn't in those days much field for comparison, but now that I have ranged and roved I believe that the more you travel the more you feel these things, and when you have known many cities you know that some among them are lovable and others are not. Some are bright with worldly splendor, some are cold and gray, and there are young cities that should be beautiful, but are garish and unlovely. Chicago is a man's town—"there's power in the air," and Charleston is a woman's town. Natchez is a slattern, and Philadelphia's a snob. Some cities are dowdy. Others are squabbly and scraggy. And there are cities that are grim and bleak as narrow, unwed women. And when you spend the night in them, it rains and dinner is awful; you go to the movies and the picture is dreadful, and your room is on a court, with one dirty window and thin, hard blankets on the bed.

Boston and New Orleans are as different as baked beans and jambalaya, and each in her own way is satisfying. Boston, as everybody knows, was founded by Puritans, and Louisiana by Latins. And the colonizers left their everlasting marks. People are always falling in love with both cities. Boston, slightly on the frigid side, preserves her civic chastity, and never bats an eyelash. New Orleans, more the seductive type, flaunts her beauty and views the minor vices with gallic tolerance. She is no better perhaps than she should be, but she is merry and wise, and she has an indestructible chic and a gaiety that Boston never knew. She goes to Mass and tells her beads, and wears azaleas in her hair, and has champagne for breakfast.

New Orleans has lived through wars in which her sons and lovers bore arms against each other. She has survived yellow fever and bubonic plagues, and if she had not the fatal gift of lasting beauty she would be a dreadful hag by this time, because she has really had a rather terrible past. She was once the richest city in America, and the gayest. Men called her "The City That Care Forgot," and she led the maddest, gladdest, damnedest existence of any wicked seaport in the country. Then she went to war and was beaten, and after that she was destitute and her beauty faded. But she lifted herself up and bound her wounds, and her Creole lovers said, "My dear city is poor, but I would not leave her for a richer one." And then she wore her wounds proudly and covered them with her laughter.

Poets have loved New Orleans, artists and dreamers, and people like you and me, and others will go on loving her because she is mellow and tender and kind. Writing words like these reminds me of a funeral poem by Victor Plarr that said some lovely things about a girl who had died. These are the first and last lines, and I guess they haven't much to do with New Orleans—but aren't they wonderful?

> Stand not uttering sedately
>   Trite oblivious praise about her!
> Rather say you saw her lately
>   Lightly kissing her last lover.
>
> O for it would be a pity
>   To o'er praise her or to flout her;
> She was wild and sweet and witty—
>   Let's not say dull things about her.

To understand New Orleans it is best to go back to the beginning—to men who loved the land and dreamed its destiny, to the Frenchmen who shaped the young city and to the Spaniards who made her beautiful. We could go back a long way—to the Old World, and the ancient régime in Europe when France was the richest and most cultivated nation in the world, and the sun had not yet set upon the empire of the king of Spain. But when people buy a book like this, they expect to cover a couple of centuries and a good deal of territory in a few pages. So we will start with the men who made history in the New World—with Pierre Le Moyne, Sieur d'Iberville, and his brother Jean Baptiste Le Moyne, Sieur de Bienville. The first time I had oysters Bienville at Arnaud's, I am ashamed to say I hardly knew who Bienville was. The next day I went to the library, and by the time I saw Iberville's name on a street sign I had a rather warm feeling for the brothers, especially for Bienville, who was quite handsome. You probably know a great deal of what I am now going to tell, but you may be glad to refresh your memory since most people have a way of forgetting—even learned people like Andrew Lang, who was a regular encyclopedia. Mr. Lang wrote a ballad in which he said:

> Here stand my books, line upon line
> They reach the roof, and row upon row,
> They speak of faded tastes of mine,
> And things I did, but do not know.

Of course, everybody knows that the Spanish discovered Louisiana, and also the Mississippi River. But sixteenth-century Spaniards were so blinded by the gold and silver of Mexico and South America that they paid no attention to the possibilities of the Mississippi Valley, and after a while France moved in. La Salle, a French adventurer who had an estate near Montreal, accompanied by countrymen and Indians, descended the Father of Waters to the Gulf of Mexico, and on the shore near the river's mouth he took possession of the "entire tributary system of the Mississippi" in the name of Louis XIV. He named the land Louisiana in honor of his king. Some years later the king sent the brothers Iberville and Bienville to make settlements in the new country. Iberville founded the first permanent settlement at Biloxi. He became known as the "Father of Louisiana," and died in 1702. Biloxi was an ill-fated place, and in 1717 Bienville moved his headquarters some hundred miles up the river. In a clearing in the marshes he set down sixty-eight men and raised the fleurs-de-lis of St. Louis. This new settlement—destined to be the capital of France's colonial empire—he named La Nouvelle-Orléans, in honor of the Duc d'Orléans, a *most* unmoral man.

The duke, one of the most notorious rakes in history, was a younger brother of Louis XIV, who had died two years before, and he ruled France as regent for the little five-year-old king who succeeded his grandfather. Almost everybody mixes up the Louis and I, for one, mix up their mistresses. Louis XIV—Le Grand Monarque—was the one called the Sun King. And his principal mistresses were Louise de La Vallière, who was his "morning star," Madame de Montespan, his "noonday star," and Madame de Maintenon, his "evening star" who brought up his seven illegitimate children. In the lobby of the Cabildo (which is now the State Museum) there is a giant statue of Bienville, standing in his lusty manhood beside a portrait of the dissolute Sun King, with sword and scepter and his hand on his hip, in a black wig and an ermine robe embroidered with golden fleurs-de-lis, posturing and posing and pointing his toes like a chorus girl.

When New Orleans was laid out, Bienville, perpetuating his name forever, named a street for himself, and a hundred years later the Americans named one for his brother. The other streets were named for patron saints of the royal family, for nuns, a princess, and for the illegitimate sons of the old dead king. The original city, which was small and laid out like a checkerboard, became known in later years as the Vieux Carré, which means Old Square. Most of the streets still bear the same names they did in the beginning when the settlers were wading around in the mud, building little log huts and thatching them with bark. It was so swampy then that the streets became ditches, and the ditches filled up with mosquitoes and alligators, who bit the colonists and gave them malaria and gangrene. There were no white women around, so the men took to chasing Indian squaws, who were fat and extraordinarily dirty, through the ditches and into the woods. The men came down with fever and many of them died, and it was all very discouraging.

But back in Paris the Duc d'Orléans had become friendly with a Scotch promoter named John Law, who persuaded the duke to give his royal blessing to a scheme calculated to put the struggling colony on its feet. The scheme, subsequently known as the Mississippi Bubble, was to invent and publicize glamorous propaganda about life in the Mississippi Valley. Before there were twenty huts in New Orleans, Law drew up posters showing eight hundred beautiful mansions. He represented Louisiana as a paradise on earth—a land of gold and silver and fabulous pearls—where wine flowed like the Mississippi and men were surrounded by Indian maidens, all slim and clean, with jewels in their hair and wraps of local mink and muskrat. The floors of the mansions, said Mr. Law, were carpeted with furs "lying so close together that the boards could not be seen," Louisiana ladies were "dressed in the style of the French court," and peasants lived like kings. Law's agents spread the lies through France and Germany. Bourgeois businessmen sold everything they owned to invest in Louisiana real estate and colonists flocked to the new Utopia.

Then the duke, who was always broke, bought himself a palace in Paris, and a country place for his mistress, with a gilded pagoda and a hundred monkeys. Law became a financial magnate, and his Mississippi Company issued an unlimited amount of paper money. But soon the Mississippi overflowed, Indians massacred the colonists, and the survivors came down with malaria, and after a period of wild excitement it was found that the company's money could not be exchanged for either coin or property. Then the duke, to save his face, broke with Law, and all through France there was collapse, failure and ruin. Law fled to Venice. And the speculators' dreams were like bubbles and, like bubbles, they burst.

But Nouvelle-Orléans was there to stay. The people made a levee to keep out the river. They killed a great many of the Indians and made friends with the rest. They asked the duke to send them con-

"I like a city that is worn and old . . ."

victs to drain the marshes and chop down the trees. Indian slavery having proved impractical, they bought black slaves from Africa, and in the face of great obstacles they went on building until they had sixteen little crisscross streets, with houses on them of cypress logs, plastered over to keep out the miasma.

None of the first houses remain, but on Chartres Street there stands the old Ursuline Convent, temporary home of the celebrated "casket girls." It was a custom of the times for the king to send women to console his soldiers who were stationed abroad and bachelor colonists in distant lands. When Iberville was having his troubles at Biloxi, he implored Louis XIV to "send me wives for my settlers, for they are running in the forests after the Indian girls," and Louis did. Shipments of the "king's girls" arrived regularly in Canada to become the wives of farmers and soldiers, and everything worked out nicely. But the Duke of Orleans, who had no taste about such things, sent to Louisiana a shipload of women picked up on the streets of Paris and taken from the houses of correction. With them he sent a midwife nicknamed Madame Sans-Regret. The women, distributing their favors among Indians, convicts and sailors, kept the midwife busy. But hardly anybody married them, and the whole thing turned out to be a very bad idea.

A number of highborn ladies came to the colony to join their husbands and, outraged at the goings-on, petitioned the duke for some respectable girls. Complaisant as usual, he remedied matters by ordering an immediate shipment of peasants, and orphans from the asylums of France. These girls were guaranteed virtuous—not by his Highness—but by their own parish priests or, in the case of the orphans, by the nuns who had reared them.

Each girl, in her small casket, carried a dowry from the king, including four sheets and a blanket, two pairs of stockings, six headdresses, and a pelisse. They were met at the ship by the mother superior and taken to the Convent of the Ursulines where, in due time, they were permitted to receive suitors who knew that they were good little girls, anxious for husbands and willing to take a chance. Most of them could read and write and sew a fine seam. Those who could not, stayed with the nuns until they had learned. And as time went on they proved to be such good wives that it became a Creole boast that "great-grandmama was a casket girl."

Of the first shipment it is recorded that one girl took the veil, and the rest took husbands. To encourage matrimony, soldiers who married were given a plot of land, an ox and a cow, a pair of swine and a pair of fowl, two barrels of salted meat and a bit of cash. The king continued to send wives for his colonizers until 1754, at which time there appear to have been enough women to go around.

The Ursulines, eleven of them, had arrived in 1727, and in 1734 their first convent was ready. Until recently it was believed that the convent on Chartres Street, which has been called the oldest building in the Mississippi Valley, was the original building. But it now appears that there was an earlier one, and the convent that stands now was not built until 1752 or '53, so that it definitely is not the oldest building in the valley.

Next door to the convent is an old church, where the hearts of all the dead archbishops of the diocese are said to be buried beneath the altar. But I do not believe it, because who ever heard of carving up an archbishop?

I lived across from the convent one spring, in the old Beauregard House, and around the corner on Ursuline Street there is, or was the last time I was there, a place where they sell the best spumone and cassata this side of Naples. There are many Italians living in the Vieux Carré, and I guess they all like spumone. I have heard that the Italian population of New Orleans is so huge that more spaghetti is made in the city than anywhere else outside of Italy, but I am not sure that this is true. The Italians did not arrive until a century or so after the city was begun, but they multiplied as usual very rapidly.

Leaders of the dreaded Mafia established a powerful organization and there was once a dreadful Black Hand slaughter in Beauregard House, of which I shall tell you later.

From the front gallery of the house I would look across at the convent and try to picture things as they used to be. Chartres Street, named for the Duc de Chartres, a nobleman of the Orléans family, was the commercial thoroughfare of the old city. On the corner of Esplanade there was a slave market and later there were fashionable stores, among them Mr. D. H. Holmes's, which moved later to Canal Street. Mr. Holmes used to close his store annually while he went abroad on a shopping trip. He bought all over Europe, but it was what he brought back from Paris that the Creole ladies liked best. After the War Between the States, the Red Light District took over the Vieux Carré. But before that Chartres was a busy and a prosperous place, and in the beginning it was a pious little street, with the nuns at one end and the Church of St. Louis at the other.

The Convent of the Ursulines was built in plain and honest style, as enduring as faith. The shutters, faded now to bluish green, are nice against the pale walls, and the steeply pitched blue roof is pleasing against the sky. For the nuns' chapel, slaves hammered an altar rail as exquisite as lace, delicate balusters for the stairs, and beautiful gates for the garden. The slaves planted a myrtle grove on the waterfront, and in the garden they planted orange trees and roses that the nuns had brought from France. The balustrade the slaves made is still in the deserted convent, and there is an old wrought-iron grille in the window at the front of the stairway. But there is nothing in the garden now but desolation.

When the convent was completed, the women of the town decorated it with their handiwork. Great ladies spread altarcloths embroidered with gems, and poor women brought laces from their needles, and they all brought flowers from their gardens. The priest came with his jeweled miter that the Bishop of Orleans had sent from Paris, which sparkled with diamonds and sapphires. Troops ranged themselves on either side of the governor's house. And as the convent bells rang forth, the nuns marched out in their black gowns and their big white bonnets. A parade formed, led by the governor, wearing a wig, followed by twenty-four little orphans, wearing hand-me-downs. And they all began to sing as the procession moved joyfully down the muddy street.

There was a girl named Madeleine Hachard, a young postulant in the Ursuline Convent in Rouen, who came with the nuns to New Orleans and became secretary to the mother superior. Madeleine kept the annals of the order and recorded a vivid description of that happy day when the Ursulines took possession of their first convent. It was on the 24th of July in 1734. The occasion was attended by "all the distinguished citizens and almost the entire population." Following the orphans in the parade were "over forty of the most respectable ladies in the city, bearing lighted tapers and singing pious hymns." Next came twenty-five little girls dressed as angels. Following the angels marched "St. Ursula," in a mantle of silver tinsel, with "ribbons in her hair of diamonds and pearls," on her head a "superb crown," and in her hand a heart pierced with an arrow. Ursula had eleven companions dressed in white gowns and veils, all carrying palm branches. The eleven represented the eleven thousand girls who had marched with Ursula, and the palms they carried symbolized their ancient victory over the sinful Huns.

St. Ursula, in case you do not know, was an Englishwoman who raised an army of girls to march from Britain to the Holy Land. Ursula was a spinster and the girls were virgins. There were eleven thousand of them, which seems a great number. But that was eighteen hundred years ago, and times have changed. You wouldn't, for example, find girls today putting on Olympian games, but when Ursula's virgins reached Rome they staged all-star tournaments that included foot races, high jumping and discus throwing. When the meet was over, they resumed their march on the Holy Land. But they had not gone far when they were set upon by a horde of Huns, and forced to defend their virtue with their lives. Those who were taken captive flung themselves upon their spears, and died for virtue's sake.

After the girls came the nuns, bearing lighted tapers, and after the nuns, the clergy carrying the Blessed Sacrament beneath a canopy of cloth of gold, embroidered with the lilies of St. Louis in shimmering seed pearls. On either side of the procession were soldiers and townsmen with fifes and drums.

The greater part of New Orleans's original population was made up of soldiers and rough workmen. Men who married the hardy little casket girls had become the fathers of Louisiana's first Creoles. With a new generation growing up, the colony was becoming rich and fashionable, with snow-white dresses for little girls who marched in processions and diamonds and pearls for fine young ladies. Artisans were busy, and shopkeepers prosperous. There were wine sellers and a baker on the Rue de Chartres. Seigniors swaggered through the little streets and great ladies picked their way through the mud. There were soldiers and Indians and African slaves, and Jesuits from Montreal. As in all French towns, there were widows in black scarves who tucked warm loaves of bread under their shawls and scurried through the town, and the good smell of the fresh bread mingled with the smell of wine and the exquisite fragrance of tea olive as it floated over the convent walls.

In 1743 a new governor was sent to the colony, the Marquis de Vaudreuil, a gentleman of patrician birth. The marquis and his lady loved splendor and gaiety, and wished to model the social life of the town after Versailles, so they brought with them many of their friends from court. And they all brought their fine furniture and ancestral plate, and their Gobelin tapestries and Aubusson carpets. Upon their arrival they bought great numbers of slaves. When the slaves had learned to cook and serve, the ladies began to entertain, and each sought to outdo the other in the splendor of her affairs. The French had always a flair for such things. France, since the age of chivalry, was Europe's chief instructor in the ways of polite society, and the

Great Marquis set an example for gracious and beautiful living that was exciting and extravagant.

The marquise was a lady of great chic, and Nouvelle-Orléans learned from her how to wear a tiara and a beauty spot, how to speak Parisian French, to give lovely parties, and to do things with an air. The marquis and his lady taught the young city both wisdom and nonsense. They practiced the philosophy that holds that men live only once and should enjoy each day before it becomes history. It was at this time that the tradition began which has become so much a part of New Orleans—the tradition of pleasure.

Ladies dressed in the style of Versailles, although it was a dreadful nuisance in streets where one could scarcely walk for water and for mud. Skirts were enormous, six and eight feet across and eighteen feet in circumference, for panniers and farthingales were beloved of the king's mistresses, and courtesans set the styles in those days as movie stars do today. Overskirts opened in front to show exquisite underskirts, and were held back with artificial flowers and jewels and bows. The ladies wore scarves over their shoulders, gossamer in the summer and mink in the winter.

Gentlemen carried canes and wore magnificent waistcoats that reached to their knees. They sent to Paris for lacy cravats, and buckles and butterfly bows to wear on their shoes. Some of them wore petticoat breeches instead of doublet and hose, and under their arms they carried hats trimmed with laces and plumes.

On all formal occasions both ladies and gentlemen wore wigs. Louis XIII, growing bald, had set the style a full century before and it had taken such hold that an eighteenth-century gentleman felt immodest if seen without his perruque. In fact Louis XIV, who performed the most private acts in public, used to wear his wig to bed, and pass it modestly from behind drawn bed curtains when he was ready to go to sleep.

Pompadour, the favorite of Louis XV, originated the style of hair-do that bears her name, and in their towering hair-dos New Orleans ladies stuck every exotic thing they could get their hands on. Pompadour herself once wore a full-rigged ship with jeweled spars and silken sails. Wigs were uncomfortable in the summertime, so that fans were an important accessory, and in New Orleans there were always slaves to carry the fans.

Frivolity stopped short at the convent, but even the nuns had slaves—squaws in the kitchen and bucks on the ground. An early prospectus sets forth the "primary object kept in view by the Ladies of the Institution": "the adorning of the pupils' minds with knowledge and the forming of their hearts to virtue." The nuns had "a suite of bathing-rooms, twenty-five in number," and the prospectus extolled the luxury of "refreshing baths during the bathing season."

It was considered a dangerous practice to bathe in the winter. The nuns did not, of course, countenance bathing out of season, but in April they permitted foot baths on Saturdays. In May, for all-over baths, they distributed muslin gowns with drawstrings at the necks, and the pupils donned the gowns once a week and soaped them until the suds went through. Les dames religieuses considered it indecent for a woman to see her own body, and little girls were taught to undress without so much as a glance at themselves. Womanly modesty was a Creole virtue right from the beginning. Convent girls were traditionally "gentle as doves" and "innocent as babes unborn," and this may explain why, as time went on, they often played second fiddle to the celebrated Quadroons.

The Ursulines were very strict about the color line, and never accepted a pupil who was not pure white. The Quadroons, barred from New Orleans' fashionable boarding school, frequently went abroad to be educated, and when they returned from Paris, with pretty Continental manners and trunks of beautiful clothes, they completely eclipsed the convent-bred Creoles whose modest innocence was, by comparison, on the dull, pale side.

2

LISTEN TO THE MOCKINGBIRD

Camellias in New Orleans begin to flower in January. Azaleas, co-operating with the Chamber of Commerce, burst into joyous bloom for Mardi Gras and blossom in February, all up and down the city streets. Oleanders, to please the Garden Club ladies, wait until March, and flourish for Spring Fiesta. Magnolias bloom in May when the oleanders fade. And when the trees are filled with flowers the mockingbirds go mad with glee.

The things that most people want to do in New Orleans are eat in the famous restaurants, visit the old houses, see the Azalea Trail with all its blossoming flowers, and listen to the mockingbirds.

One day in Audubon Park a mockingbird flew into a magnolia tree and perched on a bough where he could look down upon an ornithologist, sitting in the pleasant shade made by a big hibiscus. The ornithologist—a man from the London Zoo—didn't think much of mockingbirds. He thought English songbirds were the sweetest in the world. But he had heard about how the mockingbirds sing in the park, and had gone to hear what he might hear. Then the mockingbird began to sing. Melody upon melody rushed from his little throat—an overture from the meadow-lark, a robin's roundelay, and a song of his own. The high sweet notes poured forth, showering the shining leaves and pelting fragrance from the flowers, until Keats's nightingale would have died of shame. The mockingbird imitated thirty-two different birds and ended with an aria of pure ecstasy. Although this may have been pure exhibitionism on his part, it was a marvelous experience for the astounded ornithologist, who could hardly believe his ears. The next day he wrote a letter to *Life* magazine, and *Life* could hardly believe it either. But they sent a man to investigate, and a photographer to get pictures. The photographer found some mockingbirds, pleased no doubt with the publicity, who posed quite charmingly because mockingbirds love the limelight and always play like mad to the gallery.

They are friendly creatures, fonder of people than most birds, and they build, too trustingly, near the ground, usually in a pretty place like a scarlet hibiscus or a flowering acacia. Sometimes, in the nesting season, males beat up marauding cats and dogs, and New Orleans editors, in tribute to the little fellow's fighting heart, put the story on page one.

Once I saw a fox terrier barking up a pink oleander. A mother bird flew from a crybaby tree to the little dog's back, and pecked him so savagely that the neighbors came to rescue him. He ran away howling, with his tail between his legs, and the triumphant mother, chattering like a shrew, chased him down the street.

The female is a busy, bustling bird with a singing spirit, but a comparatively small voice, who sits with her gray wings folded, humble and enthralled, when her mate comes home to sing their brood to sleep. He is a handsome fellow with a fine white breast and white patches on his slate-gray wings and tail. When summer comes and the magnolias fade, he stops singing. He starts again in the fall, and stops when winter comes. In the fall they separate. I have been told that after she is deserted, the female sings a plaintive little song. If this is true, I think it is rather sad. New Orleans has no winter to speak of, so they never go out of town. You can hear them in December, chirping blithely in the hedgerows.

Audubon Park is a popular place with mockingbirds, and another of their favorite places to give a concert is City Park. If you are not likely to get so far from the city you might drop around at Pat O'Brien's patio bar on St. Peter Street, but go before dark because a

". . . and sometimes they sing all night."

mockingbird wouldn't be caught at Pat O'Brien's after the place gets busy.

The best time to get acquainted with the birds is at daybreak, when the stars begin to fade and the eastern sky turns pink. All birds are happiest at dawn, but mockingbirds seem happiest of all. Sometimes in rapturous joy they topple out of chinaberry trees, turn a tumbly somersault, and come to earth still singing. All day they mimic other birds and scold and work themselves into rages until, at twilight, they go home to take a nap and visit awhile with Mrs. M. and the babies. When they have rested they often start singing again when the moon comes up, and sometimes they sing all night.

Visitors arriving in New Orleans for Mardi Gras often stay for Spring Fiesta, when homes in the Vieux Carré and the Garden District are open to visitors. Then life turns back for a century and more while visitors linger in the patios and wander through old, old houses that remember when Nouvelle-Orléans was young and gay. Many ladies and gentlemen wear beautiful clothes of long ago. The men wear ruffled shirts and tall hats, and the ladies drift in pale organzas, like garden beds of posies, while little girls in shimmering hoop skirts go bouncing all about. And they all ride in old barouches through the narrow streets of the Vieux Carré.

It was during Spring Fiesta that I went hunting for a pink house, with an iron lace balcony and a patio filled with bright blossoms and moonbeams, where I could work in the daytime and have a wonderful time nights. I thought that next to New York, and maybe Paris, I had rather live in New Orleans than anywhere. It is anticlimactic to add that none of the pink houses were for rent. So I stayed in all the hotels in town, and then at the Orleans Club. When I left the club I lived for a month in the Beauregard House, where the Great Creole's ghost pokes around nights looking for a pair of boots. It seems they buried the poor man in his stocking feet and, being a meticulous dresser—especially when in uniform—he cannot rest until he finds them.

Most cities claim a ghost or two, but New Orleans has more than most places, and it is probably because the poor souls hate to leave town. While I was living in Beauregard House I never caught even a glimpse of the general. But one night a friend saw the ghost of Paul Morphy, the great chess player, sitting in the patio with a chessboard in his lap. Morphy was born in the house, and when he was a little boy he used to play chess in the courtyard. When he was nineteen he became world champion chess player. And then he became queer, but I will tell you about that later. When my friend saw him, Monsieur Morphy was listening to a mockingbird that was swinging from the topmost spray, singing, in the moonlit oleanders.

*   *   *

The first day I was in New Orleans I had three Ramos gin fizzes, and it turned out to be a beautiful day. Ordinarily the last thing I would think about the first thing in the morning would be a drink. But a Ramos gin fizz is not much stronger than an ice-cream soda, which is what it looks like. So that one drink led to another until there were three. And three Ramos gin fizzes are balm in Gilead. The sun was shining, the azaleas were blooming, the mockingbirds were singing, and that was the day I fell in love with New Orleans. In the morning I met two honeymooners from Texas. The bride's father was a professor at Baylor, which is a Baptist university, and her mother was president of the W.C.T.U. Naturally, the girl was a teetotaler. But the man she married was a low character who loved gin.

"Darling," said the Low Character, as they sat at breakfast in the Coffee Shop of the Roosevelt Hotel, "I want you to taste a milk shake that is a speciality of the house. It has the white of an egg in it." The innocent bride tasted it and she loved it.

In New Orleans, people have cream cheese for breakfast with Louisiana strawberries, and pecan waffles with syrup, and they drink quantities of Creole coffee that is mixed with chicory.

"I don't want to eat," said the bride, pushing away her beautiful breakfast. "Darling," she said to her husband, "I just want some more of those lovely milk shakes." And that was the day that the bride also fell in love with New Orleans.

Everything was romantic and exciting, the old houses in the Vieux Carré with their dreamy courtyards, too romantic to be true, and the lacy balconies that shade the narrow streets.

There was a poet from Donegal, with the beautiful Irish name of Cathal O'Byrne, who visited New Orleans and loved the Vieux Carré, who wrote a poem about the iron work:

> When Vulcan irked the jealous Jove,
>   In womanish disgrace
> He banished him to New Orleans,
>   And set him making lace.

It is fun roaming through the little streets of the French Quarter, under the balconies, and through the flowery patios, in and out of shops that are housed in old mansions, antique stores with crystal chandeliers and shining treasures, restaurants and art galleries and bookshops. On Bourbon Street, jazz floats through the swinging doors of cafés and bars that seem gayer in New Orleans than anywhere else. On Chartres Street are the old Cathedral and the Cabildo and Presbytère, which are now museums, and the Pontalba buildings on either side of lovely little Jackson Square.

On that first day I went to Antoine's for luncheon and had two orders of oysters Rockefeller. I visited the Cathedral, and sat in Jackson Square, eating pralines while the Angelus rang and the mockingbirds sang from one blossoming bush to another. That night I dined in Count Arnaud's, which is the restaurant I came to prefer above all others. The count suggested the menu, and I remember everything we had. First there were huitres Bienville, then there was filet de triute meunière amandine, with sauterne from Bordeaux, suprême de volaille en papilotte, and a green salad, crêpes Suzette Arnaud for dessert, because I like things that flame at the table, and café brûlot, fragrant with brandy and spices, that blazed in a silver bowl. After dinner I went to the Little Theatre where pretty girls served Creole coffee between the acts, in a patio that was filled with magic and moonlight and the sound of running water. Then we went to the French Market for café au lait, because that is where nearly everyone goes between midnight and dawn—and that was the end of a perfect day.

It would have been beautiful without the Ramos gin fizzes, but I think they helped, because fizzes sort of gloss over everything that is unattractive, and the truth is there are a number of ugly places in the Vieux Carré, and some terrible smells that I did not even notice.

The Roosevelt Hotel bought its celebrated fizz recipe from the man who made it up, whose name was Mr. Ramos. And the hotel pays a royalty to the Ramos heirs on every fizz it sells. Although there are many persons who dislike gin, I never knew anyone who did not like a Ramos gin fizz. But if you are an Alcoholic Anonymous, or just someone who doesn't touch liquor, you could leave out the gin, and it would taste practically the same. Or you could double the gin, and let a few drinks creep up on you in the gentlest sort of way. Then you would understand why Mr. Ramos' fizz became so famous. Here is the recipe which was given me by Paul Alpuente, dean of the Roosevelt bartenders and one of the original Ramos mixologists. Mr. Alpuente, whom everybody calls Doctor Paul, went to work in the old Ramos bar in 1890 and stayed until Prohibition closed the place in 1920. When Prohibition was repealed and the Roosevelt secured the right to make the fizzes, Manager Seymour Weiss sent for Alpuente. Doctor Paul has mixed about a million fizzes and the secret of their success, he says, is accuracy.

ORIGINAL RAMOS GIN FIZZ

1 jigger of gin
1 jigger of milk
1 egg white
1 teaspoon of powdered sugar

1 generous teaspoon of lemon juice
1 scant teaspoon of lime juice
5 or 6 drops of orange flower water.

Shake with cracked ice until you can feel the mixture getting fluffy, then strain into an 8-ounce glass.

Being a woman who never leaves well enough alone and convinced that prodigality would improve a bar drink, I used to make my fizzes with heavy cream, which did not help any. It made them too frothy. Even light cream is sometimes too heavy. Milk is best, but it should be rich. If you have used the top-of-the-bottle for coffee, get a jar of light cream and use half milk and half cream. I have also experimented with more lime and lemon juice than Doctor Paul uses, and that was another mistake. Trying to improve an expert's recipe is like Shakespeare said about gilding the lily and throwing perfume on the violet, a "wasteful and ridiculous excess." Properly mixed, a Ramos fizz has a faint and lovely fragrance with no distinguishable flavor and has, upon occasion, been enjoyed by innocent teetotalers. One White Ribbon sister, refreshed by two "nice cold fizzes" ordered by an unregenerate grandson, scraped her glass with a spoon.

"Heavens to Betsy!" she said. A reminiscent smile illumined her kindly face. "Listen, Georgie. It's a poem I learned when I was a little girl:

'Brain and heart
Alike depart
From them who favors gin or brandy'

Now what," she said, "do you suppose made me remember that?"

A nice thing about fizzes is that you can put them together at your leisure and keep the mixture in the refrigerator until time to shake and serve.

When Huey P. ("Kingfish") Long was a power in the land, he visited the Hotel New Yorker in Manhattan where he ordered a gin fizz that didn't fizz. It didn't have any flower water in it, and it was made with lemon juice and no lime. The Kingfish was shocked. He telephoned the Roosevelt in New Orleans and Seymour Weiss sent his head bartender, Sam Guarina to New York on the next plane. Sam brought along a quart of orange flower water and a bushel of green limes. During the remainder of his stay in New York the senator served Ramos gin fizzes to everyone who wanted one.

Shortly afterward, the senator was assassinated, and now he is a sort of legend in Louisiana. Even the people who hated him most admit he did many good things for the state. Most visitors go to see the famous Huey P. Long Bridge, three and a half miles above the city, that was built during Long's administration as governor. It is almost four miles long, with double railroad tracks, motor highways, and a sidewalk on either side.

For half a century, engineers had dreamed of a great bridge to span the Mississippi, but it took the Kingfish to build it. Back in the nineties, men of practical vision were planning a combination carriage road and railroad bridge for the Southern Pacific. They met to talk about it in the saloon across from the old State Capitol where Mr. Ramos—his first name was Henry, Henry C. Ramos—mixed drinks for politicians, and invented his famous fizz. Plans and prospective financing dragged on for generations. Then Long became governor and secured the necessary advance of $13,000,000 to start and complete the bridge. He put a thousand men to work, and in three years it was finished. During Long's administration the magnificent State Capitol also was built.

On September 8, 1935, as he was leaving the governor's office, the senator was shot, supposedly by a young dentist named Weiss, who had attended Mass that morning and spent the next few hours at a quiet family picnic with his wife and baby, to both of whom he was deeply devoted. His purported motive for the murder was an alleged remark of Long's about Weiss's father-in-law, a county judge.

In the confusion that followed, Weiss was riddled with sixty-four bullets by Long's bodyguards. Whether it is the sort of local story that inevitably springs up after such a spectacular event or whether Weiss was the innocent victim of a deeply laid plot, there is a tradition that somebody else killed Long and, in the wholesale shooting that followed, the conspirators planted the pistol that fastened the crime on Weiss. No autopsy was performed to ascertain whose gun fired the fatal bullet. The senator's body was rushed to a grave in front of the Capitol and buried beneath tons of cement in a beautiful sunken garden. The tomb, authorized by legislative appropriation, cost $50,000. On it is a 12-foot bronze statue for which Long's son posed, and on either side of the statue are miniatures of the Capitol and the Huey P. Long Bridge.

When Huey was a presidential aspirant, writing *Every Man a King* and *My First Days in the White House,* he promised, facetiously, to promote Ramos gin fizzes from the White House. When Huey was sixteen and selling a lard substitute, he put on a cake-baking contest at Shreveport that was won by Miss Rose McConnell with a gold cake. Three years later Huey and Rose were married. When her husband mixed fizzes, Mrs. Long would often take the yokes for a gold cake, and frost it to please Huey, like the cake that won the prize. The story of the Kingfish has made several books and a movie, and I should like to tell you more of his violent young life, but if I don't get back to Mr. Ramos we will never finish with this gin fizz business.

New Orleans politicians persuaded Mr. Ramos to move from Baton Rouge, so they would not have to wait so long between drinks. He bought the Imperial Cabinet at the corner of Gravier and Carondelet streets, where the Sazerac Bar is now, and stayed there twenty years, doing a wonderful business. Then he bought the Stag from Tom Anderson, the "King of the Tenderloin." The Stag was on Gravier Street opposite the St. Charles Hotel. It was a high-class place because Tom Anderson was fabulously rich and liked to do things in the grand manner. Anderson owned the most elegant brothel in the Red

Light District, and another saloon on Basin Street, called Arlington Annex, and known as the "Town Hall of Anderson County."

Many women who lived in the district are still around town. Some of the girls became madams, and the wages of sin weren't death, but nice houses uptown. One ex-madam has a limousine and liveried chauffeur. She went to work for Josie Arlington when she was fifteen, in a five-dollar bordello. Josie was said to be the ritziest madam in the country, and to have the youngest and prettiest girls. But when Josie died, the girls quarreled with the new madam, and the one I met ended up after a while in one of those dreadful 50-cent houses. Before she had been there long she was befriended by a prosperous madam who took her back to Basin Street where the two of them went in business together, and now they are both respectable dowagers, with good cooks and money in the bank.

After Tom Anderson sold his Stag to Mr. Ramos, he devoted himself exclusively to his holdings in the district, until he got sick and almost died. Then he took the pledge and became very pious. He even gave up swearing, and when he died he left his widow $120,000, all made in sin and booze.

Mr. Ramos, meantime, was making the Stag a famous place, and he was making money too because, as Mr. Emerson said about a mousetrap, if a man makes a better fizz than his neighbor the world will beat a path to his swinging door. In the Stag there was a very long mahogany bar, and during Mardi Gras there were thirty-five boys who shook fizzes twenty-four hours a day. They stood in line and passed the shakers over their shoulders, down the line from one to another, all shaking like mad. In those days, with no electric gadgets, a fizz was shaken *con amore*. Now there are Waring blenders, which are not as picturesque as shaker boys, but more convenient. They make a lovely fizz and if, as you sip them, you think of liquid flowers, it won't be the gin making you rhapsodical but only the orange flower water.

The first time I tasted orange flower water was in the bazaars of Algiers, where it is sprinkled in hot tea to make the tea fragrant. I brought some home, and after it was gone I bought various bottles labeled "Orange Flower Water." But it was always horrid stuff, and I never again had anything pleasant until I found the real thing in New Orleans. Solari's on Royal Street, and most of the better liquor stores, carry an essence distilled in Grasse. (Shopping note: At Christmas, fill bitters bottles with Eau de Fleurs d'Oranger for the tea-drinking ladies of your acquaintance.)

When you hear of the thousands of fizzes that are made every day in New Orleans you may wonder, if you are a practical person, what becomes of the yolks.

At home, when I have a run on fizzes, I scramble the yolks when the company has gone and I am eating by myself. And I get pretty darn sick of them. If I had more time I suppose I might make a gold cake with six yolks and a coconut frosting. But they can't do anything like that in a bar, and being a New Englander and a thrifty soul ("Willful waste makes woeful want") I had wondered. One day I asked a barman, "When you use an egg white, Joe, what do you do with the rest of the egg? Yolks must be an awful nuisance," I said. But not to Joe they're not. Joe has solved the yolk problem by leaving out the white.

"Add a squirt of soda water," said Joe. "Nine times out of ten nobody knows the difference."

Anybody who never had a fizz mightn't know, but it is a horrid thing to do because an egg white is very important to a fizz.

"Yard eggs" are cheaper in New Orleans than in most places, and usually plentiful. In the old days a market man, when asked if his eggs were fresh, would break one to show, and then toss it into the gutter. Mr. Ramos made omelettes with his spare yolks, and served them free, which was the pleasant habit of the day. Barroom lunches in the Crescent City were prodigious in ante-bellum times, and fa-

mous up to Prohibition. I have the diary of a man who stayed at the
St. Charles in 1859 who could hardly believe his eyes.

"The barrooms," he wrote, "hold a thousand people. There is set
out every day—free to all comers—soups, fish, roast, roast joints, fowls
and salads, with hot French bread and cheese. You eat as much as
you like, and the dime (or picayune) which you give for the mint
julep or sherry-cobbler pays for everything." The gentleman was
charmed, and no wonder.

"Roses bloom, bananas ripen, golden oranges cover the trees in
January. People say, There is no place like New Orleans—and there
is no doubt about it. Men drink a great deal (it is said the climate
makes it necessary), but they drink magnificently. They say they
would rather be broke in New Orleans than own New York, and
have to live there."

Lafcadio Hearn, fresh from Cincinnati, wrote that it was better to
live in New Orleans in sackcloth and ashes than to possess the whole
state of Ohio, and there are any number of persons—even Ohioans—
who feel the same way. Hearn had a room in a moldering mansion
on St. Louis Street, where he lived for three dollars a week in an
atmosphere haunted by romance. That was in 1877, twelve years after
the War Between the States, and New Orleans was desperately poor.
Hearn was a reporter on the *Item* at ten dollars a week. After work,

he sat in the neglected courtyard of the old Creole house, where the sun fell and the leaves were green, and he wrote to his friends in wintry Cleveland of the beauty all around him—"a strange, tropical, intoxicating beauty, with sweet perfume-laden air":

> I don't really care a damn whether I make money or not. Life here is so lazy—nights are so liquid with tropic moonlight—days are so splendid with green and gold—summer is so languid with perfume and warmth—that I hardly know whether I am dreaming or not.

3

*G*OD BE THANKED FOR ALMONESTER Visitors

to New Orleans are concerned with bars and jazz and Mardi Gras
rather than with old, unhappy, far-off things, and battles long ago.
They are more interested in topical personages than in historical
characters. Count Arnaud is undeniably more fascinating than the
Duke of Orleans, and Dear Dorothy Dix means more to newspaper
readers than the Baroness de Pontalba does. Roy Alciatore's father,
Jules, invented oysters Rockefeller, and Roy, grandson of the original
Antoine, is the third generation of his family in the restaurant business. No epicure ever visited New Orleans without dining at Antoine's. On Bourbon Street Marty Burke and his wife Santa have a
famous bar. Marty boxed more rounds with Jack Dempsey than any
man in the world. Pete Herman, the blind prizefighter, has a club
on Conti Street, and every old-time sports fan wants to shake hands
with Pete. People on a holiday are more interested in Louis Armstrong, the King of Jazz who learned about music on Basin Street,
than they are in the Marquis de Vaudreuil. Mayor Chep Morrison
means more to most folk than Jean Baptiste Le Moyne and Sieur de
Bienville, and the legends of twentieth-century Storyville are indubi-
tably livelier reading than the *Code Noir* of 1724. Most visitors, however, want a bit of background to heighten their enjoyment of New
Orleans, and since hardly anybody likes to study history on a holiday, I am going to tell, as briefly as I can, what was happening in
Europe in the days when New Orleans was the richest city in America. Then I will tell how the Spaniards came to Louisiana, and if you

are not already familiar with the story, you will better appreciate the Vieux Carré and the culture of the old French-Spanish city.

Europe in the middle of the eighteenth century was almost as confusing as it is today, especially after Frederick the Great of Prussia, having defeated the Allied Forces of Europe, split the spoils of the Seven Years' War with George III, the mad old king who lost America, who had lent him ships and money. France, impoverished by wars and the enormous sums Louis XV spent on his mistresses, was in a bad way. Frederick had obliged France to cede to England both Canada and Nova Scotia, to say nothing of India. England would have had Louisiana too, except that Louis, by secret agreement, had made a gift of the country, which included the entire Mississippi Valley, to his cousin Charles III of Spain. This was in 1762. It was not that Charles especially wanted Louisiana, but the cousins were agreed that it was too bad to let England get everything in sight. Spain accepted the gift, but did nothing about it. Louis neglected to inform his subjects of the change in monarchs, so naturally they went on feeling French, and when the secret agreement was discovered, as secret agreements always are, there was the usual hell to pay. (I will tell you more about this in a minute.)

In 1792 the Convention in Paris declared the end of royalty, and in 1793 Louis XVI and his queen were guillotined. In 1798, when Napoleon was conquering Europe, the dead king's brothers visited New Orleans. In 1801 Napoleon contrived the return of Louisiana from Spain to France, and in 1803 he sold Louisiana and all the Mississippi Valley (almost a million square miles) to Thomas Jefferson for fifteen million dollars (which was about four cents an acre). Then came the War of 1812, and the Creoles, who were then Americans, fought against Great Britain for the dearly bought freedom of our country (won by the thirteen colonies, 1775-1781). The greatest battle in American history was the Battle of New Orleans (January 8, 1815), when Andrew Jackson and his tattered forces, defending the city and the river, beat the pick of the British Army, and the British Navy took their great general, Sir Edward Pakenham—who had hoped to be Earl of Louisiana—home on the *Plantagenet,* pickled, poor man, in a hogshead of rum.

Sugar and commerce made New Orleans very rich, and until the War of Secession she grew richer every year. The first shot of the War Between the States was fired at Fort Sumter at the command of General (The Great Creole) Beauregard. The war lasted from 1861 to 1865. When it was over, the eleven seceding states were reconstructed as members of the Union, the slaves were freed, and New Orleans was bankrupt. . . . There, in chronological order, are all the important dates you should know, and if you forget them now you know where to look.

Louis XV, in 1763, turned the colony over to his cousin Charles. The French governor was recalled and thrown into the Bastille. Louis sent a director-general to tell the people, a year or two after it happened, that Louisiana had passed from his hands into the hands of the king of Spain, and eventually Don Antonio de Ulloa arrived from Havana to rule Louisiana. But Don Antonio did not assume official position. He simply anchored his vessel at the mouth of the Mississippi, and there he stayed for seven months. The people could make neither head nor tail of the matter and were puzzled and resentful, until the governor came ashore with a young wife. Then they were excited and gleeful as children, for the Creoles were always a romantic and in many ways a childlike people.

Don Antonio had waited at the river's mouth, like a lover in a fairy tale, for a beautiful bride from far away. She was a great heiress from Peru, and she came in terrific style, tripping ashore at the jetty with a tremendous retinue of fashionable Peruvians, and a train of coal-black slaves. The Vieux Carré seethed with excitement. The director-general received the newlyweds with great punctilio. He even turned his house over to them, and the whole retinue moved in. But the director-general continued to govern.

Two weeks passed and certain Creole ladies, overwhelmingly

curious, decided to call. As they waited in the courtyard, they could hear a great chattering and a clicking of wine glasses. But the bride sent word down that she was not at home. The ladies could hear the Peruvians laughing, and they could hear the governor's lady laughing the loudest of all, and they were furious, because even the slaves knew that the foreign woman had insulted them, the crème de la crème of Louisiana society!

It was a Creole custom to pay respects a fortnight after a marriage. Creole newlyweds never went away on a honeymoon but went, instead, into hiding for two weeks. Usually they remained at the bride's home. After the wedding was over, the bride's mother escorted her daughter to the nuptial chamber, and helped her don the hand-embroidered nightgown that had been made for the great occasion. Some of the brides' gowns are in the Cabildo, voluminous things with stitches so small you can scarcely see them. Girls were taught in the convent to sew like that, and every little Creole worked on a trousseau from the time she could hold a needle. After Mama tucked her child in the great four-poster, she kissed the bride good-bye—and the groom took over. For five days the couple remained in their room, presumably to become acquainted, since there had been little opportunity during their well-chaperoned courtship. Meals were brought to them by a servant, and it was two weeks before they were permitted to appear in public.

The Creole ladies, having waited a full and proper fortnight to call upon the Peruvian bride, were not only insulted by her refusal to receive them, but they knew that so ignorant a woman would never do for a governor's wife, and they rashly urged that Ulloa be banished and that New Orleans throw off the yoke of Spain.

Twelve leading citizens drew up a petition, signed by several hundred, asking the governor and his lady to leave the colony. When their request was ignored, the Creoles waited until the bridal party was aboard the honeymoon ship, then they cut the moorings that held the ship to the levee, and away it drifted. There was talk then of a republic, and shouts of "Liberté!" rang in the streets. The twelve who had drawn up the petition were heroes, and for two years there was freedom from foreign rule. Then Count Alexander O'Reilly arrived from Spain with twenty-four men-of-war and three thousand Spanish soldiers. O'Reilly marched his men to the Place d'Armes, and raised the Spanish flag of Castille and Leon where the golden fleurs-de-lis of France had flown for nearly half a century.

There was no resistance, for what could a handful do in the face of three thousand, all armed to the teeth? The Creoles, desiring peace, declared to O'Reilly that they had committed no act of insubordination against Spanish rule, because Ulloa had never actually exhibited his powers. O'Reilly assured them that "all past transactions would be buried in oblivion, and all who had offended would be forgiven." Then, treacherously, he ordered the arrest of the twelve leaders. One, resisting, was killed with Spanish bayonets. After a military trial, six were taken to Morro Castle in Havana harbor and thrown into dungeons and five were shot in the Place d'Armes, under the trees on the waterfront.

It was a dreadful beginning. But after he had ruthlessly established his power, O'Reilly became a beneficent ruler. Except for adoption of Spanish language and law, there were few changes. It was not long before O'Reilly's men were wooing French girls, and their parents were smiling on the matches. There were many marriages, and the children of the French girls and the Spanish soldiers had great dark eyes and blue-black hair, and they talked in French for Mama and in Spanish for Papa.

628830

*   *   *

Don Andrés Almonester y Roxas was a bookkeeper in Spain, and it was said that he had not a peso to bless himself with when he came to New Orleans with O'Reilly and set himself up as a contractor. Doing business with the government he became a politician, and he did very well for himself. The king made him a chevalier, and he made himself perpetual commissioner of the Muy Ilustrisimo Cabildo, which was the council that governed the city. Then Don Andrés married a Creole girl and became, in his ripe old age, the father of a daughter named Micaëla, who became the Baroness de Pontalba, and the most famous woman New Orleans ever had.

When Micaëla was two and her father was seventy-three, he died, and was buried in the Cathedral. His widow, who soon married a very young man (and I'll tell you about that later) had her husband's beneficences inscribed upon a marble tablet and set upon his grave. From this tablet we learn that Don Andrés built the Cathedral as a gift for the people, and that he also built the Cabildo, the King's Hospital, and a Hospital for Lepers.

In New York right now there are about five thousand lepers who ride in the subways and go to the movies, and eat at the Automat and the Colony like the rest of us. They get clinical injections of a sulfa drug called promin, and live to get high blood pressure, or die of old age—and never infect anyone. But in those days everybody was so afraid of lepers that the Ursulines, who nursed the poor creatures, were considered heroines.

Almonester, as a token of the people's appreciation, gave the nuns a chapel, and the nuns, as a token of *their* appreciation, gave Almonester a seat in the sanctuary. And there he sat on Sundays and holydays of obligation, his sword at his side and his cocked hat under his arm, praying away with the best of them. There is a portrait of him in the Cabildo—elegant, profligate, and a little corrupt— a substantial figure of a man, with the girth of a politician and the bearing of a caballero. This, I imagine, is the way Almonester looked when he was all dressed up for Mass.

In 1788 there was a terrible fire in the Vieux Carré which started from the flame of a little myrtleberry candle burning beneath the statue of a saint in a house in Chartres Street. The fire spread on the wind from one little house to another. On any other day the church bells would have called the people to fight the blaze. But it happened to be Good Friday, and the Capuchin friars, who had charge of the church, said that it would be a sacrilege to ring the bells on the day that Christ died upon the cross. So the bells were not rung, and half the town burned—the government houses, and the jail, homes, and stores, the parish church of St. Louis, and also the monastery of the Capuchins who would not ring the bells.

The Convent of the Ursulines, sitting back a bit from the street, escaped although flames licked at the walls of its garden, bright on that Good Friday with orange and lemon trees, and fragrant with jasmine.

When the fire was over and the people, wringing their hands and weeping, stumbled among the ashes of their dear city, Don Andrés mounted the ruins and made a fine speech. He would build a new church for them, he promised, and a new hospital— and a monastery, as well, for the Capuchins who would not ring the bells. He sent to Spain for architects, and when they arrived he had them draw plans for a Cathedral, and for a Royal Hospital. Then Don Andrés decided to build a hospital for the lepers too.

As a matter of historical accuracy, there were two fires. The second one was in 1794, and between them they destroyed nearly everything that the French had built. The Vieux Carré as we know it today dates from this period. But it is not to be supposed that the Vieux Carré changed its character overnight or became, ever, completely Spanish. There were wives and mothers who wept behind closed blinds in the changing city for the men "Bloody O'Reilly" had shot in the Place d'Armes. There were families who would have nothing to do with either Almonester or his foreign architects, and when these families built, they built as before—plain two-story houses of plaster and cypress, with hipped and dormered roofs—and no nonsense about them.

There is such a house—at 632 Dumaine Street—known as "Madame John's Legacy," that escaped both fires. It was built while

Bienville was Governor, and the casket girls were coming to town. It is one of the most photographed houses in the Quarter, and since it is neither beautiful nor particularly interesting looking, the reason for its fame must be its name, which is like a trademark every one remembers but few can explain.

The story goes back to George W. Cable, who did more than almost anyone else to immortalize the lingering legends of the Vieux Carré. Cable was born in New Orleans, although he was not a Creole. As a boy he fought with the cavalry of the Confederacy. Later he became a newspaperman and spent his spare time digging up ancient records, and talking with old people who had long memories. His first story of "Old Creole Days," published in *Scribner's,* was about a "palish handsome woman" going by the name of Madame John, who had a most beautiful daughter called 'Tite Poulette. Madame John's first name was Zalli, and she was the quadroon sweetheart of a gay gentleman whose name happened to be John. It was John who lived in the house on Dumaine Street.

"As his parents lived with him, his wife would, according to custom, have been called Madame John; but he had no wife. His father died, then his mother; last of all himself. As he was about to be off, in came Zalli with 'Tite Poulette on her arm.

" 'Zalli,' said he, 'I am going.'

"She bowed her head, and wept.

" 'You have been very faithful to me, Zalli.'

"She wept on.

" 'Nobody to take care of you now, Zalli.'

"Zalli only went on weeping.

"I want to give you this house, Zalli; it is for you and the little one.'

"An hour after, amid the sobs of Madame John, she and the 'little one' inherited the house" . . . And when you have seen it, you may judge for yourself what the Spanish did for the Vieux Carré.

"Madame John's Legacy was built while Bienville was governor and the casket girls were coming to town."

Madame John's Legacy, with its plastered first story and gallery over the street, is typical of the early French period.

The Spaniards built their galleries at the back, above patios that were filled with flowers. The street façades of the Spanish houses, although simple, were well mannered. And they were taller and grander than the houses of the French people who, except for the nobles, lived with characteristic Gallic thrift in modest little houses.

New Orleans was no longer the French outpost of a colonial empire. From the ashes of the little town rose the homes of the dons, more beautiful and stately than the French had built. The Vieux Carré began to take on the flavor of Spain, not all at once, but gradually—an arch here, pillars there, fan-shaped windows that looked down on flowery patios, Spanish roofs and Moorish tiles, balconies railed with ironwork more delicate than before. Slowly, bit by bit, Andalusia moved in on Nouvelle-Orléans, until, at last, the Vieux Carré was neither French nor Spanish but a pleasing mixture some architects call "Creole," and others "New Orleans."

Soon after the Cathedral was completed, the Casa Capitular (Capitol House) was destroyed in the second great fire. Almonester, warmed by the gratitude of the people, who were very pious and appreciative, promised to build a new Capitol that should be bigger and better than the one that had burned. The following year—the year in which Micaëla was born—it was completed, a fine big building that stood proudly by the House of God.

After a while the Casa Capitular came to be called the Cabildo, taking its name from the Spanish governing body that met in its council chamber. This is where the Louisiana Historical Society meets now. It is one of the great historical rooms of America, and I hope you will visit it. It is too bad that many people are prejudiced against museums. It may be the curators' fault because they let things get so dusty, or else lock them in forbidding cases. God knows, museums are dull, musty, and mean to visitors. Most of them, including the Cabildo, have a funereal air that is pretty depressing. I remember something that Thoreau said about museums which must have been true a hundred years ago, and it is just as true today.

"I hate museums," he said, "there is nothing so weighs upon my spirits."

Most men dislike museums and visit them, if at all, under protest. Women are more likely to go because they think they should, many women, particularly tourists, being hell-bent on culture. Children go because their teachers or parents make them. But in New Orleans almost everybody visits the Cabildo, because it is so full of a number of things and most of them interesting.

In the lobby are Bienville's statue and the portrait of Louis XIV that I told you about. What most women like best in museums are small intimate things, like babies' clothes and little girls' dolls, teacups, and ladies' best dresses. In the Cabildo are many homely mementoes of family living, and tarnished relics that gave Creole history its sparkle and charm—Mardi Gras jewels, the gowns and crowns of Carnival queens, the mantles of kings, and the shining swords of caballeros. On the walls, looking down at their treasures, are portraits of belles and grande dames and foolish young men who dueled for love, and died for honor's sake.

The late Lyle Saxon, who introduced me to Cabildo portraits, was curious to know the opinion of modern women of the Creole men with their beautiful posturing and dandified elegance.

"Look at their soft eyes," he said, "and their patrician noses. Their mouths, full-lipped like a girl's . . . and the sensitivity of their expressions. There are no such faces today." And Lyle, who was himself one of the South's most charming gentlemen, looked very sad. "Our commercial spirit," he said, "has killed the poetry in young men's faces." But I did not agree with him because I do not like beautiful young men with full lips and oil on their hair.

You must look for Julian Meffre-Rouzan, in his form-fitting coat and lovely cravat, who sat with his beautiful wife, Alix de Vezin, a belle who wore spectacles. In ante-bellum days it was chic for girls to wear spectacles, and many fashionable women sat for their portraits in ugly, steel-rimmed glasses. Among the bespectacled beauties in the Cabildo is Sophronia Claiborne, daughter of the first American governor of Louisiana and his third wife, who was a Creole girl. You would be surprised how many people look at Sophronia, and say the same thing.

"Men seldom makes passes," they say, "at girls who wear glasses," which has kept a lot of nearsighted girls stumbling around for a long time.

Adjoining the Cabildo is the old Arsenal, and next to the Arsenal are two old houses that stand on the site of old Spanish calabozo, or jail. When the calabozo was destroyed, secret rooms were found with instruments of torture that indicated New Orleans may have known the Inquisition. Friar Antonio Moreno, whom the French called Père Antoine, is supposed to have tried to introduce the auto-da-fe into Louisiana. There is not much reliable evidence to connect him with it, but since there were inquisitorial tribunals at the time in every country in Europe and since the Spanish had a special passion for them, it is not improbable that there is truth in the legend.

Atrocities of the period compare—in a small way, of course—with those of Buchenwald and Dachau. Political prisoners, taken into custody while attending a state dinner at the governor's mansion, were shot en masse in the Place d'Armes. Men were broken on the wheel, strangled beneath the scaffold, and hanged upon it afterward. Arms and legs and backs were broken, and offenders lashed upon a wheel, to expire with their "faces turned to heaven." Mutilated bodies were exhibited in the public square, and heads stuck on gate poles. Unbelievers had their tongues cut out and their property confiscated. Minor culprits were flogged through the streets, and branded. Indians were burned at the stake. For violation of discipline, soldiers were bound naked to trees, beaten until their bodies were covered with blood, then left to be eaten alive by flies and mosquitoes. For running away in the face of such horrors, deserters were nailed alive in coffins. Then the coffins were sawed in two. The eighteenth century had no gas chambers or crematoria, but with the old-fashioned tortures at their command the Creoles did pretty well.

There is another museum called the Presbytère, intended originally for a Casa Curial, or Priests' House, which was to replace the Capuchin Monastery that the friars let burn on that Good Friday when they would not ring the bells. The Presbytère is twin to the Cabildo, and stands on the other side of the Cathedral. It was begun by Almonester before the Cathedral was built, but Almonester quarreled with the Capuchins and never finished it, and it was not completed until ten years after the American occupation.

By and by, third stories with dormer windows were added to the Cabildo and the Presbytère, and both buildings were topped with mansard roofs. The roofs must be terrible because people who are learned about architecture wince whenever they look at them. But if you do not know any better you will find them charming, as everybody does but the purists.

The Presbytère is now a natural history museum, where Audubon's "Birds of America," painted and stuffed, have come home to roost. Although I like the Presbytère very much, I am afraid it is the kind of museum that Thoreau hated most of all. Museums are "catacombs of nature," he said—and I am going to copy what else he said.

"The life that is in a single green weed is worth more than all this death. . . . One green bud of spring, one willow catkin, one faint trill from a migrating sparrow," he said, "might set the world on its legs again."

Audubon was at the height of his glory when Thoreau wrote that, and in another chapter I am going to tell you about Audubon and his famous birds.

$\mathcal{H}$E SANG, HE FOUGHT, HE KISSED

FIVE HUNDRED DOLLARS
REWARD

To be paid to any person delivering Jean Laffite to the Sheriff of the Parish of Orleans, or to any other Sheriff in the State, so that the said Jean Laffite may be brought to justice.

Given under my hand on this 24th day of November, 1813.

by the Governor (Signed)
William C. C. Claiborne.

Jean Laffite, handsome in crimson coat and black velvet breeches, a tricornered hat on the back of his handsome head and a flutter of lace at his throat, swaggered down Bourbon Street. He stopped at the Old Absinthe House where this notice was posted above the banquette, and laughed as he read it. Then he went in and had a drink.

Three days later Claiborne, sauntering down the same street, also stopped. But Claiborne did not laugh, and his face grew red as he stared at the wall. For there, pasted above his offer for Laffite's arrest, was Laffite's counteroffer:

FIFTEEN HUNDRED DOLLARS!

to be paid for the delivery of
William C. C. Claiborne
to Grande Isle

Jean Laffite

Grande Isle was the pirates' hideaway. When the people heard the story, they thought it very funny.

Claiborne was their first American governor, and the Creoles resented him. It was difficult for them to think of themselves as Americans. They felt no loyalty to a government that imposed tariffs on European commerce, and they were glad to buy from anyone whose goods were duty-free.

That was how Jean Laffite got his start.

Laffite came from France. It was rumored, and may have been true, that he was the son of a nobleman. He was known as a gentleman, and is said to have been handsome. In 1813 he was about thirty-two years old. He spoke, besides his native French, Castilian Spanish and excellent English, as well as the patois of the Baratarians. The women of the town were mad about him.

> And many a maid at Holy Mass,
>   All bonneted, pelissed,
> Dreamed o'er her beads of the wicked man,
>   Who sang and fought and kissed . . .

He went to the quadroon balls, a gallant, ruffled rover, and attended the opera in bottle-green tails which nobody had ever seen before, and a flower-spangled waistcoat from Paris. But it is improbable that Laffite, for all his lovely manners, was ever asked anywhere for dinner. Under Spanish rule, men who were esteemed as honest citizens were often smugglers and privateers, but, if well born, were socially acceptable. But with the coming of the Americans, life in New Orleans had taken on a puritanical tinge, and Creoles felt obliged to draw the line at Baratarians.

In the beginning, Jean and his brother Pierre had a smithy on Bourbon Street where slaves swung the sledges and shod the horses, and the brothers stood around like gentlemen. The smithy was their first front for smuggling. Later they established a luxury shop on Royal Street where fine ladies went for silks and velvets, for china and silver, and smuggled jewels. Pierre kept in the background. Jean, who was the charmer, was the front man. For a partner they had a big, silent creature, more the cutthroat type, known as Dominique You.

The Laffites sailed under letters of marque from the republic of Cartagena, which was fighting for her independence from Spain. Jean claimed that his men attacked only Spanish ships, which was proper enough under the law. And proper, in any case, with the French Creoles.

Grande Isle guards the mouth of Barataria Bay, some fifty miles south of New Orleans. To Grande Isle the pirates—or privateers, as Jean preferred to call them—brought their captured ships. It was not difficult to smuggle their cargoes from Grande Isle to the Creole capital. Feminine fripperies were the least of the Baratarians' goods. The Laffites handled "black ivory" too—Negroes seized from Spanish slave ships and sold at a dollar a pound. The Creoles were glad to get them; why should a man pay $1,000 for a "nigger" when Laffite would sell him one for $200? At the slave market in the Vieux Carré big bucks were usually bid up to $1,000. Wenches were cheaper, and Jean had some nice little wenches dirt cheap.

In a swamp near New Orleans there was a slave farm where blacks fresh from Africa were kept until they were tamed or killed. Those who survived, and learned to plow or handle an ax, were brought into the city and sold at auction. There had been an insurrection at Pointe Coupée of these swamp blacks who had fixed upon a date when all whites in the parish, except the women and girls, were to be killed. But the leaders quarreled among themselves, and one of the slaves revealed the plan to his master. The principal plotters, including three white men, were arrested. The white men were banished from the province, the Negroes were placed upon a boat which drifted slowly down the Mississippi. At every parish between Pointe Coupée and New Orleans the boat stopped and one of the Negroes was hanged from a tree.

It was hoped that this would be a lesson to "swamp niggers," but it was not surprising that many planters preferred to buy their slaves from the barracoons on Grande Isle. Laffite's "niggers," they said, usually turned out pretty well.

On Grande Isle, Jean Laffite ruled a thousand cutthroats, directing their sea activities, dividing their loot and banking their cash. When necessary, he hired the best lawyers in the South, and with high-class legal talent Laffite managed to keep his men out of jail, and off the gallows.

When Claiborne sought to arrest him, Laffite captured the governor's revenue men and took them to Grande Isle, where he had a table set upon the beach with fine linen and beautiful silver, and a Sèvres dinner service that had been made, so it was said, for Madame de Pompadour. Slaves served the dinner—without much style, to be sure—but with an astonishing variety of choice wines and fine old brandies. When the meal was finished, Laffite loaded his guests with gifts and sent them, quite drunk, back to Claiborne. It made a good story and the Creoles, loving audacity, admired the young outlaw who made the governor apoplectic.

But times were changing, for both Creoles and pirates. Since the Louisiana Purchase the population of New Orleans had tripled and the city kept growing richer and richer. Nine years later America was at war with England and the war was going badly. The British had completed a blockade of eastern ports, and marched on Washington. President Madison and his Cabinet fled on horseback. The British fired the Capitol and the President's Palace. Dolly Madison, when she knew the redcoats were coming, stood on a chair and cut from its frame the portrait of Washington that now hangs in the East Room of the White House. She rolled it up in a tablecloth, and then Dolly Madison ran like hell. That was in August.

In September a ship from his Majesty's fleet dropped anchor in Barataria Bay, and two officers were rowed ashore to see Jean Laffite on Grande Isle. They had come, they said, with an offer from the king. If the Baratarians would join the British attack on New Orleans, the king would give Laffite a commission of captain in the Royal Navy, and bestow upon him and his men grants in the territory of Louisiana ... If they should refuse, the Royal Navy would blow the Baratarians into the sea.

Laffite poured the officers brandy from a decanter set with jewels, and assured his visitors that their proposition was interesting. He would like a little time, he said, to consider.

"Would two weeks be enough?"

Laffite refilled the glasses. "Quite enough, gentlemen," he said.

When the officers had gone, he sent a message to Claiborne. In return for amnesty to the outlawed Baratarians, he and his men, Laffite said, offered their services to the governor, and would lay down their lives for America.

Claiborne's answer was a fleet of gunboats, the schooner *Carolina,* and three barges loaded with men and ammunition. At first, because the ships approached from the Gulf, the Baratarians thought the British were returning and, dragging their cannon to position on the beach, they prepared to set them off. But when they saw the American colors, the pirates turned and fled. There was not a man among them who would fire upon the Stars and Stripes.

The Americans landed without resistance, and took a hundred prisoners, including Dominique You. But the Laffites and nine hundred men got away in pirogues, scurrying through the bayous to Grande-Terre. It was on Grande-Terre that they kept most of their ammunition.

The soldiers broke open the warehouses on Grande Isle and took more than $500,000 worth of captured goods. They burned forty houses of different sizes, and seized nine ships and twenty cannon. When the Americans were through Laffite had lost his empire, and a fortune besides.

It took the troops nearly a week to clean up and raze the place, and when they sailed back to New Orleans with a hundred prisoners and all the beautiful loot, General Jackson, who had arrived to take charge of the defense of New Orleans, congratulated the governor on the action he had taken.

"We need not hellish banditti to join us in our glorious cause," declared Old Hickory a bit pompously—and erroneously too, as you shall see.

Two days before Christmas, a messenger galloped into town with word that the enemy was encamped on the de Villère plantation, nine miles down the river. Their coats were red as blood and their bayonets gleamed in the sun. For the day of attack the countersign was "Beauty and Booty." No wonder the Creoles were nervous!

That afternoon General Jackson, desperately ill and swaying in his saddle with fever, reviewed the American troops—700 regulars, the Bataillon d'Orléans, a Creole organization commanded by Major Jean Baptiste Plauche, and an assortment of free men of color, Choctaw Indians, flatboatmen, and fierce black men from Santo Domingo. They were 2,139 untrained men, divided by hatreds and several languages. Most of them had never seen action. Pakenham had 9,000 seasoned veterans, trained under the Duke of Wellington, who six months later defeated Napoleon at Waterloo.

The town was in a panic. Banks were closed and business suspended. Jackson declared martial law and issued a proclamation that every able-bodied man prepare to fight. Slaves were brought in from river plantations to throw up the earthworks which began at the levee on the Plains of Chalmette and vanished into the cypress swamps. At almost the last minute some 2,000 Tennessee and Kentucky sharpshooters arrived in the city, after a long march through swamps and over mountains. But Jackson still lacked ammunition, and cannoneers, and ships to guard the water flanks of the town.

One day there appeared at the house where the general was staying a tall, slender man with golden hoops in his ears—Jean Laffite, with a price on his head! The general stared. Laffite bowed with Creole grace.

"Forgive me for intruding, sir," he said, sardonically polite. "I have come to place at your disposal my men, my ships, and my ammunition."

Old Hickory squared his thin high shoulders. He had come by his nickname at the beginning of the war when his men, short of supplies, found their commander under a hickory tree making his dinner on nuts.

"Ahem!" said Old Hickory, and made an instant decision. "I accept your offer, sir," he said.

That day a new proclamation issued by Claiborne appeared on the streets, and it was posted everywhere that the offer for Laffite's arrest had been posted. The Baratarians, it said, having expressed a desire to serve the common cause, would henceforth be accepted as fellow patriots.

Then the pirates came to town, and swaggered in and out of the bars, with red bandannas on their heads and dirks at their waists. The day the motley little American army marched forth to meet the British, the Baratarians marched up front. They were the only artillerists that Jackson had.

For two weeks there were skirmishes along the River Road. On the 6th and 7th of January the women of New Orleans prayed both day and night before the miraculous statue of Our Lady of Prompt Succor, in the Chapel of the Ursulines. The mother superior made a vow that if the Americans won a Mass of thanksgiving would be sung before the Lady's shrine on every anniversary of victory. The women were on their knees at dawn on the 8th, when the Battle of New Orleans began. At 8:30, two hours and fifteen minutes later (the official time of action), the British had lost 700 men, including three generals, 1,400 more British were wounded, and 500 had been taken prisoner. Jackson reported his losses in the main assault as six killed and seven wounded. These figures explain why the Battle of New Orleans is listed among the greatest battles of history.

In the afternoon, while the women were still on their knees, a messenger dashed into the chapel shouting the news of victory, and the women cried with joy to hear him. The Ursulines have never forgotten the Masses the mother superior promised. And if our Lady smiles sadly on the 8th of each January, it may be that she is remembering the Treaty of Ghent.

At noon on the day of the battle a truce was arranged. All that afternoon and by torchlight the enemy tended their wounded. But it was another ten days before they had finished burying the dead and retired to their fleet. When the British left the Plains, the Americans marched back to the town.

Then the most heartbreaking thing that happened was the news that came too late. On the day of the Battle of New Orleans, England and America had been at peace for sixteen days. The boys from quiet English towns who spent their blood along the bayous had died—as young soldiers often die—for nothing. Not even for glory. The Treaty of Ghent had been signed on Christmas Eve.

Upon his return to the city, General Jackson and his staff, accompanied by Jean Laffite, went to the convent to thank the nuns for their prayers. And little Creole angels up in heaven laughed to see Old Hickory and the pirate genuflecting before the statue of their gentle Lady.

"The General," wrote Jackson in his official report, "cannot avoid giving his warm approbation to the manner in which these gentlemen [Laffite and his crew] conducted themselves, and of the gallantry with which they defended the country."

A victory ball was held, and Old Hickory, with a crown of gold upon his grizzled head, stepped a reel to the tune of "Possum up a Gum Tree," while Jean Laffite danced with the prettiest girls in town. Yankees and Creoles were friends at last and Jean Laffite was the toast of the town. It would be romantic to tell that he fell in love with a "frail flower of pure womanhood" (which is what Creole girls were), sheathed his sword and settled down forever, but the truth is that Jean Laffite was not made for respectability.

Soon after the battle, the ships and contraband seized at Grande Isle were sold at auction. Laffite, through an agent, bought the ships back, and within a month he and Pierre and Dominique You were on the prowl again. They moved to the Texas coast, and established a colony called Campeche on Galveston Island. Some of the women of the waterfront went along, and for a while everything was fine. But when the loot ran out, the women drifted back to New Orleans. Then the impoverished pirates, irked by their desertion, decided to defy Laffite and go after American shipping.

Laffite had bought a schooner in New Orleans with which to operate outside the jurisdiction of the United States, and he sent a crew of sixteen to bring it to Campeche. The crew, against his orders, attacked a Spanish vessel in American waters. While they were looting it along came one of America's new revenue cutters, and caught them redhanded. The pirates were captured and taken to New Orleans, where they were tried and sentenced to hang. The Laffites hired the best lawyers in the city, who appealed the decision. But the most the lawyers could manage was a pardon for one and temporary reprieves for the others. When the reprieves expired, the fifteen were hanged in the Place d'Armes, and all their lights-o'-love turned out to watch.

Jean returned to Campeche and continued operations until one day a brig put in the harbor with orders from Washington that the pirates must evacuate at once. There was nothing to do but obey. That night Laffite divided what little gold there was among the few members of his colony, and in the morning he sailed away. But where he sailed to no one knows.

$\mathcal{S}$EE, THE CONQUERING HERO COMES! Chal-
mette Battlefield, six miles from the heart of the city, is where the
Battle of New Orleans was fought. Almost everybody goes to see
the Plains, so I went too, although I hate battlefields. Visitors climb
Chalmette Monument, which is a copy of the Washington Monument, only not so high, and when they reach the top they look
down, and reconstruct the battle scene, and I did what everybody
else did. But I could not make much of it, and maybe it was because
I am a pacifist and conditioned against such recreational jaunts.

There is a slight depression and elevation, along which a row of
moss-hung hackberry trees stand, and that is where the breastworks
were. Most people think that the breastworks were made of cotton
bales, which is what the schoolbooks used to say. But it seems that
they were made of earth, and that was much better because the
British artillery just buried itself in the mud.

The siege of New Orleans began with a gunboat battle, in which
the British captured the American ships that had stormed the pirates
out of Grande Isle. There was a sort of poetic justice about that, although it was tough on the sailors. Then came the invasion. There
were three battles before the one at Chalmette which is known as
the Battle of New Orleans. After the battle, Jackson became the
hero of New Orleans, and Jean Laffite and Dominique You were
almost as popular as Errol Flynn and William Bendix.

If you go to the Cabildo, look at the painting of *The Battle of
New Orleans,* a huge picture hanging on the second floor in the

Louisiana Transfer Room, where the biggest real estate deal in the world was transacted. In the Louisiana Transfer Room the Spanish governor turned the province back to France, and twenty days later France sold it to us. Papers were signed at a desk that stood in the window overlooking Jackson Square, only it was the Place d'Armes then, because that was before Jackson became the Conquering Hero.

In the painting are the celebrated earthworks, with the Americans crouched behind them. Across the Plains of Chalmette come the British—*into the jaws of death, into the mouth of hell*—brave as the Light Brigade. And there, on a white horse, rides Pakenham at the head of his troops. As you watch, he falls from his horse. And the men behind the earthworks load, and fire again . . . and the star-spangled banner waves in the breeze.

Legend has it that Pakenham was struck by a cannon ball fired by Dominique You, and when the general's men saw him fall, they swore they would burn New Orleans for his funeral. It was thought that they carried him to Versailles, the near-by plantation home of the de La Rondes, and laid him under the live oaks, now known as the Pakenham Oaks, that grow along the road to the river. But the truth is he was bleeding so badly that they put him in the shade of a pecan tree. And there, in the roar of a lost battle, the general who expected to be Earl of Louisiana died, a most disillusioned man. And after he died his men took his heart and buried it on the field where he fell, because that was the grim custom of the times. His body they took home for burial.

The painting in the Cabildo of *The Battle of New Orleans* was done by a Frenchman, Louis Eugène Lami, who was a little boy in Paris when the battle was fought, and who was never in America in his life. Lami started as a lithographer. But he achieved great distinction while he was still very young with his portraits of Parisian society. Louis Philippe thought he was wonderful, and commissioned him to do some important oils of French battles and other historical subjects. With all his orders from the king, how he ever found time to paint *The Battle of New Orleans* I cannot imagine, particularly since he had to check on the earthworks, and do any amount of research besides. But I expect that after the Restoration, many Creoles went to France for a visit, and among them were probably veterans of the battle who told Lami all about it.

The Battle of New Orleans was painted in 1837, twenty-two years after it was fought. Andrew Jackson, the Hero of New Orleans, was then president of the United States, and Mr. W. W. Corcoran of Washington City was running a drygoods business across from the White House. Forty years later Mr. Corcoran, then a multimillionaire and a patron of the arts, bought Mr. Lami's painting for $20,000 to hang in the newly established Corcoran Art Gallery in Washington. But someone persuaded him that he should give it to New Orleans instead, and so he did.

Mr. Corcoran was always doing nice things. Another thing he did—which has nothing to do with New Orleans, but I will tell you because it is interesting—he brought home from Africa the body of John Howard Payne, who wrote *Home, Sweet Home* and died in Tunis.

Mr. Corcoran sent a silver coffin to Tunis, and when the coffin came back to Washington (with Mr. Payne inside), Mr. Corcoran was waiting at the depot, accompanied by the president of the United States with all his Cabinet, and the Marine Band playing *Home, Sweet Home*. A hearse drawn by four white horses proceeded to a hillside where Mr. Payne used to sit in his youth, which Mr. Corcoran had bought for the occasion. And there Mr. Payne was buried beneath the trees he had loved. Mr. Corcoran wrote a verse for the gravestone:

> Sure, when thy gentle spirit fled
> To realms beyond the azure dome,
> With arms outstretched
> God's angels said,
> "Welcome to Heaven's Home, Sweet Home."

A few years later Mr. Corcoran died, and was buried in the cemetery he had bought for Mr. Payne. And when he reached heaven, I hope he was met by Mr. Payne and the celestial choir, all singing *Home, Sweet Home.* (Monsieur Lami was still in Paris.)

* * *

There is a guide in New Orleans who tells a weird story about the Pakenham Oaks. There are fifty-two live oaks all hung with moss, and perfectly magnificent (you *must* see them). The guide says that Monsieur de La Ronde, the master of Versailles, was a cast-off lover of Catherine the Great. According to the guide, the empress taunted him with the prowess of fifty-two lovers who had preceded him, and in grim obeisance to his betters he planted on his birthday a tree for each.

The part about the birthday is probably true, because planting trees on one's birthday is an old and charming custom. But I don't believe a word of the rest because *(a)* people always talk about rich widows, and they talked especially about Catherine, and *(b)* no Frenchman would ever admit to being a poor lover.

There are two things that almost everybody asks about the Pakenham Oaks, and all the other live oaks in Louisiana. They want to know how old they are, and if the streamers of gray moss that cling to their boughs are going to kill them. Historians think that the Pakenham Oaks were planted about 1760. Horticulturists say that the moss does not hurt the trees. It is not a parasite, they say, but an air plant. And, of all things, it belongs to the pineapple family.

Some people think the moss is beautiful, and others think it is funereal. It dreadfully depressed Lafcadio Hearn, who called it "succubus" and "vampire of the woods." I think myself that it is beautiful, especially when the setting sun shines through it, making it sea green and luminous, and at twilight when it turns gray and trembles in an eerie way as darkness falls. I love it in the moonlight when there is a breeze and it sways with a sort of spectral magic, like a dark ghost in a white night. But I hate the juicy big cater-pillars that lurk in the moss, and drop down my neck whenever they get a chance. So I keep a reverential distance, and admire moss-draped trees from afar.

The first time I saw Spanish moss was from a train as it traveled through the swamps of Georgia. I remember how the gaunt trees seemed to me like old men, like rabbis, gnarled and old and sad, with locks of gray hair and long beards. They were standing in the liquid swamps, up to their knees in dark water.

Spanish moss is a three million dollar business in Louisiana. It used to sell for two cents a pound. But when other stuffings were hard to come by, a man from the bayou country hired thirty-five pickers and made $6,000 in three months. The picking season is from November to April, when most of the trees on which the moss grows have lost their leaves. Pickers paddle around the swamps in pirogues, climb the trees like monkeys in their bare feet, and knock the moss down with poles. It is used to stuff mattresses and automobile seats, and it is used also as a mulch (which is something like peat moss) for plants that like acidity in their soil. Azaleas, en-couraged by Spanish moss, are said to do particularly well, a rumor I must check with the Young Men's Business Club that dreamed up the Floral Trail with its million azaleas (and tens of thousands of other flowering plants). Azaleas, as you may know, are frail and finicky and it would be good to know about something that agrees with them.

* * *

There is a Live Oak Society in Louisiana whose members are live oaks which are more than a hundred years old. The Paken-hams are charter members. Younger live oaks are eligible for the society's Junior League. Each member pays yearly dues of twenty-five of its own acorns, which are planted by friends who are human beings. The president of the society is a big fellow from St. Charles

Parish, 75 feet tall, with a girth of 35 feet and a spread of 175 feet. Stanley Arthur, local historian, is secretary-treasurer of the society at a fixed salary of "glory and honor, to be doubled each year." He has appointed Major Meigs Frost, U.S. Marines, retired, as military aide to the secretary-treasurer. Between them the gentlemen collect the dues and keep the minutes.

Among the society's famous members are the Jean Laffite Oaks, in whose shade the pirate made love to the girls from Barataria, and the Randall Oak, under whose boughs James Ryder Randall wrote *Maryland, My Maryland*. Mr. Randall was teaching at Poydras College in New Roads, when he heard how Union soldiers were fighting with citizens in the streets of Baltimore. It made Mr. Randall so angry that he couldn't sleep. So one night he got up and went out and sat under a live oak. And there, in the moonlight, he wrote the flaming lines that almost made a rebel state of Maryland:

> Thou will not cower in the dust,
>   Maryland! My Maryland!
> Thy beaming sword shall never rust,
>   Maryland! My Maryland!

The first time Walt Whitman saw a live oak he wrote a poem about it.

I saw in Louisiana a live-oak growing,
All alone it stood and the moss hung down from its branches,
Without any companions it grew there uttering joyous leaves of
    dark green,
And its looks, rude, unbending, lusty, made me think of myself,
But I wondered how it could utter joyous leaves standing alone
    there without its friend near, for I knew I could not,
And I broke off a twig with a certain number of leaves upon it, and
    twined around it a little moss,
And brought it away, and I have placed it in sight in my room,
It is not needed to remind me of my own dear friends,
(For I believe lately I think of little else than of them)

Yet it remains to me a curious token, it makes me think of manly
    love;
For all that, and though the live oak glistens there in Louisiana,
    solitary in a wide flat space,
Uttering joyous leaves all its life without a friend or lover near,
I know very well that I could not.

*   *   *

When I began this chapter I intended to write about General
Jackson, with whom I have been in love for some time. Jackson was
the Hero of New Orleans, and that is all the excuse I needed. But
first I had to tell about Pakenham. And then I went meandering off
about Mr. Corcoran. Then there was that business about the oaks.
And I thought you would be interested in the Spanish moss, and
the Junior League with a press agent, and particularly in the poem
I Saw in Louisiana a Live-Oak Growing because some people think
Walt Whitman's life was profoundly influenced by that Louisiana
live oak, and maybe it was. You remember those lines about *I live
not in myself, but I become portion of that around me*—and
Ulysses (through the poet's lips) said, "I am a part of all that I
have met." It would be pretty invigorating to feel identification
with a live oak, and Whitman was so lusty he probably did.

Whitman was in New Orleans for three months, in the spring of
1848 when New Orleans was a wonderful place. He worked on a
newspaper daytimes and cultivated outcasts nighttimes. When we
get to the Red Light District, I will tell you about a poem he wrote
to a prostitute. But now I am going back to the general, that wonderful Scotch-Irish roughneck who drove the British out of the
French-Spanish city of New Orleans, and loved the Creoles and
hated the British all the days of his life.

Two weeks after the battle the Creoles had a party for the general, and Mrs. Jackson came down from Tennessee. They built a
triumphant arch in the Place d'Armes, and twined it with garlands
of roses and camellias. And the Abbé du Bourg, who had offered

Mass to Our Lady of Prompt Succor on the day of the battle, crowned the general with a laurel wreath. Then there was a triumphant march to the Cathedral with Creole girls throwing flowers for the general to walk upon, and the nuns with their orphans trailing along behind. Major Plauche was there with his Bataillon d'Orleans, singing:

> Allons, enfants de la patrie!
> Le jour de gloire est arrivé!
> Contre nous de la tyrannie
> L'étendard sanglant est levé!

And the free men of color were there, and the Choctaw Indians, and the flatboatmen, and the Baratarians—all singing together. They marched to the Cathedral, where the abbé delivered an address. Then everybody sang the *Te Deum,* even Dominique You, who was a Mason. And Mrs. Jackson sat in the front pew beside Andy, and cried like everything because she was so happy.

There is the old story of Rachel Jackson's clay pipe, and how the Creoles were afraid she would pull it out and disgrace the general. But of course she did no such thing, and they all liked her enormously. They called her "Madame la Général," and I expect she was a little afraid of them. They were so beautiful, the Creole ladies in their Paris gowns, with their shining black hair and their skin like roses. The ladies used a pomade made of castor oil and beef marrow, which made their hair gleam like crows' wings. And their skin was waxy-white like gardenias, because they washed it in sour buttermilk. When they went out they swathed themselves in veils, and they never used rouge, but only rice powder to heighten their pallor.

Mrs. Jackson's skin was like leather. And her fingernails were as black as her little clay pipe, because there was no getting the dirt out of them. She was stout and plain. But Andy loved her very much, and that was all that ever mattered to Rachel.

There was a banquet the night of the celebration. Jean Laffite brought his cook over from Barataria to prepare the oysters, and there were so many courses and so much wine, and the beautiful ladies made such a fuss over Andy, that Rachel was glad when it was over. Then there were the speeches—priest and pirate, governor and general . . . Rachel had not dreamed that her husband knew so many fine words and fancy phrases. He was given to horse racing and cockfighting and the company of rough men. He was forty-seven at the Battle of New Orleans—a painfully thin man—redheaded and freckled, with a long Irish face, and a pain-racked body. His left arm was strapped to his side because Charlie Dickinson's bullet was in him, and there were times when the pain was almost unsupportable. Andy got that bullet pistol-dueling for Rachel. When she looked at his helpless left arm, Rachel wanted to cry—and not just for Andy, but for Charlie Dickinson's young widow and her baby son.

When Rachel was sixteen she had married a man named Lewis Robards, who took her to Kentucky to live. They quarreled and Rachel sent for her brother Samuel, to take her home to Tennessee. Rachel's father had been killed by Indians, and her mother was taking boarders. At the head of the table sat Andy Jackson, twenty-two—blue-eyed and redheaded—profane, dissipated, and fascinating. Andy was one of the best horsemen in Tennessee. And he had an undeniable way with the girls.

Robards went to Tennessee seeking a reconciliation, and the minute he laid eyes on the star boarder he suspected the worst. He returned to Kentucky, and filed suit for divorce.

When the news reached Tennessee, Andy and Rachel were married, and there never was a happier couple. Andy was a pagan, and Rachel strove for his unbelieving soul—adoring him, and praying for his soul's salvation until the day she died. Andy fought everybody—the Creeks, the Spanish, and the British. When he was away on his military expeditions Rachel wrote him dear illiterate letters:

I never wanted to see you so mutch in my life Let me and I will
fly on the wings of purest affecktion may God bless you and restore
you to my armes in mutuel Love My Dearer Self I must see you
My Darling you have all the prayers of your Affecktionate Wife
Rachel your Dearest Friend and Faithful Wife unto Death.

They both loved children and shortly after their marriage they
adopted two nephews of Rachel's, whom they named Andrew
Jackson Jr. and Andrew Jackson Donelson. It was like Rachel to
want both boys named for Andy.

Then word came from Kentucky that Robards' divorce had not
been granted. For two years Rachel and Andy had lived in sin.
Now, people said, Robards had named Andy and was suing again.
So Andy and Rachel waited until the decree was final and then
they married again. And that was the final that.

Andrew didn't exactly give up cockfighting and horse racing,
but he tapered off. He became senator, and was appointed to the
Supreme Court in Tennessee. He built a beautiful home for his
wife and the boys, and in the garden he built a little church that
was all for Rachel. Someday, he promised her, he would join. But
he never got around to it, and Rachel went on hoping and praying.

They had been married eighteen years when Andy heard that
young Charlie Dickinson was talking loosely about Rachel, and
challenged him to a duel. The men went with their seconds to a
field behind the town, on the bank of Red River.

Dickinson was the best marksman in Tennessee. It was said of
him that he never hit a squirrel in the body, but always took the
head off with the first shot. Jackson knew that he could not take
instant, accurate aim as Charlie was sure to do. So he decided to let
the younger man fire first. Then—if he was still alive—he would
see what he could do. It was a terrific risk, but Andy's courage was
also terrific—and, besides, it was his only chance.

When the signal came, Jackson did not move. Dickinson fired, and the bullet crashed through Andy's chest. It missed his heart, but broke his breastbone and cracked his ribs.

Jackson remained standing. Slowly—clenching his teeth—he raised his pistol and pulled the trigger. It did not snap.

The seconds examined the weapon, and handed it back. By the rules, he could try again.

Once more Jackson raised his arm. This time it was Charlie Dickinson who stared Death in the face.

When Jackson shot, Dickinson fell to the ground. The bullet had gone completely through his body. He died that night.

The duel had taken place eight years before the Battle of New Orleans. But men were never to forget it, or how Jackson emptied his boots when it was over, and the blood poured out like water. They made up a ballad called *Andy and Charlie,* and during the battle celebration you could hear it wherever you went.

There was great singing in the town that night . . . in the swamp, where the flatboatmen gathered, in saloons and gambling dens, and in the bordellos where, for six cents, a man could get a drink, a woman and a bed . . . in the Vieux Carré, where Baratarians roamed in and out of the coffeehouses on Bourbon Street and Jackson's sharpshooters swaggered through the town in high boots and coonskin hats. On one corner men sang the *Marseillaise,* and on another they sang *Yankee Doodle.* But the men from Tennessee and Kentucky sang *Andy and Charlie:*

> Come listen to my story
>   Of the dark and bloody land
> Where Andy Jackson rode one day
>   And there did take his stand.
> "Walk out here, Charlie Dickinson,
>   And load and fire," he said.
> "For slandering my wife I'll take your life
>   If you shoot me through the head."

O tum tee dee I day-dee,
   O tum tee dee I day,
Upon that dark and bloody ground
   That's what I heard him say.

So Charlie came and stood there,
   And a crack dead-shot was he,
Could bring down with one bullet
   A high and hustling bee.
"Get you ready, Andy Jackson,
   From this world to depart.
I don't waste lead on no man's head;
   I shoot him through the heart."

They measured off eight paces
   And Charlie he fired first,
When up from Andy's blue frock-coat
   There came a puff of dust;
But Andy stood there grinning
   Like as if he felt no pain.
"You can't hurt me with lead," says he,
   "If you shoot me through the brain."

"Oh, my God! Have I missed him?"
   "Get back there where you belong,
And take your turn at dying now!"
   Says Andy high and strong.
"Make ready, Charlie Dickinson,
   To spend this night in hell."
He cocked and aimed. His pistol flamed.
   Poor Charlie reeled and fell.

But Andy! Andy Jackson!
   Your boots are full of blood!
"Why, so they be—but I can get
   Some others just as good.

My blood is cheaper than the honor
  Of my wife's name," he said
"And I'd have killed that man of guilt
  If he'd shot me through the head."

O tum tee dee I day-dee,
  O tum tee dee I day,
Upon that dark and bloody ground
  That's what I heard him say.

* * *

On the first anniversary of the Battle of New Orleans, one of the veterans got a queer idea, or maybe it just seems queer to me. Mrs. Jackson thought it was beautiful. The veteran and his buddies would make a hickory mantelpiece for the Hermitage, the Jacksons' grand home in Tennessee—of *old* hickory (for Old Hickory Jackson, you see). They would work on it only upon the 8th of each January, on the anniversary of the battle. And when it was finished they would like the Jacksons to put it, please, in the dining room. They wrote Andy a letter, setting forth the plan. And Rachel was so pleased that she kept the letter in her Bible where her husband found it, by and by.

You have read of the Hermitage. Perhaps you have visited it. If you saw the second inaugural of Franklin D. Roosevelt you will remember that the President chose a model of its portico for the reviewing stand opposite the White House. Roosevelt might have chosen Mount Vernon, and honored Washington. Or he might have chosen Monticello—which would have been appropriate, since Roosevelt liked to be called a "Jeffersonian Democrat." But the home that he selected was President Jackson's Hermitage. His hero worship for Jackson was one of the nicest things about Mr. Roosevelt.

There is another Hermitage * on the Old River Road that was

* The Hermitage is open during Spring Fiesta.

built by Doradou Bringier, a rich young Creole who fought in the Battle of New Orleans, and named his home in honor of his general.

Doradou Bringier was married, when he was twenty-three, to little Aglaé du Bourg, fourteen-year-old niece of the Abbé du Bourg, who arranged the marriage with the son of his richest parishioner—and crowned General Jackson with a laurel wreath.

For a wedding present Aglaé received a doll almost as big as herself. Her descendants tell a family story of how she tore the tissues away with her quick little fingers, and turned to her uncle.

"Do you think, mon père, that this is meant for me?" she asked. "Or for my first baby?"

Then, they say, she ran upstairs crying, and that afterward, before she had a baby of her own, Aglaé kept the doll in her big four-poster bed, and played with it like a child. She had never seen Doradou until her uncle married them, and it took her quite a while to get used to him.

Aglaé had her first baby a month before the Battle of New Orleans. After that they moved to the Hermitage and she had eight more children. Then Doradou died, and Aglaé was the richest widow in Louisiana.

Sometimes at the Hermitage, which the Creoles called l'Hermitage (and Andy would never have recognized the pronunciation), there were fifty overnight guests. When they came down in the morning—two or three at a time, or trailing one by one—the slaves had fifty separate breakfasts waiting for them. Aglaé turned out to be a great manager . . . But it was of Rachel and the Hermitage in Tennessee that I began to tell—the veterans went ahead with the hickory mantel. But since they worked on it only one day a year, it naturally took a long time. In 1821, when Rachel returned to New Orleans to do some shopping, she asked how it was coming along. Since there were only six days' work done, there was not much to see.

On that trip Rachel bought a bed and armoire from Seignouret, the cabinetmaker who fought under Jackson in the Battle of New Orleans, and she bought a duchesse table from Mallard, made of rosewood, which the Creoles called violet ebony. She also bought silver and glass, a dinner service from Sèvres, and some fine brandies for Andy. Her freight bill was $273.50.

Andy had become leader of the new Democratic party. Men liked his swift daring, and his brusque, red-blooded ways. They were tired of the old conservatives, and in 1828 they swept John Quincy Adams out of office and Old Hickory in.

"Well," said Rachel, "for Mr. Jackson's sake I am glad. For my own part I never wished it. I assure you I would rather be a doorkeeper in the house of my God than to dwell in that palace in Washington."

But there was nothing Rachel wouldn't do for her husband—and gladly, if it made him happy. To do him proud, she made a trip to Nashville, for some bonnets and shawls, and a bolt of white satin to be made into a gown for the inaugural ball.

She had finished her errands and was sitting in the back parlor of the inn waiting for her carriage when she heard some people in the front room talking about her.

"What a figure she will cut in Washington!" they said.

They spoke of the old Robards scandal.

"Where there's smoke," they said, "there must be fire."

It was a shame, they said that the general was saddled with such a woman. Then, for the first time, Rachel heard what people were saying about her. Alone, in that little back room, she learned that she had become a campaign caricature.

She sat there until they went away—because, she said, they would have been hurt if they had known she heard them.

Then, with her tippet hooked high against her quivering chin and her trembling hands clasped tight in her little sealskin muff, Rachel stepped into her carriage, and went home to Andy.

She would not tell him of her humiliation, but sent for Emily

Donelson, who was married to their adopted son, and she told Emily what had happened.

"I wish never to go anywhere, and disgrace him," she said. "You will go to Washington, Emily, and take care of him. And I will stay here, and mind things until his return."

In a short while she became ill. She prayed that God would take her before her husband went to Washington. It would be better that way, she said.

The general never left her. She died in his arms. And when she was gone, he could not believe it, but spent hours trying to revive her. He ordered the servants to spread four blankets on the board where they laid her, so that "she will not lie so hard on the table." When they had dressed her in the white satin that she had ordered for that dreaded palace in Washington, Andy filled his wife's arms with roses, although flowers were not the custom at funerals then. Rachel liked them, he said.

He buried her in the garden where he knew she had been happy. And on the stone he ordered carved:

Here lie the remains of Mrs. Rachel Jackson, wife of President Jackson, who died the 22nd of December, 1828, age 61. Her face was fair, her person pleasing, her temper amiable, her heart kind. She delighted in relieving the wants of her fellow creatures, and cultivated charity. To the poor she was a benefactor; to the rich an example; to the wretched a comforter; to the prosperous an ornament; her piety went hand in hand with her benevolence, and she thanked her Creator for being permitted to do good. A being so gentle, and so virtuous, slander might wound, but could not dishonor. Even Death, when he tore her from the arms of her husband, could but transport her to the bosom of God.

On January 8, 1839, the hickory mantelpiece was completed. Rachel had been dead twelve years, but her husband knew what to do with it. On the following January 8 he had it installed in the dining room.

There are a number of portraits of the general in the house that joins the Cabildo, which is known as the Jackson House. It was built in 1842, two years after Jackson's last visit to New Orleans, and except for the portraits it has no connection with the general. The story of the man who presented the house to the city is interesting, and if the house had been furnished as he planned—the way houses were in the Creoles' Golden Age—it would be beautiful. But now it is pretty dreary.

William Ratcliffe Irby was a banker and a philanthropist—tall, distinguished looking, and rather handsome. He was not a Creole, but an Anglo-Saxon, who loved the Creole City and all its lingering legends. In the nineteen-twenties, when the Vieux Carré was quietly falling apart and no one seemed to care, Mr. Irby bought a number of its historic houses and restored them. Then he presented the houses to the city. He was not a Catholic, but he gave $125,000 for the restoration of the Cathedral, which had fallen on evil days, and he did many other things—almost always anonymously—generous and beautiful things for posterity.

One afternoon Mr. Irby went to the Athletic Club for a Turkish bath. He chatted with friends at the club, and they remembered afterward how quietly happy he seemed. From the club he went to the establishment of a funeral director whom he knew, and said he would like to select a casket. Mr. Tharp, the owner of the establishment, said that the caskets were on the second floor. Mr. Irby said that Mr. Tharp was not to bother going up with him. He would go alone, he said. A few minutes later a shot rang out. Mr. Irby had selected his casket, and put a bullet through his brain.

* * *

There are portraits of Andy Jackson in the house that Mr. Irby bought, which show him as he looked at the Battle of New Orleans, with his red hair and his long thin face—with sword and epaulets— and a pair of high black boots, in which Audubon is supposed to have posed. The story is that Jackson sat for only his face—and then the artist, Vanderlyn, persuaded Mr. Audubon, who was about the same build—to pose for the rest.

There is another portrait painted when Jackson was president—when he was sacking innumerable Whig postmasters and giving their jobs to Democrats, threatening to cut off Senator Lacock's ears, and raising hell for Peggy Eaton. And there is the one for which he posed on his last visit to New Orleans—when he was a white-haired sage, who had put aside his sword for a pen—and was going soon to Rachel.

By a rather strange coincidence, both Andrew Jackson and Franklin Roosevelt sat for portraits in their dying hours. It was sunset on a day in June when Death came into the general's room. There was a portrait of Rachel over the mantel. Andy looked at it for a long minute. Then his tired old eyes closed.

They buried him beside Rachel in the garden.

6

DOMINIQUE YOU LIVED ON LOVE STREET

Dominique You, the pirate, lived by himself in a little old house on Love Street, in the block next the quadroon sweethearts of Bernard de Marigny, who was the richest man in Louisiana until he took to shooting craps. In order to pay his gambling debts, Baron de Marigny turned a part of his plantation, which was called Elysian Fields, into a sort of suburb called Faubourg Marigny, and parceled it off in blocks. And on Rue de l'Amour he established his sweethearts, each in an identical little house.

After the Battle of New Orleans, Dominique You moved from Grande Isle to Love Street, where he lost at gambling all he had made at pirating, and died at fifty-five, reformed but impoverished. Then de Marigny with other Creole bluebloods arranged a notable funeral, and the most respectable people flocked to Love Street to honor the pauper-pirate.

De Marigny picked memorable names for all the streets in his faubourg. Next to *Rue de l'Amour* was *Rue des Bons Enfants*. Then there was *Rue des Grands Hommes,* which was called Greatmen's Street after the Américains came. There was also *Rue Craps,* which kept its name for a long time—and *Rue Bagatelle,* to commemorate the games at which the baron lost his chemise. And to comfort him when he was old, there was *Rue Solace.*

Before long a Methodist church was built on *Rue Craps*. But when the people called it the "Craps Methodist" the parishioners were so embarrassed they got up a petition to change the name, and it was abolished by City ordinance.

Rue des Bons Enfants inspired a poem by Eugene Field that was in a book I had when I was a little girl.

> Oh, days that were golden and days that were fleet
> With little folk living in Good-Children Street!

I imagined a wonderful street where the houses were filled with toys, where nobody lived but children, and every little girl had a pony —"and the sunshine of love illumined each face, and warmed every heart in that old-fashioned place."

I had almost forgotten, but it all came back—Odette and her dolly, and the army with guns painted red, with legions of soldiers—nice, make-believe soldiers—and the captain, and stick-horse that snorted and pranced. I remembered the little girl who loved Good-Children Street—the girl I used to be. It seemed strange and romantic that I had traveled half the world to find at last the street of childhood dreams. But when I asked where it was, no one knew. It wasn't the Creoles' fault that it was changed. It was the Americans who did it.

My favorite old-time streets are Virtue and Piety, Pleasure, Felicity and Desire—beautiful names that uphold the agreeable Gallic conviction that people should be good, but also have fun.

Eugene Field did not stay long in New Orleans, but he got up early and went shopping at Waldhorn's.

> In Royal Street (near Conti) there's a lovely curio-shop,
> And there, one balmy fateful morning, it was my chance to stop;
> I spied a pewter tankard there, and, my! it was a gem—
> And the clock in old St. Louis told the hour of eight a.m.

The poet bought three Bohemian bottles for his wife, "of yellow and of green" and:

> A lovely hideous platter wreathed about with pink and rose,
> With its curious depression into which the gravy flows;

Two dainty silver salts—oh, there was no resisting *them*—
And I'd blown in twenty dollars by nine o'clock a.m.

Then he had no money left to buy anything for the children, and
of course he couldn't go home without a present, so he made a poem
for them about "the angel all white who guarded the babes through
the night":

> And singeth her lullabies tender and sweet,
> To the dear little people in Good-Children's Street.

The de Marignys were one of the first great Creole families in New
Orleans. Creoles, as you probably know—though I should have mentioned this before—were the white descendants of French and Spanish in any part of the New World. In New Orleans (but not in all
colonies) any trace of café au lait meant social ostracism. The name
was derived from *criollo,* the Spanish word for children born in the
colonies. The French changed it to Creole. Creoles in New Orleans
were predominately French, although many were Spanish and some
were German and Irish.

After the Revolution the Duc d'Orléans, who fled France to save
his noble neck, set out on a trip around the world accompanied by
his brothers, the Duc de Montpensier and the Count de Beaujolais,
whose necks were also in danger. They stopped off in New Orleans,
where they were guests of the de Marignys. This was in the Golden
Age of Spanish society, and the de Marignys, French to their marrow, and anxious to impress their Spanish overlords, invited the dons
to meet the royal exiles. Everything was perfect until the night the
princes showed their hosts how to roll the dice. Presently the gentlemen were down on their knees, and the slaves were pop-eyed watching them. Next day the slaves were down on their knees. Today when
New Orleans colored men roll the bones they sing a little song:

> Look down, Rider, spot me in de dark,
> When I calls dese dice, break dese niggers' hearts.

Roll out, Seven! Stand back, Craps!
If I make dis pass, I'll be standin' pat.

Flatboatmen called the Creoles "Johnny Crapaud," because they liked frogs to eat (crapaud means frog), and when the new dice game swept the city and spread to the waterfront, the boatmen called it *crapaud* because Frenchmen played it. Then they shortened it to *craps*.

It was said that New Orleans was the pleasantest place in the world to lose money, and it probably was. But a French priest who visited the de Marignys was scandalized at the goings-on.

"Gambling is the great Creole passion," he wrote. "Men become rich or poor, and fortunes change hands at the turn of a card. When their money is gone, the Creoles play for crops and slaves. Shipowners gamble their cargoes, and planters their homes and fields."

The de Marignys, *père et fils,* were all right while they played in their own league. But when they began playing with the Americans, their luck turned. And when the Duc d'Orléans ascended the throne and invited Bernard to Fontainebleau, to repay the de Marignys' hospitality to the princes (Philippe was dead then and under the floor of the Cathedral), poor Bernard was so broke he could not go.

Next to the de Marignys, the most consistent loser in town was Colonel John R. Grymes, who resigned as district attorney to be Jean Laffite's lawyer. When the new D.A. said that Grymes was "seduced by the blood-stained gold of pirates," Grymes challenged him to a pistol duel and shot him through the hip. After which the crippled D.A. went hobbling around to the gambling houses, to gleefully watch the colonel lose his fortune. Colonel Grymes played every night and every night he lost—until at last he was as poor as poor Dominique You.

A few years after the Battle of New Orleans, Dominique You became the hero of a fantastic scheme to bring Napoleon to the Vieux Carré. To rescue the emperor from St. Helena, the Creoles bought a schooner called the *Séraphine,* said to be the fastest ship in the world, and placed her under the command of Dominique You, who recruited a crew from among the old Baratarians. The plan was for the pirates to land in the dark of the moon, and forcibly abduct the royal prisoner. Relying upon the swiftness of the *Séraphine,* Dominique You would then outwit pursuit, and carry his precious cargo straight to New Orleans.

The mayor, who headed the Committee to Bring Napoleon to New Orleans, had promised that the emperor should have his house at 500 Chartres Street, which is a rather ugly place with a Louis Quinze façade and a Mormon belvedere. It was probably better looking then than it is now, because the third story and the cupola were added at some later date. There were great preparations under way to welcome the emperor to the Vieux Carré, and the *Séraphine* was about to sail when news reached New Orleans of the death of Napoleon.

Then, instead of an expedition overseas, a solemn High Mass of requiem was sung at the Cathedral, and the Creoles who were Bonapartists cried as they prayed for the soul of their emperor, and even the cutthroat pirates were sad and blew their noses in their red bandannas. But Dominique You was the saddest of all, because he had lost every sou he had at the new Palace of Chance on Bourbon Street, and Dominique You knew the postman does not always ring twice.

* * *

Thirteen years after the death of Napoleon, a handsome Corsican with wavy black hair and beautiful sideburns stepped off a French ship, with a large bundle in his arms. The man was Dr. Francesco Antommarchi and in the bundle, which he would not put down for even a second, there was, he said, one of the most precious objects in the world.

Dr. Antommarchi was the doctor whom Napoleon's mother had chosen to share her son's exile at St. Helena. You may remember that Napoleon suffered from an undiagnosed malady, and complained that the English physicians neglected him. Public opinion forced England to do something about it, and Madame Mère was permitted to send a countryman of her own choosing to treat the emperor. She chose Antommarchi, who proudly accepted the honor and remained with Napoleon until his death.

After the emperor died, Antommarchi instructed Napoleon's valet to shave the emperor's head in preparation for the making of the death mask. Then it was discovered that there was no plaster of Paris on the island, and Antommarchi had to go looking for sulphate of lime. He was gone two days, searching a remote part of the Rock, when a terrible storm blew up, and it looked as if there would be no death mask of the emperor. Antommarchi, who had been nearly drowned, returned with the lime dust, which he mixed with chemicals to produce a plastic substance. Forty hours after Napoleon's death, the doctor succeeded in making a death mask.

Then the valet de chambre dressed his emperor in white breeches and waistcoat, with a black cravat and high black boots. Over his feet the valet flung the cloak that Napoleon had worn at Marengo. Upon his head he placed a cocked hat, and on his chest a silver crucifix.

*   *   *

Antommarchi took the mask to Paris, where he hid it for nearly ten years. Then a new revolution put Louis Philippe upon the throne. And the Citizen King, anxious to curry favor with the Bonapartists, gave Antommarchi permission to have three bronze masks cast from his precious cast. If you have been to Paris, you have probably seen the masks in the Museé Carnavalet and in the Hôtel des Invalides, and, by this time you have guessed what was in the large bundle that Antommarchi would not put down for even a second. It was the bronze death mask of the emperor—the first that was cast. Also in the bundle were the instruments with which the doctor, in compliance with Napoleon's last request, performed an autopsy on the emperor.

After Antommarchi told his story the Creoles overwhelmed him with their attentions, and in appreciation of their courtesies he said that he would like to give them his precious relic. The mayor arranged for a celebration in the Place d'Armes, and after many flowery speeches the doctor made his presentation and the mayor accepted it. Then there was a procession, headed by the Death Mask upon a satin cushion, from Jackson Square to the Cabildo, where the mask was deposited with great ceremony in the Louisiana Purchase Room.

* * *

When I was a little girl I saw Lincoln's death mask in the Lincoln Museum, Washington, and I remember that it moved me almost as though I had looked upon his face in death. I also remember, and with regret, how comparatively little Napoleon's death mask affected me when I saw it in Paris. Children have an unconscious way of subtracting themselves from their surroundings for private experiences in ecstasy. But adults, in the midst of a crowd, seldom experience emotions of solitude. With this in mind, I contrived, when I heard about the mask in the Cabildo, to recapture something of the wonder and awe with which I had viewed the mask of Lincoln.

A rendezvous with a death mask might be an adventure or a bore. But I would suggest that you go to the Cabildo in the morning, before the tourists and the guides. The effort may result in a memorable experience or it may not be worth the trouble. The mask is on the second floor, resting on a cloth of imperial red damask in a glass case, mounted on a base of ebony and gold that stands on a dais of blue velvet. Many visitors glance at the case, and do not realize what is in it. Others read the identification, but do not understand. I know this to be true because I have watched them.

After I saw the mask I went from the museum to the library to find anything that Antommarchi might have written about Napoleon, and I found a description of the death scene.

On Napoleon's bedside table there were two portraits of Josephine and one of Marie Louise with Napoleon II. Napoleon divorced Josephine because, as everybody knows, she could not have a child. And then he married Marie Louise, who had one at once. The boy was eleven at the time of his father's death. But the portrait Napoleon had was painted when the Little King of Rome was three, and Napoleon, between soup and dessert, had taught him to say, "Let's go and beat papa François." (François was the baby's Austrian grandfather.)

On the last day of his life Napoleon said of Josephine, "I loved her tenderly." On another occasion, speaking of Josephine to Antommarchi, he remarked, "I generally had to give in."

Paternal pride and affection were encompassed by Napoleon's burning ambition for his son. It was because he feared the consequence of a hereditary ailment that the emperor commanded Antommarchi to perform an autopsy.

Shortly before his death Napoleon looked about the bare room, and his lips parted in the small half-smile we see in the mask.

"It is not the splendor of the Tuileries—but no matter," he said.

That night he observed that few sovereigns had immolated themselves for their people. "A sacrifice so immense," he said, "is not without its charms."

Napoleon was fifty-two when he died, and in death he was beautiful. The mask shows a patrician nose, high cheekbones and a sweet mouth. Suffering had effaced the flesh of middle age and restored the features of youth. Napoleon in death looked like the young Bonaparte who was general of the Army of Italy at twenty-six, who loved Josephine, and set the world afire.

*   *   *

After the presentation of the mask, Dr. Antommarchi opened two offices, one on Royal Street for Creoles with money, and another in the "Napoleon House" on Chartres Street for poor people. On Royal Street he kept the instruments he brought from St. Helena—the horrid little scalpels with which he had performed the autopsy on Napoleon—all on exhibition in a shadow box. For two or three years the doctor was exceedingly popular professionally and socially. Then it was whispered that he was building his success upon the exploitation of his services to the emperor.

When he heard the gossip, Antommarchi was deeply resentful. Perhaps it was because he was a Corsican that he dramatized his humiliation. It would be impossible, he said, to live among people who could so cruelly misjudge him. He went to the Cabildo and said goodbye to his beautiful mask. Then he packed his little shadow box with its horrible little knives, and took the next boat for Cuba. Before he reached there, he died, and was buried at sea.

At that time the mask was not as carefully guarded as it is now, and during the Civil War it disappeared and fell into the hands of a junkman. One day the city treasurer, walking along Canal Street, saw it in a jumble of rags and bottles. He was so surprised that he followed the wagon along for a couple of blocks, thinking, no doubt, about imperial Caesar dead and turned to clay estopped a hole to keep the wind away—and there was Napoleon's face in a junk heap! When he could pull himself together, he offered the junkman $2.50 for the mask, and took it home under his coat.

For thirty years the city treasurer kept the mask on his library table. When he died his son's widow sold it to a collector. And when the collector heard how sad the people of New Orleans were to have lost their precious mask, he graciously offered to return it. You would think that then the curator of the museum would have locked it up securely. But apparently he didn't, because one night a man from Chicago stayed in the Cabildo until it was locked, and when there was no one around, he slipped the mask in his briefcase. The watchman, a medical student from Tulane, saw the bulging briefcase and caught the thief redhanded. After that the museum bought the ebony sarcophagus and the plate-glass case.

And now that you know about the death mask, you should hear the rest of the story about Dominique You. After the *Séraphine* project collapsed, Dominique You spent the whole time gambling. He lost everything he had, and became a ward politician. He became ill, but nobody cared, and he went from bad to worse until finally he died. Then, when it was too late, the do-gooders did one of those magnificently empty things that people are always doing after it doesn't matter.

"If the Laffites did not own or rent it, they should have."

They decided to give Dominique You a military funeral because, they said, he was really a patriot. The mayor ordered the flags hung at half mast for Dominique You, and the city bought a soldier's suit to bury the pirate in. On the day of the funeral, business houses closed and the aristocratic Louisiana Legion sent a guard of honor, all patrician Creoles, to escort the flag-draped casket from the little house on Love Street to St. Louis Cemetery Number Two. Then the Masons took over. The Masons not only paid for the lot, but they ordered a tombstone with a Masonic emblem on it, and they gave

Dominique You a fancy funeral, with Masonic trimmings. Nearly everyone in town attended and the funeral was the event of the year.

On the tomb is a verse in French from *La Henriade* of Voltaire. And here is the translation:

> Intrepid warrior, on land and on sea,
> He knew, in a hundred combats, how to show his valor.
> And this new Bayard without reproach and without fear
> Would have been able to see the world crumble without trembling.

(Bayard was a famous fifteenth-century knight, and I didn't know either until I looked him up.)

Before we leave Dominique You, let me tell you about Café Laffite on Bourbon Street where the pirates are supposed to have had the blacksmith shop that was their first front. Records show that the building (number 941) was in existence at the time that Claiborne posted the reward for Jean Laffite. But Stanley Arthur, the local historian who punctures legends, says there is no proof that the Laffites ever owned, or even rented it. If they didn't, they should have because there is a huge fireplace that would have made a fine smithy for them.

Café Laffite is a very Bohemian place. But you don't have to be a Bohemian to sit in the garden and enjoy the old-time atmosphere. Meals are good and fairly expensive. Cocktails are authoritative. The *Laffite Special*—served in an eggcup, but I don't know why—has a brandy base and the white of an egg. The *Obituary* is a dry Martini spiked with absinthe. If you are fond of cats, you will admire the Buccaneer, who stalks around the bar. And you will love Darling Nelly Gray, who purrs for ladies in the garden. There was another cat, as black as midnight, named Haile Selassie, but Haile Selassie didn't like tourists, so they let him go.

7

THE BARONESS WAS A GAUDY CHARACTER

Different people take away with them all sorts of different memories of New Orleans—the beautiful balconies of the Vieux Carré, the antique shops on Royal Street, the pretty girls at Spring Fiesta—memories of Mardi Gras, and oysters at Manale's, drinks at the Old Absinthe House, and jazz on Bourbon Street—memories of the courtyard restaurants in the blanching blaze of noon, and Jackson Square under a great white moon, of the Cathedral, and the cemeteries, of Creole lilies and candles in the sun, of live oaks and Spanish moss, memories of the Garden District, of redbirds and angels' trumpets.

But the memory I love most is of Jackson Square on a starred and stately night, with a mockingbird singing and oleanders gleaming white, and Andrew Jackson reining his horse in the grave moonlight, with his hat in his hand and his sword by his side, and his war horse rearing in the quiet of the night.

It was the Baroness de Pontalba, a great admirer of the general, who dreamed up Jackson Square, with the general in the middle astride his bronze horse, in a flowery park, all pretty and neat with tropical blossoms heavy and sweet—sunlight and space, and Andy Jackson possessing the place!

The baroness was a Creole, a home-town girl brought up by the nuns, who inherited a fortune and married a title. She lived in Paris, and was mixed up in a killing. And when she returned to New Orleans she changed the name of the Place d'Armes to Jackson Square, promoted the Vieux Carré, and lost a fortune.

First the baroness built the red-brick buildings on either side of the Square. Emblazoned in their beautiful cast-iron balconies is the lady's monogram—"AP"—entwined in graceful script, A for Almonester, because the baroness was Micaëla Almonester (daughter of Don Andrés (who built the Cathedral and the Cabildo), and P for Pontalba, because she married the baron. But before I tell about the baroness, I think I will tell you about her mother, who was a de La Ronde before her marriage, Louise de La Ronde, whose father owned Versailles and planted the famous live oaks where Pakenham died.

Louise must have been an unattractive girl because she had reached the ripe old age of twenty-nine when she married Don Andrés, and in Creole society a girl was passé at twenty. As Señora Almonester, she became mistress of a fine Spanish house in the Vieux Carré, and owner of more slaves than any other woman in New Orleans. Louise had two daughters. The first one died, and the second was Micaëla, who turned out to be an extraordinarily durable little character.

When Micaëla was born, Don Andrés gave Louise a string of pearls as big as nutmegs. The Cathedral had just been completed, and the priests and parishioners blessed him for his generosity. The lepers in their fine new hospital and the nuns in their chapel prayed for him. And the old man, basking in the odor of sanctity and accomplishment, was so pleased with himself that he would have given Louise emeralds if she had said she wanted them. He was seventy-one at the time.

But for all that her husband did for her, Louise could never forget that he was older than her father. And when, three years later, he died, she had him buried in the parish cemetery (it was a year or so afterward that his remains were disinterred and buried in the Cathedral), and almost at once she got herself a younger man.

Almonester was hardly cold in his grave when his widow announced her engagement to Monsieur Castillon, the young French consul. She was forty, and old enough to be his mother, but that was not the worst of it. Creole etiquette prescribed a long period for a widow's mourning, and Louise had flaunted tradition in an unforgivable way. She was married in the front parlor of the big house her husband left her, and she did not invite anyone to the wedding because she knew they would not come. After the ceremony she had a feast for two, and the champagne corks were popping when the charivari began.

A charivari, in case you do not know, is a burlesque serenade to torment newlyweds. It originated in France, and is given beneath the windows of widows and widowers who remarry. Originally it was a wedding custom to which all bridal couples fell victim. But as time passed it became customary to salute only ill-assorted and unpopular marriages. In the seventeenth century, the Church outlawed charivaris, and set a punishment of excommunication upon participants. But the charivari continued to exist in scattered, mostly rural spots, and was brought from rural France to Canada. Cajuns who live in the bayou country, descendants of the refugee Acadians, brought it to Louisiana. In the rough trapper country, they still have charivaris—rowdy affairs at which tin pans are beaten and cow bells rung, until the bridal couple appear and treat the merrymakers to supper. It is all supposed to be nice clean fun, and maybe the Cajuns think so. But it was certainly tough on the Castillons.

A slave reported that a crowd was collecting beneath the gallery, and the bride ordered her carriage. As the mob tossed pebbles at the jalousies, the doors of the high-walled court swung open, and Don Andrés' famous black horses plunged into the street, with the newlyweds cowering in the carriage. The crowd fell back, and the horses raced out Hospital Street to a house on Bayou Road, with the mob storming after them. Everywhere the Castillons went they were followed. They galloped in their carriage to the jetty. They crossed the Mississippi, and returned again to the city. And always the charivari was at their heels, through two nights and three terrible days. On the third night the streets were filled with people, some masked and many on horseback.

By that time the newlyweds were back in madam's house in the Vieux Carré, and the bride, peering through the jalousies, saw a coffin in a cart. In the coffin was an effigy of her late husband, in a crimson Spanish coat and a chevalier's cocked hat, like he used to wear. Sitting beside the coffin, dressed in widow's weeds and carrying an unseemly bridal bouquet was a woman, powdered and rouged like a waterfront whore. Madame Castillon fainted.

To end the charivari, Monsieur Castillon was obliged to distribute three thousand dollars of Almonester's money. Madame, furiously angry, closed her big house and sailed for France. Monsieur went along too, of course, and the Ursulines, whose fashionable boarding school had been handsomely endowed by the late Don Andrés, took Micaëla to board.

Micaëla always knew what she wanted, and seems to have got it. When she was fourteen she decided to marry young Célestin de Pontalba. He was her first cousin, and the nuns tried to talk her out of it, because if a Catholic wishes to marry her first cousin it is necessary to get a dispensation from the Pope. And even that does not make it good eugenics. But Micaëla wrote to Rome, and when the dispensation came through she wrote her mama to come home for the wedding.

The nuns made Micaëla's trousseau, and she was married by Père Antoine and sailed for France. She had three sons, and then decided to get a divorce, which was a most unusual thing in that day, and especially for a good Catholic. Micaëla went to see her father-in-law to discuss custody of the children, and this is what happened (I quote):

> There was a quarrel—angry voices, screams, shots—and then silence. The domestics came. The door was locked. They broke in. Old Pontalba and the youthful Baroness were lying on the floor— he with his brains spattered all over the fine Brussels carpet—she with a hole in her breast, grievously wounded, the finger of her hand shot away where she had sought to protect her heart. . . .

Micaëla recovered and went ahead with the divorce. Then she went to Paris, where she was living when Madame Lalaurie arrived from New Orleans. Madame Lalaurie had been Delphine Macarty, and the Macartys were a cruel lot. Chevalier de Macarty, Delphine's father, once sent a slave with a package to a lady friend. In the package was a note. *"Ma cherie,"* it said, *"this is the way to treat a renegade slave"*—and done up in a copy of *L'Abeille* (The Bee) was a bloody ear.

Delphine was married three times, and she had five children. Her third husband, Dr. Leonard Lalaurie, was a distinguished physician, and they lived in the old mansion at 1140 Royal Street that is known as the Haunted House because it is haunted by a little black ghost, the ghost of a slave girl who jumped from the roof. It is a plain and sinister-looking place from the outside, although there is still some nice lace ironwork around the balcony. But once upon a time its forty big rooms were furnished like a castle, and it was the scene of the gayest, most lavish parties in town. Madame Lalaurie is said to have chased the child who haunts the place to the roof with a whip, and the little girl jumped to escape the lash. The court records are vague. But the fact is that a child was found dead in the courtyard, the morning after one of the Lalaurie's lovely parties, and madame was fined.

A few years later Madame Lalaurie was calling in the country one day when a fire broke out, and the Cathedral bells summoned the firemen. When madame returned the fire was under control, but the Vieux Carré was in an uproar.

In the garret of the mansion the firemen had found several slaves, young boys and old men, chained in cells. In front of the cells was a long, bloodstained table spread with instruments of torture. In the kitchen was an old Negress, nearly dead from starvation, and in another room were two black girls chained to cots, more dead than alive.

"These slaves . . . horribly mutilated, suspended by the neck, with their limbs stretched and torn, had been confined for several months," declared *L'Abeille*. "They had been kept in existence merely to prolong their suffering, and to make them taste all that the most refined cruelty could inflict."

The slaves were taken on mattresses to the mayor's office, followed by an immense crowd. When it became known that the Lalauries, with the alleged connivance of the mayor, had contrived their escape, the mob streamed back to Royal Street. Meantime the Lalauries had fled in their carriage to Bayou St. John, where they crossed Lake Pontchartrain to Mandeville. From there they went to Mobile, where they stayed in hiding until a ship sailed for France.

The *Bee* continued its reports. It was yellow journalism all right. The paper did a job on madame, and there was no psychiatrist yet born to defend her. A mob stormed the mansion and began to wreck it. They began in madame's boudoir, with its rose marble fireplace and Aubusson carpet. They tore the sparkling girandoles from the brocaded walls, and the crystal chandelier from the ceiling. They smashed her little palissandre dressing table and burned it in the pink fireplace. They threw her rosewood accouchement couch out the window. With machetes they made kindling of the stately armoires and the big mahogany bed. They ripped the satin curtains and tore the velvet draperies. They smashed the mirrors and all the windows. They stole madame's jewels, and doused themselves with her perfumes. They made themselves ridiculous in her lovely lingerie, and put her fine feathers on their heads, and her sealskins and sables about their necks. For four days the hoodlums streamed in and out of the house, until the U.S. Regulars were called out. Then the hoodlums ran away.

Ten years later, while Micaëla was still in Paris, Madame Lalaurie died, and her last request was that her body be returned to New Orleans. It arrived in a box with massive silver handles, but no nameplate, and was taken at night to the family vault in St. Louis Cemetery Number One.

* * *

At that time there lived on Bayou Road a man named Peter Rabbaneck with his wife and three small daughters. One day Mr. Rabbaneck took a boat for St. Louis where he had business, and the night he went away a slave named Pauline moved into the master's bedroom. You can imagine Mrs. Rabbaneck's surprise in the morning.

"If you do not get up and go to work, missis, I will whip you," said Pauline.

So Mrs. Rabbaneck got up and went to work. Thereafter Pauline beat her mistress daily, sometimes with a cane, and sometimes with a strap, until the two oldest little girls—they were four and six—ran away and told a neighbor, and the neighbor wrote a letter to the mayor. A few days later the mayor drove out in his barouche.

Mrs. Rabbaneck, slightly disheveled, received his Honor with a black eye, and turned his solicitude politely aside. Her eye? "N'importe, monsieur. Il n'y a pas à dire. Mais n'importe, monsieur."

They exchanged a few painful pleasantries, and the embarrassed mayor was about to take his departure when he noticed that Pauline, who had come quietly into the room, was staring at her mistress in a most peculiar way, and Mrs. Rabbaneck was shaking like a cocoa pod.

The mayor asked for a glass of water and when Pauline went to fetch it, Mrs. Rabbaneck pulled herself together. Pauline had beaten her, she said, but she had not dared accuse the woman in her presence. The mayor called his coachman to summon slaves from the fields, and Pauline was soon in irons. Then the mayor packed Mrs. Rabbaneck and the children into his barouche, and drove them to town to stay with the mayoress.

When the boat from St. Louis docked with Mr. Rabbaneck aboard, the mayor was at the pier. To his astonishment Rabbaneck received the news with **unruffled calm.**

"A black eye, eh?" . . . Well, said Mr. Rabbaneck, he had given Pauline authority to run the house while he was gone. He had told her to be firm with Mrs. Rabbaneck, and had given her $200 for her trouble. Mrs. Rabbaneck, he volunteered, was crazy as a loon. She had let their baby son starve to death, and he had bought Pauline to tend to her and care for the three little girls.

Pauline, brought to trial, testified that she was twenty-eight years of age, and a Virginian by birth. She had belonged to President Monroe and worked in the White House. Her master, Monsieur Rabbaneck, had entrusted her with the care of his mad wife and helpless children. Madame had beaten the children, and she—Pauline—had beaten madame. Yes, it was true. It was true, also, that she—Pauline—was pregnant, and monsieur was her lover.

Under the Black Code which had been drawn up by Bienville any black who struck a white person hard enough to bruise or bring blood was punished by death, or imprisonment at hard labor for not less than ten years. Pauline was sentenced to be hanged.

On the day of the execution there was a public holiday, and thousands of people turned out to see the hanging. Newspapers tell of "bedizened courtesans" who came from houses of prostitution to "flaunt their charms in open carriages," as young and old streamed through the Vieux Carré to the gallows.

The gallows was erected in front of the parish prison on Orleans Street. Pauline, having confessed her sins and received absolution, was given a long white robe and white cap. Her arms were bound with black cord, and she was hanged at noon. Her body swung gently back and forth until sunset, when it was taken down and thrust into a nameless grave.

*   *   *

In 1848 there was another revolution in France, and when she saw it brewing the Baroness de Pontalba decided to return to New Orleans, which at that time was an enormously wealthy city. It was forty-five years since the Louisiana Purchase and many Americans had established themselves in the Crescent City. They had opened places of business on Canal Street, and built neo-Greek mansions in a suburb called the Garden District. The baroness could hardly believe her eyes. Mr. D. H. Holmes had moved his fine store from Rue Chartres to Canal Street, and other Vieux Carré merchants were preparing to do the same. But that was not the worst. A number of Creole families were building in the new suburb, and others were considering it. The baroness could remember when Louisiana was sold to the "Américain peegs," how the Creoles wept. She was a small girl, hardly eight at the time, but she could remember when the flag of France was hauled down in the Place d'Armes and the Stars and Stripes run up, how even the little children cried. And now they had forgotten, now the people were forsaking their dear old Square.

The baroness owned property that her father had acquired in Spanish days, on which the family had been paying taxes for seventy years—and if everyone was going to leave the Vieux Carré, what was to become of the baroness?

Business was booming. The Gold Rush had begun, and the city was filled with men waiting for ships to take them to Panama, where they would travel overland by mule train to reach other ships on the Pacific side of the isthmus. New Orleans was the last place a man could buy a pickax or a sombrero, or any other thing he fancied, and adventurers were spending like mad. The baroness, a commercially minded woman, saw business drifting away from the Vieux Carré, and determined to do something about it. She evolved a scheme to keep the Creoles in the French Quarter, where she felt they belonged, and to divert business from Canal Street back to the Vieux Carré.

She went to see James Gallier, the Irish architect who designed City Hall. (City Hall, one of the finest Greek Revival buildings in the United States, is two minutes' walk from the St. Charles Hotel, and of course you should see it.) She told Gallier of her idea, a sensational housing project, a combination of modern apartments with de luxe shops, and he agreed to make the plans.

Mr. Gallier had a son who was also named James and, as that was before the day of "Junior," the two were known as Gallier the Elder and Gallier the Younger. It was the father who designed the St. Charles Hotel, which was the first great hotel in the country, and also the Boston Club, where the Queen of Carnival sits on Mardi Gras and reviews the parade from the gallery. When I first saw the Boston Club, I imagined that it was built for some Bostonians who went to New Orleans to live. But it was originally a Creole mansion designed by the great Gallier, and taken over by the Boston Club, a group of gentlemanly gamblers who spent their spare time playing a game of cards called boston, which originated with British troops during the siege of Boston. Gallier the Elder designed the most elegant neo-Greek mansions of the Garden District and was greatly in demand. But by the time he finished the Pontalba Buildings his sight had failed and he was obliged to retire. His son was then commissioned to undertake the famous French Opera House. Shortly after the Opera House was completed, the father, returning from France with a troupe of French opera stars, was drowned at sea, and a little later Gallier the Younger also died, at the height of his career.

The baroness's property ran along two sides of the Place d'Armes, from Chartres Street to the river, and the Place at that time was a bleak and muddy place. The baroness urged that it be beautified and renamed Jackson Square, and she began campaigning for a monument to the Hero of New Orleans.

The baroness was about forty when she had her ample figure laced into whalebone stays, and donned a girlish creation of mousseline de soie with enormous sleeves and many pink ribbons, to pose for Monsieur Jacques Amans. Dr. and Mrs. George Ronstrom found the portrait in a shop on Royal Street, and recognized the baroness at once. The picture shows a florid, rather handsome woman, with small, appraising eyes, a heavy chin and puffy hands, overweight and overdressed. The Ronstroms also have a portrait of Baron de Pontalba, who was slight and sensitive with wide eyes, delicate features and beautiful patrician hands. Looking at their pictures, you are not surprised that the two did not get along, or that the baroness survived the shooting and came home to reorganize life in the Vieux Carré.

After Jackson's last visit to New Orleans, the City Council offered a prize of $1,000 for the best portrait of the General submitted within six months. Every artist in town went frantically to work. And Amans (who painted the baroness) and Theodore Moise went to work together. Their collaboration won the prize, and the painting hangs now in City Hall.

While workmen were tearing down the old buildings on St. Anne and St. Peter streets, the baroness was out canvassing for a statue to put in the park. The buildings, which had been constructed by her father, were rented to untidy people with big families who ran stores downstairs, and lived upstairs. On one corner was the famous Café of the Sucking Calf, where none but persons of quality were served. All the other places were dirty and shabby.

What the baroness had in mind was an arcade of elegant shops to be rented to a select list of distinguished merchants, who would live in the grand apartments overhead. There were to be sixteen apartments on either side of the square, and each street was to be a little Rue de la Paix. The buildings—of red brick, with galleries embroidered with iron lacework—were erected at great cost. The baroness sent to France to have her monogram entwined in cast iron, as delicate as vines. The apartments were elegant, original, and extremely exclusive. The tragedy was that nobody wanted to rent them and the baroness, who had longed to reclaim the Vieux Carré, lost a fortune.

As years went on, the buildings fell into disrepair until they were nothing but neglected tenements, with taxes unpaid, and rats and cockroaches running through their splendid rooms. Then the city bought the ones on St. Peter Street, and the ones on St. Anne Street were bought by Mr. Irby (that generous man I told you about who committed suicide in the undertaking place). Mr. Irby gave them to the state, and nearly a million dollars was spent (under the WPA) to make them habitable.

I had a chance to rent one of the apartments, and I think it was the one in which the baroness lived and which she turned over to Jenny Lind, when the Swedish Nightingale sang at the St. Charles Theatre. I should have loved living there, but I had the Beauregard House at the time, and I couldn't live in two places at once. I went to call, however, and when I read a piece in the *Daily Delta* written almost a century ago, I felt that I could vision everything as it was when the baroness moved out and Jenny moved in.

It was probably all a publicity stunt that the baroness thought up, or maybe it was Mr. Barnum. Anyhow there were the Pontalba Apartments empty when Jenny came to town—and the hotels filled to overflowing. The baroness had just moved in, the carpets were down and the curtains hung, the mirrors and silver polished, and the rosewood furniture waxed. In the drawing room Don Andrés's portrait looked down from one wall, and Madame Castillon's from another. In her bedroom the baroness's four-poster had a new silk canopy, and her little altar a petticoat that matched. On the rosewood washstand was a hand-painted bowl and pitcher, a gift from the nuns. And there was an armoire big enough to hold the wardrobe of even Jenny Lind.

Did you know that it was Barnum, the circus man, who brought Jenny Lind to America? He had never seen or heard her, but she was a sensation in Europe, and Barnum offered to pay all her expenses, and the expenses also of a secretary, a traveling companion and a maid. He promised to pay her pianist $25,000 and her baritone $12,500. And, on top of everything, he guaranteed Jenny $175,000.

Jenny signed the contract, and Barnum flooded the country with publicity. He christened Jenny "The Swedish Nightingale," and said she was the most beautiful woman in the world, and had the sweetest voice.

In the Latin hearts of the Creoles nothing could take the place of music. When they heard that Barnum was bringing his songbird to the Crescent City, steamers were chartered to bring people from every city and town in the Mississippi Valley, and when it was evident there would be a shortage of hotel rooms, the baroness announced that six hundred to eight hundred persons might be accommodated in her new apartments—if some person of enterprise, she added, would furnish the rooms to rent out. Nobody responded, and the baroness had another idea.

She wrote a letter offering her own "sumptuous apartment" as "a nest for the warbler." She had a silver door plate made with Jenny's name upon it, and a golden key. The editor of the *Delta* sent one of his bright young men around for an interview, and the next day there was a story on the front page.

The story began with the view from the gallery—the Place d'Armes, the Cathedral and the gay and crowded levee, with the crowd pouring back and forth from the French Market, and the forest of masts in the Mississippi. The baroness exhibited her "four handsome parlors and eight or ten sleeping rooms, furnished new and elegant, but not gaudy."

Two days later Jenny arrived, and thousands flocked to the wharf in front of the Place d'Armes to greet her. She was quite plainly dressed in black silk with a slate-colored bonnet. The crowd, slightly disappointed, trailed her carriage up St. Peter Street to where the baroness, all bows and smiles, was waiting on the gallery. Jenny retired at once to her nest, and the Great Barnum stepped forth. Miss Lind, he said, was pale and panting for rest, and must withhold for a while the light of her countenance. But the crowd clamored, and finally Jenny bounced out and bowed thirty-one times.

Seats for the concert, sold at auction, brought as high as $245. Society editors wrote of white necks and heaving bosoms, of glowing eyes that dimmed the brilliancy of jewels. Jenny, they said, wore blue silk, cut low to expose fine shoulders and a noble bust. Her arms were tolerably well shaped for a lady of her size, and gleamed with jeweled bracelets. Her hair was interlaced with flowers. About her neck she wore a simple diamond. "Certainly she was not ugly," conceded the man from the *Delta,* "but neither is she pretty."

The music critics were more enthusiastic. Nothing, they agreed, could have been more exquisite than the way Jenny sang. There was an amazing composition—*The Trio*—that had been written especially for her—for her voice and two flutes. Jenny was applauded to the very echo.

When the concert was over, the baroness took the Queen of Song and her party to the French Market for coffee. But the place was so crowded that they went back to St. Peter Street and had champagne in the drawing room, with the jalousies drawn and the crowd shouting hosannas in the square below.

The French Market, a stone's throw from Jackson Square, looks now almost as it did when Jenny Lind saw it, only then the roofs were made of tile and now they are slate. It is an arcaded place, built in the old-fashioned way—of brick plastered over—with flagstone floors, and overhanging roofs to shade the banquettes. There is one market for meat, another for vegetables, and one for fish, and many vendors sell flowers. Every day when I was living in the Beauregard House I went to the French Market to shop, and it was quite a smelly place. Mostly it smelled of hens and fish, but there was also the smell of coffee, and sometimes the fragrance of lilies. The things I liked best to buy were shrimps, flowers and gumbo filé, which is powdered sassafras leaves, and is used to thicken gumbo.

Creole cooks also use okra for thickening. They would never dream of using flour as Northern cooks do. And everyone who ever had a Creole gumbo knows that it is the best soup there is. In my New

England books, I said there was nothing so good as a New England clam chowder. But when I said that I had never had a Creole gumbo or a crayfish bisque, which goes to show that one should not be so opinionated, because now I think that a gumbo filé (made with chicken and oysters and ham) is the best of all possible stews. And another thing—in my Cape Cod book I said that Cotuit oysters were the best in the world. Now I believe that Louisiana oysters are better. I do not mean that every restaurant serves superior ones. But if you go to a really good place—the Smile, for instance, on St. Charles or Manale's (which is uptown) and have the oysterman open the oysters at the bar and eat them right then and there, I think you will agree that they could not be better. You can't eat oysters in the French Market. You can only buy them to take home.

The market goes back to the days of the Indians, when Choctaw squaws used to paddle down the river with the precious ingredient for the Creoles' first filés. The squaws gathered the young leaves of the sassafras, and when the leaves were dried the squaws pounded them into powder, passed the powder through a hair sieve and brought it to New Orleans, to sell for medicinal purposes. The Creoles soon discovered its culinary charm and originated their famous gumbos.

In order that the Germans who lived farther down the river might have a place to trade, the Spanish set aside that section of the levee where the Indians traded as a sort of market place. At first there were only the squaws, who sold furs and baskets as well as sassafras, and the Germans who sold vegetables. Each morning they arrived before sunrise, and spread their goods for early risers bound for Mass at the Cathedral. As time went on, the fishermen joined them and then the vendors of fruits and meats. Until the market that had been set aside for Indians and farmers became also a bazaar for merchants, who imported bales of fine silk and barrels of wine and olive oil from Spain and France, and—by and by—delicacies of all sorts. Then Creole ladies and gentlemen and Cathedral monks rubbed shoulders with sailors and convicts and slaves in a market that was extremely cosmopolitan, and as bizarre as the people who frequented it.

At the market there were cuisiniers who set up braziers of charcoal to make coffee. And from the very beginning the aroma of that strong Creole brew drifted over the stalls and filled the air with its fragrance. Coffee is served in two ways in New Orleans—café noir, as black as night, to wake you up in the morning, and café au lait, morning, noon and night. Café au lait (with hot milk) is the great breakfast drink, while black coffee is more generally the before-breakfast and afternoon drink. Everybody in New Orleans loves coffee. If you say that it keeps you awake nights, they say that is a silly superstition, because coffee is good for whatever ails you, even insomnia. Coffee, they say, makes people live a very long time. If you doubt this, they point triumphantly to the oldest people you ever saw on two legs, all having a beautiful time. "Créoles pas mourri, ils desseches," they say. (Creoles don't die, they dry up.) Black coffee, they believe, is one of the best preventives of infectious diseases—it is also a brain food, and the greatest stimulant in the world.

At the coffee stands in the French Market people drink café au lait, which is served with fried cakes that are something like doughnuts, only they are square, and they haven't a hole in the middle. And unless you eat them at once, they capsize and are not very good. Naturally then, you eat them at once, and then they are excellent. Café au lait with three fried cakes costs a dime.

The only better value in the food line is a poor boy, which costs fifteen cents, and is a whole loaf of French bread cut lengthwise, with roast beef, ham, cheese, tomatoes and lettuce between. If this is more than you can believe, you can buy one at the French Market Lunch and see for yourself. Another Creole specialty is a peacemaker, which is a French loaf scooped out in the middle, buttered liberally, and filled with hot fried oysters. Men who are out late, proverbially take home a peacemaker, and wives hungry with waiting melt at the thought of the oysters bedded in the warm crusty bread—or that's the theory.

There are two coffee stands in the French Market, one at either end, with all the produce stalls between. In the beginning the coffee stands were just for marketmen, so they opened at ten o'clock at night and closed at noon. But about a hundred years ago visitors began saying how colorful the French Market was, and how good the coffee was, and now the stands are open day and night, and they are more of a tourist attraction than the battlefield.

Across from the coffee stands is a very old Creole restaurant—Tujague's—where meals are good and reasonable, but the place is not very clean. And next to Tujague's is Buck Fulford, whose grisly accomplishment brought him to the attention of Believe It Or Not Ripley, and resulted in a cartoon that paid off in advertising. Mr. Fulford can kill, pluck, cook and eat a chicken in one minute and fifty seconds. To save time, he dunks it from the boiling grease into ice water, and eats with both hands. In more leisurely fashion, Mr. Fulford fries three hundred chickens a day, and sells them to eat on the premises, or to take out. One chicken, he says, is enough for four persons—less ravenous persons, obviously, than Mr. Fulford.

In the old days, before Decatur Street was built up, it must have been beautiful looking down from the Place d'Armes to the river, when there were no railroad tracks or wharf sheds. When Jenny Lind was in town, Tujague's was there, and before Buck Fulford, there were colored women frying chicken over charcoal pots, and making gumbo filé and jambalaya.

There were Creole gentlemen marketing in French fashion, and doing something a little like Buck Fulford and the way he tears a chicken apart. They were buying papabottes, which I think were hummingbirds—or anyway they were little birds, which the marketwomen roasted and the gentlemen ate, bones and all. Creole gentlemen were inordinately amorously inclined, and papabottes were considered a great aphrodisiac. For the same reason, the amorous gentlemen drank a concoction made from "Spanish flies," and ate black cock oysters. They usually did the marketing for the family, and were accompanied from stall to stall by slaves carrying reed baskets for their purchases, exactly like the baskets that are sold today in the market. There were the same beautiful things then as there are now—red and yellow bananas and orange persimmons, scarlet pomegranates and sweet pineapples, shrimps and turtles and strawberries and roses. And there were pretty quadroons who sold the gentlemen boutonnieres of jessamines and carnations and violets.

* * *

It was thirty-six years since the Battle of New Orleans, but nobody had forgotten Andrew Jackson. He had been dead five years, and all over America men were still planting hickory trees in his memory. Congress had made an appropriation for a statue of the general to be erected in Washington, and the contract had been awarded to a man named Clark Mills, on the basis of a miniature plaster model that showed Jackson on horseback on the day of the Battle of New Orleans.

Mills was a common laborer who knocked about the country, drifting from job to job. He knew nothing about horses. He had never seen an equestrian statue, and had never worked in bronze. He worked in South Carolina as a plaster molder, and had drifted on to Washington where Congress was debating the monument appropriation. Mills borrowed money and bought a horse—a Virginia thoroughbred named Olympus, and set about teaching him to stand on his hind legs. Olympus got so used to rearing that he forgot how to trot. Mills succeeded in making the miniature he had planned, and after he was awarded the commission he spent two years on the plaster model. After that came the biggest problem—casting in bronze. Mills built a shack in Maryland and using equipment scoffed at by experts, guided only by books, he began his gigantic

"Olympus looked like a horse on a merry-go-round and the general's 'seat' was bad, the critics said. But most Americans liked the statue and the baroness adored it."

task of making a bronze Jackson, astride a bronze horse. Working by trial and error, it took him five years.

On the anniversary of the Battle of New Orleans the statue was unveiled in Lafayette Square across from the White House. The President was there, with justices of the Supreme Court and members of Congress—and the Baroness de Pontalba, up from New Orleans. Stephen A. Douglas was the orator of the day, and Mills was so overcome by emotion that he could not say a word. When called upon for a speech, he could only point at the statue, while tears ran down his cheeks. Almost everybody blew their noses and cried a little, even the baroness. They all thought the statue was wonderful, and the baroness hurried back to New Orleans to persuade the city to order a replica for Jackson Square.

Art critics called the statue a prodigious joke, and a number of other things that grieved Mr. Mills and made the baroness angry. Olympus, they said, looked like a horse on a merry-go-round, and the general's "seat" was bad. While the controversy was raging, Thackeray visited Washington, and Charles Sumner took him for a sleigh ride. When they passed Lafayette Square, Sumner leaned forward so that Thackeray could not see the statue. The story was broadcast over the country, with a mean statement from Sumner about how ashamed he was to let an Englishman discover how little Americans knew about art. Most Americans, however, liked the statue very much, and the baroness adored it.

Three years later she secured a replica for New Orleans, and had it unveiled at a great ceremony in Jackson Square. In the best of all possible settings, the general's statue, she liked to say, was the most magnificent of statues, and his horse the best of all possible horses.

Twenty-five years later, Nashville ordered a second replica. Nashville is where Andy and Rachel lived in the Hermitage, and died, and are buried in the garden. After all the insults he had suffered, the Nashville order made Mr. Mills feel pretty good.

On the base of the statue in Jackson Square is an inscription that was not put there by the sculptor, and is not on the monuments in Washington and Nashville. It says THE UNION MUST AND SHALL BE PRESERVED, which is a strange sentiment to find in a state that seceded from the Union. But that is another story, and I am going to save it for another time.

8

PEOPLE SAID MR. AUDUBON WAS NO GOOD

John James Audubon was the son of a French sea captain and a girl from Haiti named Muguet (Lily-of-the-Valley) Rabin. A French priest in Port-au-Prince told me that he has seen a baptismal record from the parish church of Aux Cayes, which showed that Muguet Rabin's son was christened Petit Fougère, which means Little Fern.

There is no doubt about Audubon's illegitimacy. His grand-daughter claimed that he was the Lost Dauphin. She said that after Louis XVI and Marie Antoinette were beheaded, the little prince was taken from Paris straight to Louisiana.

"And the prince was Grandpapa. Grandpapa," she declared, "was Louis XVII!"

Bernard de Marigny, who was the father-in-law of Sophronia Claiborne (the girl who wore glasses), said that Audubon was born at Fontainebleau, the de Marigny's plantation, and that he (Bernard) was in the room at the time, which does not seem probable, as Bernard was then a small boy. Audubon, who told conflicting stories about his birth, sometimes said that he was born in Louisiana, and there was once a plan to turn Fontainebleau into a memorial park and call it the "Birthplace of Audubon." But the sponsors, getting wind of old scandals, dropped the idea.

After Muguet's death her lover took the child to France, where he was brought up with the rest of the Audubon children, who dropped his fanciful name and called him John.

When he was a young man Audubon came to America to open a store in Henderson, Kentucky, and there he married a girl named Lucy Blakewell. They had two children, and when the store failed the young husband had to go hunting to fill the cupboard. Wild life fascinated him and soon he was shooting birds of all species, and toting them home. He wired the pitiful crumpled things before their colors faded, and stuck them in lifelike positions to paint. Poor Lucy, stumbling over dead creatures, was always telling the children, "Don't touch! Papa spank!"

They lived in one room, and you can imagine what a mess it was with dead birds molting all over the place. They were so poor that for two months one winter Audubon had to give up keeping his journal because he had no money to buy note paper. But he kept on shooting. Some days he shot as many as two hundred birds, which would certainly, in this day, have got the S.P.C.A. down on him. But the way Audubon societies have perpetuated his name with bird sanctuaries, you would think he was some sort of scientific St. Francis.

While he was struggling for recognition, Audubon lost three years' work to a family of rats. He had about two hundred drawings of nearly a thousand birds tucked away in a closet, when a pair of rats, bent on raising a family, came along and gnawed the drawings to bits, and raised their family in the tatters. Audubon tells in his journal about how when he found the rats' nest, "a burning heat too great to be endured" passed through his brain.

"He slept not for several nghts, and the days passed like days of oblivion." But his courage returned, and one day he took up his gun and went to the woods "as gaily as if nothing happened." . . . "I felt," he wrote, "that I might now make better drawings than before."

That was the year that Vincent (*Anthony Adverse*) Nolte, who also kept a journal (for Hervey Allen), wrote that Audubon was an "odd fish." "He wore a Madras kerchief knotted about his head."

The two met at supper in an Allegheny mountain inn, and, taking their horses aboard a Mississippi flatboat, shared a cabin. Audubon, in kerchief and woodsman's clothes, might have been an "odd fish" to the elegant Anthony Adverse, but to himself he was "quite a handsome figure."

He naïvely described himself about this time as of "fair mien, with large, dark and rather sunken eyes; an aquiline nose and a fine set of teeth . . . five feet ten and a half inches, with hair of soft texture and luxuriant, divided behind each ear, and falling in ringlets to the shoulders."

In the Presbytère there are reproductions of every known likeness of Audubon. Among them is a portrait by Henry Inman that shows him in his prime. He *was* (as he said) a handsome figure, and Lucy thought so too. There is another portrait with dog and gun that was painted by his sons, and one for which he posed after he had lost his fine teeth and bobbed his thinning ringlets. With his big beak and feathery sideburns, he looks rather like an aging eagle.

Beneath his bronze bust is displayed his monumental work— *The Birds of America*—an original elephant folio edition of 435 copper engraved, hand-colored plates. Near by is a poster stating that the four volumes are worth $15,000. They are really worth more, because every time a set is sold, a new value is established.

Most of the birds—and there are 1,085 of them—were from Louisiana, because there were birds of more species in Louisiana than anywhere else. The Delta was always heaven for ducks and geese. Wild turkey roamed the woods, and in the deep marshes and along the reedy shores were most of the loveliest birds in America. The way in which Audubon found and painted them is a fascinating story, and if you do not know it, you might not properly enjoy the museum—so I am going to tell you.

Audubon had no faith in genius. He believed that a man with energy and determination could make himself what he pleased, and in fantastic fashion he set out to prove it.

He was living in Ohio with Lucy and the children when he approached a flatboat captain with an extraordinary offer. In exchange for his passage to New Orleans, Audubon guaranteed to feed the ship's passengers with game birds that he would shoot along the way. The captain took him up, and Lucy said that she would get a job teaching while he was gone.

The bayous were full of birds, and when Audubon had bagged the cook's quota for the day, he would fill his hunter's bag with personal prey—golden warblers and meadow larks, and nests of ruby-throated hummingbirds with babies in them no bigger than bumblebees. He shot snowy heron, for the white aigrettes that ladies wore on their hats, and plucked the pink tail feathers of flamingos, for Creole girls to pin in their hair. He hunted roseate spoonbills for their shining wings, and killed Louisiana heron for their sky-blue plumage.

When he reached New Orleans, he took a room on St. Anne Street, and there he met Mrs. James Pirrie, who heard that he had some lovely feathers for sale, and went to see them. Mrs. Pirrie came from the Felicianas, the rich cotton-raising land of Louisiana, and she had journeyed to New Orleans to find a tutor for her fifteen-year-old daughter Eliza.

Audubon hoped to do some portraits, but there were several fashionable artists in town, and competition was too much for the shabby woodsman. In those days there was a vogue for European artists who charged $1,000 a portrait. But there were also a few New Orleans artists, among them John Jarvis, who were well thought of, and Audubon went to Jarvis seeking employment. Jarvis told him that he might as well give up painting.

"You will never be an artist," Jarvis said, which goes to show the mistakes people make.

That was the day Mrs. Pirrie came to town seeking a tutor for Eliza, and Audubon made his second extraordinary offer. He would go to Oakley, he said—Oakley was the Pirrie plantation near Bayou

Sara—if he might take a helper along, and teach Miss Eliza on half time. For sixty dollars a month and keep he would instruct her for four hours a day in drawing, music and dancing. But the Pirries must board his helper, and promise not to interfere with their hours together. Mrs. Pirrie agreed and the arrangement for a time turned out beautifully.

Feliciana was next door to heaven. Audubon wrote Lucy that he was surrounded by "Thousands of Warblers and Thrushes, and intoxicated with the Odoriferous Blossoms of the Rich Magnolias." The intoxication never wore off. Audubon did his best work in Feliciana. He immortalized its warblers and thrushes, and painted them against the shining green leaves and waxy-white blossoms of the magnolias he loved.

Before dawn, he and his helper were out in the woods or paddling through the bayous. After breakfast Miss Eliza had her lessons. In the afternoons Audubon painted, and in the evening he taught waltzes and cotillion steps to young people from the neighboring plantations.

Between times he painted Miss Eliza's portrait, which is now at Rosedown, the near-by plantation house of three old, old ladies who are the granddaughters of Miss Eliza—Miss Sarah, Miss Nina, and Miss Belle Bowman. Rosedown is one of the saddest places I have ever seen, because once it was so beautiful. The three old sisters putter among their old-fashioned roses in a garden gone almost to bush, and—charging admission now—show visitors through the beautiful, shabby rooms of the mansion where, long, long ago, they were young and gay.

Rosedawn was built in 1835, while Eliza Pirrie was a young woman, and she often had tea in the drawing room where her portrait now hangs. Audubon painted her in a high-waisted gown, with prim little curls about her oval face. The old ladies say that she grew up to be a tremendous belle, and married three times. Her second husband was a young minister from Pennsylvania, the Rev.

Mr. William Bowman who established Grace Episcopal Church, the second Protestant church in Louisiana.

Grace Church is of gray brick, and sits in a grove of ancient oaks that are hung with gray moss, in the old gray town of St. Francisville. A strange unearthly light filters through the trees, and the gray moss weaves a Druid charm as it sways over the grave where Eliza rests with her second husband. (I have seen much beauty in Louisiana, but Grace Church with its graveyard is the most beautiful of all I have seen.)

Eliza died when she was forty-four, the same year in which Mr. Audubon died, and it is pleasant to know that they remained friends until the end, although Audubon had quarreled years before with her mother. Eliza in those days was ill. Audubon expected to be paid just the same. But Mrs. Pirrie said *no work, no pay*. And Audubon, in a great huff (he was always quarreling with people), packed his trunk, and sent for Lucy.

Lucy got a job at a Louisiana plantation called Beech Woods and supported the family with her teaching, while Audubon roamed the woods. Until at last, with a bulging portfolio, he set out to seek a publisher. He went to Philadelphia, New York and Boston, but he had no success. Lucy sent him his return fare, and he went to Beech Woods to live.

People said that Mr. Audubon was no good—running around in the woods like a wild Indian—shooting birds and daubing with paints—while his poor wife supported him. But Lucy knew what she was doing—or perhaps it was only that she loved him. At any rate, she scrimped and saved, and the next year there was money enough for her husband to go to Europe. In London Audubon found an engraver, Robert Havell, who was willing to promote his beautiful dream. The first step was to finance it. If this could be done, Mr. Havell promised to make copper engravings for elephant folios—big enough to hold a full-grown turkey, or an albatross in flight—and to publish all of Mr. Audubon's birds "on a scale of elegance never before attempted in England or in any other country."

Audubon stayed in London to prepare a prospectus for possible customers, while Lucy continued to teach. According to the prospectus, for a thousand dollars subscribers to *The Birds of America* would receive eighty numbers of five elephant folio plates, copper engraved and hand colored. These numbers might be bound, piecemeal, by the subscribers; or they could be kept unbound, until a set was completed, at which time they might be returned to Mr. Audubon, who would bind them, at his own expense, in buckram with a tasty red morocco back.

While the prospectus was at the printer's, Mr. Havell pulled a few wires and Audubon was invited to court, where the king made a great fuss over him, and Queen Adelaide placed a subscription. And so did Sir Walter Scott. The records show that Sir Walter paid, but the queen expected hers for nothing.

During his success in London, Audubon wrote to Lucy: "It is Mr. Audubon here and Mr. Audubon there, until I am afraid poor Mr. Audubon is in danger of having his head turned."

Then he was elected to the Royal Society of Edinburgh, and he wrote Lucy again:

Dearest Friend,
    The honors I have received enable me, I assure thee, to be respected and well received in any portion of the Civilized World . . .

Then he asked his "Dearest Friend" to share his glory. She was to give up teaching, he wrote, and buy herself some clothes.

After three years, Audubon returned to Louisiana for Lucy, and they sailed for Europe and success. Meantime, 175 subscribers had been secured at $1,000 apiece—$175,000 was a good deal of money, but manufacturing costs are said to have exceeded $100,000. There were also the Audubon sons—John and Victor—to be paid. Lucy had taught them to paint, and the boys did most of the hand coloring and the backgrounds for the elephant folios.

The work took twelve years. Audubon and Havell were not only as good as their word—they were better. They had promised 400 plates and they furnished 435, each plate depicting a different species of bird: tall heron waded through the marshes, bald-headed eagles posed on rocky crags, and saucy chipmunks laughed at big hoot owls. Redbirds flitted through the cedars, mourning doves nested in the dogwood, and cuckoos cried in the magnolias of Feliciana. There was a hawk, with a popeyed fish in his mouth flying over a Louisiana bayou, and a snake at Oakley attacking a mockingbird's nest that made Miss Eliza cry. All the birds were life size, and they were all doing the things they do in everyday life.

Audubon had traveled across the entire country. He climbed mountains to find his birds, and lived in swamps. He found 435 *different* kinds of birds, and painted them against their proper backgrounds of leaves and flowers, grouping them in such original patterns of design and color that the paintings are as decorative as they are instructive. The enormity of the task, as breath-taking as its beauty, proved his contention that a man with energy and determination could make himself what he pleased.

The New York Historical Society owns all but three of the Audubon water colors from which the famous engravings were made. They are on occasional exhibition, and people who listen carefully can hear the woodpeckers quarreling, and the wild turkeys gobbling. Once I heard a woman say that she could plainly hear a rustle of wings, and she looked so happy I expect she could. Her pleasure reminded me of something the late Frank Chapman once said to me.

I had gone to Barro, Colorado, where scientists were studying the ways of wild animals in a virgin forest, and Mr. Chapman took me into the jungle to hear the birds' evening song. When I said goodbye, I tried to tell him how much I had enjoyed the concert.

"Yes, I understand," he said. "Everyone is born with a bird in his heart. That is why we love them."

And that, I suppose, is one reason why Mr. Audubon goes on and on, and gets more famous every year. Another reason is that after the copyright ran out, a popularly priced edition of *The Birds of America** sold over 200,000 copies, and is still going strong. The success of the book inspired decorators to launch a vogue for Audubon prints, which attained such proportions that a girl I know received eighteen for wedding presents. Macy's, she thinks, was overstocked that June, and marked them down.

The original water colors, which are said to be priceless, were bought by the New York Historical Society for $4,000, and the story of their purchase involves loving long-suffering Lucy, who outlived her husband by twenty-four years. Audubon lost his sight and was pitifully feeble. His wife read to him, walked with him, and fed him. When he died at sixty-six, she went back to teaching. Her son Victor died and a few years later John died. The following year Mrs. Audubon, "aged and debt-burthened," offered her husband's paintings for sale.

The Historical Society raised $4,000 among its members, and Mrs. Audubon sold the society all but three of the original watercolors for *The Birds of America*. What had happened to the three missing paintings nobody knows.

In the New Orleans *Bee* of February 20, 1853, there was an advertisement:

Chances on
THE BIRDS OF AMERICA
Complete Elephant Folio
One of the Greatest Works Ever Published
$1.00 Each

---

* Macmillan, $6.95.

The last public sale of the elephant folio brought $15,600 at public auction in the Parke-Bernet Galleries in New York. The last known private sale, as reported by Rosenbach, was to an American in London for $25,000. . . . And wouldn't it be nice to know who in New Orleans had the lucky number back in 1853—and what happened to the prize?

9

*A*ND THE WIND SIGHED   When I went house hunting in New Orleans, renting agents had lists of applicants as long
as their arms or maybe longer, and there wasn't a house to be had.
Everybody said I was lucky to have a nice hotel room. But I was
restless and sick of nice hotel rooms, and I wanted a place of my
own.

New Orleans has been in the hotel business a long time. The St.
Charles, "the pride of Dixie," was the first Grand Hotel in America,
and it is still doing business at the same old stand. The St. Charles
has marble pillars and grand staircases, and an old-time flavor that
is very nice. When the hotel was built, its mirrors were the largest
ever imported, and its bronze chandeliers were the biggest. Each
chandelier had 120 gas burners. There were gold and silver table
services—and "a water-closet on every story!" When the hotel was
destroyed by fire, the Creoles raised money to build another exactly
like it. But when it came to the furnishings they resolved to do
even better, and a committee went to Paris and had practically
everything made to order.

The St. Charles, as it was in the beginning, is now, and always
will be, is an elegant place to stay. Next to the St. Charles comes
the Roosevelt, with its Ramos gin fizzes and turkey poulettes. Then
the New Orleans, the Jung and the Monteleone. What I especially
like about the New Orleans is the wonderful Creole cream cheese
they have for breakfast. At the Jung I like the absinthe frappés and
the little blonde hairdresser who calls me "hon" (me, and everybody

else). Many Northerners dislike being called "hon" by perfect strangers. They say that sweet talk is cheap and insincere. But to me the friendliness of southern girls is like a fragrance. It may be artificial, but so is Arpège, and I love it.

New Orleans is a city of pretty customs and fragrant memories. When camellias are in season, Solari's sells them on the vegetable counter, pin and all, for a dime. I was living at the Monteleone when I discovered Solari's pecan waffles, and began going there for breakfast. And I usually bought a camellia, because they cost three dollars at Max Schling's, next to where I live in New York, and it did my heart good to save $2.90 on a ten-cent purchase.

The Monteleone, a nice handy place to live, is on Royal Street, in the middle of the Vieux Carré where the antique shops are. Around the corner are the famous restaurants. One block away is Bourbon Street where honky-tonk tourists buy drinks for fancy ladies, and the musicians all play jazz. And up and down and all around are the old, old houses with the beautiful ironwork and the famous courtyards.

My room was as quiet as the St. Louis Cathedral. From my windows I could see the Mississippi, and I could lie abed and see the moon and the stars above it, and the lamps of Algiers burning gold beyond it. In the daytime tugboats went blowing up and down, and big ships anchored at the wharves. And the wind carried the fragrance of coffee from the ships unloading at the piers, and the hot, sweet smell of tropical fruits and rum from the Indies. And in the bar there was a man named Pete who could shake a lovely gin fizz.

In many ways hotel life is pleasanter than housekeeping, and it is indisputably easier. New Orleans hotels are pleasant and good enough for anyone. But I am a domestic model and when I live too long in hotels I get tired of the best of them.

I wanted to try my hand at Creole cooking, and have some people in for dinner. I wanted to buy a big market basket to hang on my arm, and shop for gumbo filé and soft-shell crabs, and beautiful red watermelon at the French Market. I wanted a Seignouret bed to sleep in, and a flowery patio to sit in. But most of all I wanted a little kitchen to cook in.

And what did I get but the Beauregard House, with a kitchen as big as a baseball diamond—with two stoves and two refrigerators, and a sink out in left field. And pretty soon I was mashing anchovies and washing spinach—for oysters Rockefeller. And I was making mint juleps, to drink in the courtyard—and sleeping at night in one of those beautiful beds I had been dreaming about.

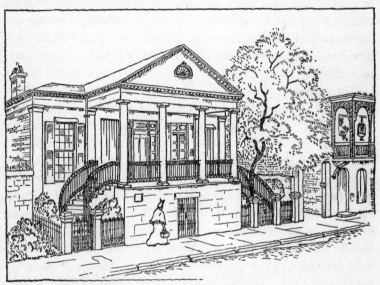

"And what did I get but the Beauregard House."

The tradition of southern hospitality is said to have originated with the Creoles' big beds—always room for one more. Beside the bed, there was a Seignouret armoire to hang my clothes in that had a mirror in each door—"one for the master," as Monsieur Seignouret used to say, and "one for the dame." But this dame had it all to herself.

Beyond my bedroom was the dining room. The dining room opened on a gallery that was a lovely place to make café brûlot. And the gallery looked down on a patio where rose of Montana climbed the old slave quarters, and banana leaves rustled in the breeze.

The Beauregard House at 1113 Chartres Street belongs to the city and is maintained as a memorial to "The Great Creole," which is what his fans called the general. When I moved in all I knew about the general was that he had something to do with Sumter—or maybe Manassas. And I knew that he was famous for his juleps, because I had read in an old letter of a julep to "cool or assuage the heat of passion"—a julep served by Monsieur le Général Pierre Gustave Toutant Beauregard, and the first thing I did was plant some mint in the garden. Then I bought a pot of rosemary for the gallery, because there is a Creole superstition that rosemary brings luck to a house, and I am always pushing mine pretty hard.

The way I got Beauregard House was an act of God, aided and abetted by Mrs. Frances Parkinson Keyes who wrote *Crescent Carnival* and *The River Road*. I had noticed that the house was empty, and learned that Mrs. Keyes, who usually lives there, had gone away. So I wired her in care of her publishers in New York, asking if I might rent it. A few days later I had a reply—from Louisiana, of all places—from "The Cottage" on River Road, where Mrs. Keyes was writing another book, saying not only that I might have Beauregard House, but that Mrs. Keyes would put me up at the Orleans Club until the house was ready.

The Orleans Club is a handsome place—one of the old nineteenth-century mansions on St. Charles Avenue—where there are mockingbirds in the garden and crystal chandeliers in the drawing room. And breakfast is served in bed, on an old French tray, set with silver and Sèvres—and the beds are four-posters so high you have to climb steps to get into them.

Living at the club was a delightful experience, but I kept thinking how good it was going to be to have a house of my own. Meantime, I was reading about the general, and I had met his great-granddaughters, who told me stories that their grandfather had told them about his father, the general. I loved the idea of entertaining in rooms where once the "chivalry of southern manhood" had toasted the "flower of southern womanhood." I was also looking forward to sleeping in the general's bed, though Mrs. Keyes had preceded me there. Later I learned it wasn't the general's bed at all, but only an antique that the landlady picked up—which reminds me of something Dorothy Dix said. Dorothy Dix, who is Mrs. Elizabeth Meriwether Gilmer in private life, is president of Le Petit Salon and the grande dame of New Orleans society. But what Dorothy Dix is most famous for from Spoon River to Sumatra is her advice to the lovelorn. I interviewed her for *True Confessions* at her home on Prytania Street, which is furnished with treasures she picked up all over the world, and the bed in which she sleeps is the grandest bed you ever saw.

"It was Pompadour's," she told me. "And I'll bet," said little old Dorothy Dix, "that I am the only respectable woman who ever slept in it."

But getting back to the general—there is a portrait of him in Beauregard House that made me a little sad, because he seems so sad himself. One of his biographers said that he looked like "a poet in uniform," and I expect that he did. But a quite dashing poet. In City Park (right at the entrance) there is a statue called *The Great Creole* of a mournful little man upon a mournful little horse. I don't believe that Beauregard ever looked like that. After the first Confederate victories when the Yankees were badly beaten, northern papers said he was a madman who rode a mad horse, and he became a sort of fierce legend—so fierce that some people said his horse didn't have any head! Southern papers hailed him as the "Colossus of Manassas," and one of them printed a poem on the front page that began:

Then Beauregard came
Like a tempest of flame
To consume them in wrath
On their perilous path.

And I am sure he never looked like that meek man in City Park astride the rabbity little horse. His great-granddaughter told me that people began collecting for the statue the day the general died. But New Orleans was so poor after the war that it was twenty years before they got together money enough to lay the cornerstone.

On the stairway in the Cabildo there is another portrait that shows the general after he ordered the shot fired on Fort Sumter, and he looks very Creole with his heavy-lidded dark eyes and his silky little mustache and goatee. It was a fashion then for men to have whiskers. Girls said that a kiss without a mustache was like an egg without salt. The bigger the beard, they said, the better the lover. Even society writers advocated beards. A lady in Boston wrote a book called *Success in Society,* and "Nothing so adds to native manliness," she declared, "as the full beard, if carefully and neatly kept."

In the Union Army young men grew ferocious mustaches as symbols of virility, and the generals all wore beards. But in France, Napoleon III wore a mere tuft of hair upon his royal chin, and Beauregard, admiring court fashions, copied the emperor's small neat beard. His staff, known as the Elegants, followed suit, and the restrained hirsute touch was in fastidious contrast to the ostentatious displays of the hairy enemy.

Ladies true to the Confederacy went into ecstasies over the "little-bittee" beards of their Creole general and his staff. Beauregard was always a great beau and popular with the ladies, and after the first Battle of Bull Run he became the idol of the South. Button snipping was then a sport of Dixie bustle-girls, and the general was their favorite victim. To keep her husband tidy, Mrs. Beauregard sent a box of buttons to his orderly, with instructions to keep a supply of spares always on hand. She was the general's second wife, and people said that for Pierre it was a mariage de convenance.

His first wife was Marie de Villère, whose grandfather was the first native-born governor of Louisiana. It was on the de Villère plantation that the British camped before the Battle of New Orleans, and it was under grandpère's pecan tree that Pakenham died. Marie was a pretty girl, whose young husband spent an unconscionable time studying the campaigns of Napoleon. In her portraits she has sad blue eyes and hungry lips.

There is a story they tell about a Creole bride who was going to have a baby. It was practically unforgivable in those days for a pregnant woman to appear in public. I do not know that this particular girl was Marie, but it might have been, so I will tell you the story. The Creoles were passionately fond of music. At the end of a musical performance the men would stand up in the theater and wave their arms, and fill the air with their bravos. There were boxes enclosed with loges grilles, where femmes enceintes could sit in privacy and clap until their hands hurt. The opera one night was *Faust,* and there was a bride who lost herself under the spell of the music, until, in the middle of the performance, she turned quite suddenly to her husband.

"I am desolated, mon cher," she said. "But I am afraid," she said, "that I cannot wait for the ballet."

Marie had two children—René, and a daughter. When the girl was born, she died. Pierre, as was customary, went in mourning for a year. And after some time he married a plain, matronly woman named Caroline Deslondes. There were nine of the Deslondes sisters who, inevitably, were called the Muses. But the truth is that Caroline was no beauty. She died during the War Between the States, and her funeral was the first one ever attended by Creole ladies.

The general and his army were fighting in Florida, and in the absence of their husbands the ladies took entire charge of the funeral. They escorted the casket from the house to the Cathedral, marching with military precision in rows that extended the width of the promenade publique—under the live oaks and the magnolias—down Chartres Street to the Cathedral. After Mass they marched to the cemetery with muffled drums beating and the Confederate Stars and Bars flying. People said it was the most impressive funeral New Orleans ever had. Mrs. Beauregard was buried from the Beauregard home on Esplanade Avenue. Before the general bought the place on the avenue, they had another house in town. But the Beauregards never lived on Chartres Street.

Heaven knows I hate to spoil a story, and if I were to write as I should like, it would be about how romantic it was to live in the general's old house. I enjoy creating scenes of long ago, and I would like to tell how I used to think about Pierre when he was a young officer home from West Point and Marie was a bride, in the Creole days of long ago . . . or later, when he had become commandant of West Point . . . and Marie was dead and in her grave— because then there was Caroline. But it wouldn't be true, because by the time I got settled in the so-called Beauregard House, I knew that Marie never so much as crossed the threshold—or Caroline either.

It would be pleasant to write about Mrs. Beauregard rustling around in taffeta and crinoline and a little tight bodice, while Pierre and his cronies drank mint juleps under the oleanders in the courtyard . . . about ante-bellum parties in the big white ballroom, when Mrs. Beauregard and the general greeted their guests under the master's portrait that hangs in the hall . . . and the general wore his golden epaulets and a silver sword . . . about René taking his sweetheart to the gallery, while the white moths fluttered around his mother's tuberoses, as he held his Creole girl in the moonlight . . . and the crystal lusters on the girandoles trembled when he kissed her . . . in the Creole days of long ago.

But the truth of the matter is that no Beauregard ever had a party in the old house. It was not until the war was over that the general went there to live, and he was then a lost and lonely man.

A lady at 1113 Chartres Street was taking roomers, and the general rented a bedroom. He wanted privacy, and so she gave him a room on the courtyard, and, shutting himself in, he began the book that he hoped would justify his military tactics and explain his defeats. As he wrote, the great tattered leaves of the banana trees rustled mournfully in the February rain. The wind sighed in the oleanders. And the dead, dried fronds of the courtyard palms made a sad and lonely sound like the wind and the rain together. Eighty years later I read the general's book in the courtyard where the banana leaves still rustle, and began this one of my own about the Creole city that he loved and the house where he was so unhappy.

The general hardly went out that winter because New Orleans was a heartbreaking place for a Creole gentleman, with carpetbaggers all over the place and Negroes running for Congress. In the spring he went to live with his son René, who had found a house at 934 Royal Street. Over the entrance to the courtyard was an ironwork grille, with two doves pecking at a bowl of pomegranates. And the doves and the pomegranates are still there.

10

'TIS ALL A CHECKERBOARD

Living in Beauregard House was a beautiful adventure for a girl who had fallen in love with New Orleans. But keeping house in the Vieux Carré was not all sunshine and roses or moonlight and magnolias. It was fun, but it was also a lot of work and not as romantic as you might suppose. The price of love (the poet said) is this, a crown of thorns for your head and vinegar to your kiss, and the price of loving the Beauregard House was blisters and fatigue, and the cockroaches that infest the kitchen were thorns and vinegar.

Houses of the Vieux Carré in their day and age were modern homes for modern living. La famille was the core of Creole life, and the old homes, with utter disregard for the outside world, were built so that the front of every house was in the back. Then family life and parties centered in complete privacy about the courtyard which, at the time, was a nice idea, for life in those days was ample and leisurely and a hostess didn't get blisters toting mint juleps around the flagstones, because slaves were a sou a dozen. Time fell asleep in the afternoon sunshine, and nobody hurried and nobody cared.

Life is not like that any more. It has changed in many ways— not all for the better nor all for the worse. But gone are the julep passers and the sunlit leisure of ante-bellum days. Creole houses without servants are a mockery and a delusion, and a flagged courtyard a snare to blister a lady's feet.

Beauregard House is not so very big. But it is far-flung—fifty-seven feet wide by seventy feet deep, not counting the galleries, front and rear—and a 150-yard dash from the courtyard to the telephone, and the leg work adds up. There are not many rooms, but they are extraordinarily large, and a cocktail party was a marathon, what with rushing canapés from the kitchen and passing hors d'œuvres around the ballroom. Dinner parties began with drinks in the courtyard, proceeded up a flight of stairs to the dining room, and ended with café brûlot on the gallery. And it was all very pleasant, but definitely fatiguing.

The worst, however, of keeping house in the Vieux Carré are the cockroaches. Creole cockroaches have squatters' rights in the French Quarter, because their ancestors came over on the first ships. And they mosey around the old kitchens and courtyards as if they owned them. Cockroaches are nocturnal creatures. Most of them, Greenwich Village cockroaches, for example—scuttle like mad when you put on the lights and surprise them. But Creole cockroaches just wave their whiskers (which are unusually long and revolting) and go on about their business. And it doesn't make any difference what a wonderful housekeeper you are, or where you hide the food. There they are, and there they stay. It doesn't even make any difference how much insecticide you use.

New Orleanians say you are squeamish to let such little things bother you. But Creole cockroaches are not little things. They are peculiarly BIG things. And they make themselves at home in even the private dining rooms of the most famous restaurant.

*　　*　　*

A house, we are told, should be designed for the way a family lives, and the old homes of the Vieux Carré were designed exactly that way. Many of them are beautiful and they all have charm. But for modern living almost anyone would swap a ballroom for automatic heating—or a garconnière for a guest room with bath.

A garconnière was where the sons of the family slept. It was a wing of the house that extended along one side of the courtyard. When a boy was big enough to stay out nights, he moved from his little-boy bedroom into the garconnière, so that his mother would not sit up waiting for him and worrying about what time he got in. Many Creole youths before marriage (and sometimes afterward) had Quadroon mistresses. Their mothers knew about the beautiful colored girls who lived in little houses along the ramparts. But pure flowers of southern womanhood were not supposed to mention such matters, and to keep peace in the family it was customary for white women to practice a technique of dissimulation. (I am going to tell about the Quadroons and their famous balls in another chapter.) The garconnières where the bachelors slept were also used for guests who were not exactly friends of the family and were not persons of social importance. They were for business agents and people like that.

Beauregard House is not as grand as the Haunted House where Madame Lalaurie tortured her slaves and the little black girl leapt to her death from the roof, or as big and pretentious as some of the other mansions in the Vieux Carré. But it has an enduring elegance, with its white columns and the grace of its curving granite staircases. Iron gates open to the court—and the courtyard is almost as it used to be, with the slave quarters in the back, with the garconnière on one side, and the kitchen and service rooms on the other, with the rose of Montana climbing the old walls and the tattered leaves of the bananas forever rustling in the breeze.

Jeanne de Lavigne, who wrote *Ghost Stories of Old New Orleans,* thinks that the Beauregard House is "the most beautiful house in the Vieux Carré." "It stands intensely solid," she says, "mute, brooding and inscrutable." *Inscrutable* is a word that beautifully expresses its quality. But I do not think that it is beautiful. I used to wonder when I lived there about the Le Carpentiers, who built the old place, and Paul Morphy, who was born in it, and about General Beauregard, who stood on its granite steps on an

April day in 1866 and spoke to a group of men in tattered gray uniforms. And I used to wonder about Pietro Giacono who shot three men to death. They were men of the Mafia, and in the morning when Mrs. Giacono took in the milk, she found a fourth who was badly wounded, lying under the banana tree.

People say that if you spend a night in Beauregard House with the candles unlit and the doors barred, the night closes down tightly until about two o'clock, and then the most terrible things happen. Miss de Lavigne (who wrote the ghost stories) says that people, laughing bravely at midnight, have hurried away at dawn with white faces and tales to chill your blood. But I think that Mrs. Keyes frightened the ghosts away—or exorcised them, perhaps, with Father Murphy (who wrote *The Scarlet Lily* and *Père Antoine*)— because there were no such happenings while I was there.

The legend is that the furnishings of the place dissolve like fog, and every room becomes filled with things of another century. There are a number of old things in the house now—General Beauregard's armoire and his portrait, and Mrs. Keyes's bed, old sofas of rosewood, crystal chandeliers and gilt-framed mirrors. But everything that is not old is said to disappear—cocktail tables, I suppose, the deck chairs on the gallery, and Mrs. Keyes's big desk. Then everything in the courtyard is supposed to burst into blossom, gardenias and jasmine, roses and fleurs-de-lis. The hibiscus blooms like mad, and the banana plants burst into fruit and big purple blossoms. Slaves move across the old flagstones, and up the white staircase to the gallery.

From the ballroom comes the general, and around him spring the silent dead—thousands of them—some with their faces shot away, some with no legs. They fill the house and the back gallery and the courtyard. They are the dead who died at Shiloh. The general straightens and salutes, and the dead grow dim, and slowly fade away, and when the dawn comes creeping down Chartres Street the flowers fade and the general disappears.

There was a house in Dominica in the West Indies where I used to visit, and the man who lived there—and also his servants—sometimes saw his mother's ghost standing behind my chair at dinner. It distressed me because I could not see her, and when I heard that the Beauregard House was haunted I was delighted, because, although I have always been interested in ghosts, I had never seen one and I thought that now I might be more fortunate since I was to be alone and ghosts are said to appear oftenest to people when they are alone. It grieves me to report that although I sat on the gallery nearly every night, waiting and hoping, not one ghost ever appeared to me.

Beauregard House was built in 1827 by Monsieur Joseph Le Carpentier, the celebrated "double-tongued" auctioneer of the Vieux Carré—which meant that his English was as good as his French, and what he auctioned was slaves. Enriched by the rising tide of ante-bellum prosperity, the Le Carpentiers desired a home to eclipse the neighbors'.

One-story houses had given way to more elegant structures known as courtyard houses, built in solid blocks, with flat façades, and not a bit of what you might call "front interest." The Le Carpentiers, influenced by the Greek Revival, decided upon what is known as "the raised basement single-story type"—a little like Madame John's, but more stylish, with a wide front gallery, white pillars, granite staircases, and nice ornamental ironwork. There was dignity to a white-pillared mansion, a combination of magnificence and restraint.

Inside there would be high-ceilinged rooms—a central hall, flanked on one side by the drawing room and ballroom, with elaborate frescoes and rich cornices, and beyond the ballroom a powder room—across the hall the bedrooms. The dining room at the end of the hall would open, through three great doors with fanlight transoms, on the back gallery above a courtyard, with a fountain surrounded by tropical flowers.

The Spanish called them patios—the courtyard gardens that are an inseparable part of Creole architecture. But the Le Carpentiers were French, and theirs was a courtyard. Against the slave quarters, so they could enjoy it from the gallery, they planted rose of Montana. Since almost anything would grow in a courtyard, they also planted a clump of bamboos and a date palm, a fig tree, camellias from China, and French roses.

Monsieur Le Carpentier found some black African marble for the fireplaces, and Madame Le Carpentier had the floors carpeted in rich crimson. Many of the Creoles had their walls papered, but the Le Carpentiers decided on whitewash, as being more effective with the red carpets.

Before the house was finished, Monsieur Le Carpentier sent for a great quantity of variegated seeds. He had the ground harrowed along Chartres Street to the corner of Ursuline, and sent his slaves to the swamps for wild iris and lilies, and clumps of ginger with dark leaves that looked as if they were polished. These were planted along the banquette, with a variety of woodland ferns. When the seeds came, the slaves scattered them among the swamp plants all the way to the corner where the land was open to the street with no wall to shut it in. Nobody had ever before seen a man's garden, unless they knew him well enough to sit in his courtyard. But when the Le Carpentier flowers blossomed everyone could enjoy them, because Chartres Street was the main thoroughfare where almost all the stores were. Everybody thought it was a charming thing that Monsieur Le Carpentier had done.

The Le Carpentiers had a daughter—Louise Thérèse Felicité Thelcide. The Creoles all had long names, and because of the size of Creole families several members often had the same name. But they were shortened to pretty alliterative nicknames like Dedée and Mimi and Popo and Zaza, so that it was less confusing. Almost everybody in the old days had a petit nom, and Louise was Loulou. Loulou Le Carpentier married Alonzo Morphy, and became the mother of Paul Morphy, world champion chess player, who was born at 1113 Chartres Street. Long before the place became known as the Beauregard House, it was famous as the birthplace of Paul Morphy—whose name, as you might guess, was originally Murphy. The way the Murphys became Morphys was no doing of their own.

Many people change their names these days, but an Irishman would never do such a thing at all. It was what happened to an ancestor by the name of Michael O'Murphy, who went from Ireland to Spain where the people called him Don Miguel Morphy, and Morphy it was from that day to this. Michael married a lady from Castile and the children took after their mother's side of the house. He had a son, Diego, born in Madrid, who came to New Orleans and founded the Creole branch of the family. There was a Morphy debutante I met in New Orleans, more Spanish than Irish and a great belle, with liquid dark eyes and a Latin air.

Although the Creoles were mostly French and Spanish, many of the Spanish had a good dash of Irish in them. The first Spanish governor, you remember, was an O'Reilly, and there were the Spanish Macartys whose daughter became Madame Lalaurie and tortured her slaves in the Haunted House.

There were also German Creoles—notably the aristocratic and enormously wealthy Labranches, who were once the Zweigs. Johann Zweig, the first of the family in New Orleans, came from Metz. Johann's son, who was also Johann, fell in love with a girl named Suzanne Marchand. When Johann proposed, Suzanne accepted him upon condition that he change his German name. Johann agreed, and the priest who married them twisted *Johann* to *Jean,* and *Twig* to *Branch.* The Labranches had a son—Jean—who made a fortune in sugar, and built the beautiful Labranche mansion at the corner of Royal and St. Peter streets that is known as the Lacework Building, and is now the House of the Artists. Along the cast-iron balconies, oak leaves are entwined with acorns in a pattern of *zweigs* or *branches* that is one of the nicest designs in town, and the jacket on this book is the way it looks to John O'Hara Cosgrave II.

If you are interested in ironwork, there is a shop at 603 Royal Street where you can buy almost anything from a gallery railing or a porte-cochere to a flowerpot holder, all cast in authentic old designs. The company has been in business on Prytania Street ever since New Orleans became famous for its cast iron, and the shop is a sort of showroom for the foundry.

In the beginning, the ironwork in the Vieux Carré was hand wrought. Some of it was brought from Spain, and some was made in the colony. There is not very much of the first iron left, and although wrought iron sounds somehow more romantic, the cast iron was usually more beautiful. When a pattern was created for a customer—such as the acorn design for the Labranches—the manufacturer kept the mold, and used it again, usually for people who lived out of town. Most of the old patterns are now for sale at the shop on Royal Street, the tulip and rose vine patterns, the morning-glory and the maize. The live oak is generally considered the most beautiful. There is a grape design that I prefer, but connoisseurs say it is "busy," and not as "chaste" as the others.

But to get back to the Morphys—when Louise Le Carpentier married Alonzo, they went to live with the bride's parents, in the house on Chartres Street with the lovely garden. While they were living there Mrs. Morphy had a baby, and as he was born on St. Paul's day, they called him Paul. He was a sickly child, and the Morphys continued to live with the Le Carpentiers so Loulou's mother could help with the baby.

Paul's father, who was a Supreme Court judge, used to play chess in the courtyard while the little boy watched. One day at the end of a game Paul, who was five at the time, remarked, "You won, Papa, but you made the wrong move with your knight."

"Who taught you to play!" exclaimed the judge.

"Nobody," said the child. "I just watched."

"Sit down, mon petit chou," said the judge, "and show Papa."

So the little boy sat down and showed his father, and defeated him so easily that the judge was the proudest man in the Vieux Carré. The next day he took Paul around to the New Orleans Chess, Checkers and Whist Club to meet some real players. The gentlemen laughed when the judge proposed a game with his son, but their laughter soon changed, for only the best of them could beat the little boy.

Before Paul was eleven, he had beaten the greatest chess players in the South. When he was twelve, Herr Loewenthal, the celebrated Hungarian, visited New Orleans, and Paul beat him too. The master was so impressed that he embraced the child and prophesied that he would become the greatest player in the world, which is exactly what happened.

The Morphys were sensible people and kept their little Quiz Kid under blankets. He was permitted to play only on Sundays, and never more than three games at a time. Mrs. Morphy was an accomplished pianist, and the judge a great scholar. The whole family played chess, and talked brilliantly and with equal fluency in four languages. All Creoles talked French and had a smattering of Spanish, and after the Purchase most of them had learned English. But the Morphys knew it all the time. Mrs. Morphy had a salon that helped to form the thinking and the culture of the Vieux Carré, first on Chartres Street and later on Royal Street. Wherever there were Morphys the fashionable literati gathered.

When Paul was small, the judge bought the Louisiana Bank Building, and the family moved upstairs. Living above stores and over offices seems strange to most Americans. But it was a Creole custom, and even the wealthiest and most fashionable people did it. The judge bought the building, the loveliest casa grande in the Vieux Carré, at auction for $35,000, and spent as much again to make it even lovelier. Now it is a restaurant called the Patio Royal where tourists dine in the Morphy courtyard, while guides point out the L.B.'s in the wrought-iron balconies. "L.B." stood for Louisiana Bank.

The special drink of the restaurant is called patio royal. It is really a Sazerac, and about as good as you are likely to get, especially if you are a woman because women can't go to the Sazerac Bar where the best ones are made. But a patio royal is a good drink, particularly when served in the shade of the old magnolia tree where the Morphys used to sit (most likely) and listen to the mockingbirds.

Paul was at college when his father died and he came home and passed his bar examinations. He was nineteen and knew Louisiana's civil code by heart. Since he was too young to practice, he accepted an invitation from the Manhattan Chess Club to enter America's first Chess Congress. The Manhattan Club is the second oldest chess club in the country. The first one was the New Orleans Chess, Checkers and Whist Club, where the judge took his little boy to play. It is now called the Paul Morphy Chess Club.

While Paul was in New York, the Manhattan players asked him to sit for a portrait to hang in their club room. The club is on Central Park South, in the block where I live, and since I was writing about Paul I went around to see what he looked like. The painting is an oil in a big, baroque frame and unless the artist flattered him, Paul was a beautiful boy, like the young Byron, and the lines Emerson wrote about his son:

> The hyacinthine boy, for whom
> Morn well might break and April bloom,
> The gracious boy who did adorn
> The world whereunto he was born.

Paul's features were sweet and proud. He was slight—five feet four—with soft, wavy hair, a high forehead and a gentle mouth with full lips, a Creole patrician to his fingertips.

In New York he defeated every master, beating his strongest rival by the crushing score of 5-1, and capturing the prize silver salver, pitcher and goblets. The New Orleans club was so proud that the members took up a collection and presented Paul with a set of antique Burmese chessmen. They wanted to send him abroad, to play at club expense in London, Paris and Germany. Paul was not interested, but his mother persuaded him to go. He should spend his own money, she said, in order that everything should be quite correct.

In Creole society it was a principle that no gentleman should earn money except in certain occupations. The professions were acceptably genteel. In business a gentleman might be a planter, a banker or a merchant. With discretion, he might venture into politics. A gentleman could not, of course, engage in manual labor, because that was what slaves were for. Well-born persons were sometimes obliged to earn their living in stores and shops. But a *real* aristocrat was never seen in public without coat, cravat and gloves.

In Manhattan, men had played chess in their vests, and when the Creoles heard about it they were shocked. Paul, warned that the New Yorkers might be common, had set an elegant example in striped trousers and swallowtail, with a stiff white shirt, an extremely high collar, and a crimson cravat of Persian silk. There was something, he was afraid, a little vulgar about the game—nothing on which he could quite put his finger. But if chess was not a gentlemen's game, Paul wanted no part of it.

With misgivings he kissed his mother and sisters good-bye and sailed for Liverpool. In London, where he played brilliantly, Paul was so undemonstrative that even taciturn Englishmen were astonished at his restraint. They took him to Buckingham Palace, to Westminster Abbey, and to Simpson's for luncheon.

And all he said was "I am sure it is very nice."

His ambition was a match with Howard Staunton, the leading

English player, who was past his prime and reluctant to meet the young master. Time and again Staunton presented excuses. While Paul waited, he met and defeated all comers, until he had become the first (although unofficial) world champion. Staunton continued to avoid the match that would have made the title official.

During his stay in London Paul gave a blindfold exhibition on eight boards, and astonished the press by reading a book while his opponents pondered their moves. Finally, despairing of a match with Staunton, he went to France, where he was flattered by men of genius and asked to dine with dukes. The great Lequesne begged him to sit for a marble bust and when it was done, Lequesne sent it to Mrs. Morphy who kept it on a rosewood table in the front parlor, under a portrait of the judge.

During his triumphant tour Paul defeated every famous player who would meet him, and became the undisputed King of Chess. When he sailed for America, he had three trunks filled with trophies and gifts for the family.

His ship docked in New York and he was given an ovation at the pier and escorted, like a returning hero, to the Union Club, where he was crowned with a wreath of silver laurel. The next night there was a banquet where he was presented with a set of precious chessmen and a magnificent gold watch. The chessmen were of pure gold and silver set on carnelian pedestals, and the eyes of the figures were rubies. After the presentation the chessmen were exhibited in Tiffany's window, and the watch was exhibited at R. Rumrill's on Broadway.

Paul, who always played deadpan, received his honors with quiet composure. It was known that he disliked to have chess spoken of as a profession. To him it was an art, but one of the lower arts. When an unfortunate toastmaster in Boston referred to him as an "honor to his profession," he launched into angry protest. The occasion was the presentation of another extraordinary watch, on which the numerals were jeweled kings and queens and bishops and rooks. After an embarrassing moment, Paul apologized and accepted the gift with his best Creole manners.

Word of his European triumphs was telegraphed from New York to "a highly respectable gentleman of the Vieux Carré," who carried the news to *L'Abeille,* and the editor published it on the front page.

Shortly after his return there was a performance at the French Opera House and Paul, attending with his family, renewed acquaintance with a childhood friend who was making her first appearance that night. There were no debuts in Creole society. When a girl finished at the convent her family rented a box for the opera, and that was her bow to society. Wearing a gorgeous gown, carrying a bouquet of roses and a lovely lace fan, she received between acts. Everyone in the house kept count of the number of men who visited her box, and the girls prayed to St. Joseph to send them a crowd. Thereafter they were in circulation, and ready for beaux.

Paul chatted for a while, paying his respects to her mother and tantes. The next day he sent a friend as intermediary, to ask permission of the girl's father to call. Thereafter on Wednesday evenings he played dominoes with her father, while her mother and tantes plied him with questions about acquaintances and fashions in Paris. He was never, of course, alone with the girl for a moment. Such an impropriety would have been shocking.

One evening as he took his departure, Paul told the family that he was journeying north on a matter of unfinished business. The next day he left for New York where he signed a contract with the *Ledger* to edit a chess column, for which he was paid $3,000 in advance. Then he went to Boston for a testimonial banquet at the Parker House, where he was honored by America's great men of letters. The Quaker poet Whittier sat at one end of the table, and Mr. Longfellow at the other. Down the long board were Lowell and Dr. Holmes and Agassiz, and old Mr. Alcott, Richard Henry Dana and young William Dean Howells. Between toasts, the

Brahmins crowned Paul with a golden crown. He was then twenty-two years old.

That night he wrote his mother of the distinguished men who had done him honor, and told her of his desire to marry and establish himself in the Vieux Carré. Upon his return to New Orleans, Paul sent the friend who had previously acted as intermediary to ask for the hand of the girl he wanted. Her father received the young man and listened attentively as he pressed Paul's suit. The girl, of course, was not consulted. But it happened that Paul's friend heard an exclamation that drifted in from the gallery as mother and daughter listened beyond closed jalousies to the conversation in the parlor, and he told Paul what he heard.

"Mais, mon Dieu, maman!" exclaimed the girl. "Popo is a *chess player!*"

That was the end of Paul. He had known from the beginning that chess was a mistake, for he was as much of a snob as the girl. Because he had violated the tenets of his Creole world, he determined then to re-establish himself as an aristocrat, and resolved to be a great lawyer like his father. He would also be a man of letters.

He broke his contract with the *Ledger,* and gave away or destroyed his chessmen and trophies—his golden crown and marble bust, and the beautiful watch that was given him in Boston. Collectors would give a fortune for Paul's gold and silver chessmen, or any of the chessmen with which he played.

Chess collectors are a fanatic lot. There was an Englishman who had one of the finest chess collections in the world. He spent every dollar he had getting sets together. And then he was broke and had to sell them. He sold the collection to Gustavus A. Pfeiffer of New York for $90,000, and pretty soon he started collecting once more. In a few years he had spent the entire $90,000. Then he cabled Mr. Pfeiffer to ask if Pfeiffer would buy him out again.

Mrs. Morphy took Paul's chess table when her son started throwing things away, and used its compartments for her sewing. After her death, the table was handed down in the family until Mrs. Regina Morphy Voitier gave it to the Metropolitan Museum of Art, where it is now in the American Wing.

Very few women play chess—perhaps because they have better things to do, or maybe because it involves a lot of keeping quiet. Players never talk when playing. They just snarl occasionally. Reporters covering a grand tournament in New York said that six contestants were not on speaking terms at the beginning of the tournament, and all eleven had stopped speaking before it was over. Addicts often have nervous breakdowns and sometimes, like Paul Morphy, they become queer.

Once when his opponent—the celebrated Paulsen—sat for fourteen hours without making a move, Paul broke down and cried. A number of people thought it was about time.

Nowadays such a nerve-racking thing could not happen. In twentieth-century chess, players are given an allotted period in which to make a specified number of moves. If they do not make the required moves they automatically lose. Tournaments are played with two clocks on the table. As soon as a player makes a move, he presses a button that stops his clock and starts his opponent's. Paul was a fabulously quick thinker, and Paulsen's calculated deliberation was a trick to wear him down. He apologized for his tears, and pulled himself together. The match was a draw. A chess player's nerves, like an athlete's legs, are the first thing to go, and great players are proverbially temperamental. But Paul was so mannerly and considerate that he was known as "the chivalrous Bayard of chess."

Capablanca, who at his death in 1942 held all the major world records, was once charged with tampering with tournament time clocks, so that his own ran slow while his opponent's ran fast. The promoter of the same match accused the challenger of smoking cigars that made Capablanca, and also the promoter, sick at their stomachs. Chess is obviously not always a gentleman's game, and that was one reason why Paul hated it.

At twenty-two his phenomenal success was over, and the rest of his life—twenty-five lonely years—was misery. He opened a law office, but although he knew the Napoleonic Code backward, his practice never amounted to anything. If clients mentioned chess, he lost his temper and drove them away.

"I wish never to hear of chess again!" he told them.

Although he was a genius, he was immature and belonged to the aristocracy of the sensitive who are easily destroyed. Finally he gave away his lawbooks and declined cases. He developed a persecution mania, and brought causeless suit against his brother-in-law. Fearing that enemies sought to poison him he refused to eat anything prepared by the servants, and his mother or sister had to cook his food.

At last the family decided to send him to a sanatorium called the Louisiana Retreat. Paul obligingly drove to the door with them, and there, he summoned the superintendent and discussed his rights so convincingly that the nuns who ran the place refused to accept him.

Every day at exactly noon he went for a walk down Royal Street, swinging a little Malacca stick. Shopkeepers in the Vieux Carré set their clocks when they saw him pass. In the evening he threw an opera cloak across his shoulders and strolled through Jackson Square to the levee, wearing a tall silk hat and looking every inch the Creole gentleman.

This went on for twenty-five years until there came a very hot day in July when Paul was forty-seven—and Death made the final move. He had taken his morning walk and returning home, drew a hot bath. The Creoles did not believe in bathing when the body was overheated, and nobody was surprised that Paul died in the tub.

He was buried in St. Louis Cemetery Number One, where most of the old Creoles sleep. On his grave it says:

Paul Morphy
ne le 22 Juin 1837
decede le 10 Juillet 1884

This stanza from the *Rubaiyat* would be a nice epitaph for him:

> 'Tis all a Chequer-board of Nights and Days
> Where Destiny with Men for Pieces Plays:
> Hither and thither moves and mates and plays,
> And one by one back in the Closet lays.

Paul Morphy was the first American sportsman to attain world fame, and he was internationally so much more famous than General Beauregard that it seems strange his birthplace should be named for the general. But if Paul knows anything about it, he would be the soul of tact and courtesy, and he may have told the general, as they stroll the Elysian Fields together, that chess was a dreadful mistake and all he wants is to be forgotten.

11

THE VIEUX CARRÉ

There is so much to tell about the Vieux Carré that it is hard to know where to begin. There is the temptation to be sentimental, to write about "houses too beautiful to be true" and "dreamy patios filled with moonlight and roses." The best thing probably is to stick to history and facts. There are the narrow streets and iron lace balconies that you have seen in magazines and the movies and the patios where, in books you have read, Jubal kissed Mimi in the moonlight. The flowery courtyards are restaurants now, and patio bars. And some of them are shops where colored mammies make pralines, and white women sell dolls dressed like old-time Creole characters, the Baroness de Pontalba, Marie Laveau, and Jean Laffite and Père Antoine.

The old houses, grim and a little arrogant, stand with their backs to the banquette, and although you may sit in the courtyards, the only time you can visit the houses of the Vieux Carré and also the old houses of the Garden District is during Spring Fiesta, when they are open to visitors. During Fiesta, many plantation homes along the Mississippi also are open, and there are tours from New Orleans all the way to Natchez.

Spring is a darling season in New Orleans. Then the Vieux Carré is the representation of a dream world. And there is re-created that wonderful age of security and Creole aristocracy when men were born with gold spoons in their mouths and girls with satin in their hope chests, when life was upholstered with mammies and juleps.

And all the men were brave and all the girls were fair, and nobody ever dreamed of plumbing or bombs.

Oliver La Farge once opened a novel with the line, "New Orleans was a mystery and a promise," having in mind the Vieux Carré on a warm night. "The hot nights (said Mr. La Farge) stirred you until you had a cat's longing to prowl, down streets turned utterly silent, by doors that gave out snatches of music, and the blocks where the whispers and the eyes of the whores behind the shutters made a false promise of romance."

That is the kind of writing, and also the kind of prowling, that I love. But there are many people who would never, in this world, get a cat's longing to prowl, and they would not be found dead (I should hope!) in the blocks where the whores and shutters are. There is not a Red Light District any more. But there are a few blocks that are given over to bars and jazz where blondes and sailors meet, and seedy characters drift in and out of the shuttered houses, and I expect that is what Mr. La Farge had in mind.

He also mentioned the trolleys. Anything could happen, he said, in a town where the signs on the trolleys say *Desire*. In Havana it used to say *Jesus* on the trolleys, and that seemed sacrilegious. But of course it wasn't sacrilegious. It was a proper name like Desire Street, which was originally Rue de la Désiré, and named by a lovesick Creole long ago.

There used to be a great deal of gambling in the Vieux Carré. There were slot machines in every bar, and people playing for money at the tables. Mayor deLesseps Story Morrison, who was elected on a reform ticket, wanted to regulate gambling, and tax and zone it. But the voters defeated his proposal, and now the mayor is enforcing laws that were never enforced before.

If you want to gamble, you can drive to either Jefferson or St. Bernard Parish where it is permitted, where there are smart night clubs with gaming tables, and croupiers like Monte Carlo. Where ladies wear evening gowns, and men watch the tables through peepholes in the walls, with their two eyes glued to one hole and a machine gun to another. But the casinos are nowhere near the Vieux Carré where there isn't, these days, even a slot machine.

Physically the Quarter has not changed much of late, except for the transients, the young men who wear whiskers and berets and corduroy pants, the poets and playwrights in the coffee shops, and the artists with their easels on balconies and banquettes. The Bohemians make the place seem a little like Greenwich Village or Paris on the Left Bank, and occasionally the young men upset a trend. For years the most photogenic landmark in the Vieux Carré was the Brulatour courtyard. But now it is a girl called Stormy who does a strip tease at the Casino Royale. Next year it may be another girl, or it may be the Brulatour courtyard again.

The Brulatour courtyard is part of the mansion where François Seignouret lived, who made the big beds that are sometimes for sale on Royal Street. Its patio is so favored by artists that the charming sketches and tinted photographs are exceedingly tiresome. But before pointing out courtyards, it might be better to tell you something about Creole architecture, which is completely puzzling until it is explained. Then you can wander around by yourself, taking pleasure in the quaint streets, the ironwork, and the sun. If you prefer company, there are buses and tallyhos, and guides on every corner. For a more appreciative approach, you might try getting in touch with a lady whose great-grandmama's mantilla is in the Cabildo, Mrs. Henry Fish Reynick, a quite special guide. If you are a hound for details, buy Mr. Stanley Arthur's comprehensive directory, *Old New Orleans.* If you are in New Orleans during Spring Fiesta, go to Fiesta headquarters in the Pontalba Building, and pick yourself a nice ladyguide. Miss Laura Simons is a nice one. And so, I suppose, are ever so many other ladies whom I do not know.

The Vieux Carré is about a mile square, and its narrow stone streets are hard on the feet. It doesn't make any difference how comfortable your shoes are, the Vieux Carré is going to wear you out. If you want to see it all in one day, get an early start, and break the day with luncheon in one of the courtyard restaurants. Rest awhile in mid-afternoon in Jackson Square, and go at sunset when the long cool shadows hover to Pat O'Brien's patio for a mint julep. If you don't like mint juleps, go to the Courtyard Kitchen for homemade ice cream, or just a cup of tea. Then if you want some perfume, to remind you of New Orleans when you are far, far away, go to Mrs. Hovey-King's in the next block for sweet olive toilet water that smells almost like the real flowers.

It is possible to see the Vieux Carré in a day. But it is pretty fatiguing, and nothing I would recommend. Anything short of three days is something of an endurance test. But if your time is limited, you can plan accordingly. If you have two days, I would suggest wandering around the streets the first day, and saving the second day for the Cabildo, the Presbytère, Jackson Square and the Cathedral.

Every visitor should have luncheon in at least two courtyards, the Patio Royal, the Court of the Two Sisters, or the Courtyard Kitchen. They are all beautiful, but the Courtyard Kitchen, I think, is the most beautiful. It is also the most expensive, the least crowded, and there is no liquor served there. The Patio Royal and the Court of the Two Sisters are open for dinner, and there is dancing at night in the Court of the Two Sisters. The Courtyard Kitchen serves only luncheon and tea.

It would be a sin and shame to visit New Orleans and not have dinner at Arnaud's, Antoine's and Galatoire's. There is also La Louisiane, which was a Creole mansion and is now a beautiful restaurant. Then there is Broussard's, where there is a statue of Napoleon in the courtyard. When brandy is served, a bell is rung, the lights go out, and the poor silly waiters salute the statue. Some people think the statue was an award for distinguished food. But it was really a prize in a Napoleon brandy selling contest.

The Vieux Carré is a good, small restaurant, specializing in excellent French dishes. Most of the restaurants are French or Creole. But

Jimmy Moran's is Italian. Jimmy's specialty is meat balls and spaghetti, but his crayfish bisque is almost as famous as shrimps Arnaud or oysters Rockefeller. Tujague's, opposite the French Market, is inexpensive and colorful. When you have dined, go to the Little Theatre if there is a play, have a drink afterward at the Old Absinthe House, and then go to the French Market for café au lait.

"The Vieux Carré looked like Hell's Kitchen."

The Vieux Carré has had its ups and downs for more than two hundred years, and now it is one of the greatest tourist attractions in America. First it was the little village of a bourgeois aristocracy. In the second and third generations the Creoles became wealthy, and for over a hundred years they maintained a tradition of elegance. During the War Between the States they were ruined, and after the war the Vieux Carré became a slum. Carpetbaggers and Negroes moved in. Italian immigrants moved up from the waterfront, and loose ladies moved down from the north.

Ironwork was ripped off, fireplaces and mantels torn out. Archways were bricked up, and courtyards boarded. Patios were roofed with tin, advertisements were nailed over hand-forged gates, and lacework balconies were covered with plaster. Then the Vieux Carré looked like Hell's Kitchen, but it still had *something*.

In the thirties, the local government appealed to the federal government. The WPA remodeled the Pontalba Buildings, and Mr. Irby (the man I told you about who committed suicide) paid for the reconstruction of the Cathedral, the Patio Royal, and a number of other old buildings. In 1936 an amendment was added to the state constitution for the preservation of Creole antiquities, and a commission appointed to watch over the Vieux Carré.

It was a fortunate circumstance that under French and Spanish rule builders were obliged to file plans and color sketches for everything they built. The old painted sketches show the exact color of every house and building. Ironwork was usually green, but sometimes black. Buildings were soft pinks and twilight blues, pale greens and yellows, and some were white.

The commission, with access to these plans, secured legislation which forbade building and painting that does not conform to the established customs of the Vieux Carré. Empowered with extraordinary strength, the commission has secured the arrest and directed the prosecution of offending builders and painters, and the courts have ordered unauthorized structures demolished. Now, if Mr. Rockefeller, or someone else with a golden wand, would reconstruct le Vieux Carré de la Ville as colonial Williamsburg was reconstructed, it would be as beautiful and even more interesting, because there never was, before or afterward, anything in America like New Orleans' French Quarter.

Architecture to be good must be honest, and there is no doubt about the integrity of the houses in the Vieux Carré. They are a symbol of the character of those who built them. Creole families were large, and their houses were large enough for comfortable living and vast entertaining. Built without regard for what went on in the streets, the backs of the houses are flush with the banquettes. Projecting balconies protect pedestrians from rain and sun, and are frequently ornamented with fine ironwork.

In the courtyards, where they could live outdoors ten months of the year, the builders planted trees and flowers, and brought birds in bright cages. To the Creoles, within their garden walls, belonged the earth and kingdom of heaven. There was no home in the Vieux Carré, grand or humble, without its courtyard, except in the very beginning when there were only huts, and it goes without saying there were no courtyards then. After the huts came the small houses of which I have told you, one-story cottages like Café Laffite, and two-story houses like Madame John's Legacy.

There were two great fires, you remember, and after the fires there was more beautiful building than before. Fine houses were built from the beginning of the nineteenth century, but not in great numbers until 1825.

Then came the big houses with their thick brick and stucco walls, and tunneled portes-cocheres. Courtyard gates were usually of thick wooden planks, although sometimes they were of beautiful iron. And the domed passageways were very high because the Negro coachmen always wore towering beaver hats.

On the ground floor of the houses there was always some sort of business transacted. If the owner was a planter, it was his counting-house. Lawyers and doctors had their office on the ground floor, and so did commission merchants and brokers. Architects had their draft-rooms, and merchants their storerooms. And in one beautiful house there was a gentleman who bought raw furs and made a fortune like John Jacob Astor, only not as large. Wealthy gentlemen were never, except in the case of the fur buyer, actually "in trade."

Drygoods and groceries, restaurants and saloons were for the bourgeois, whose wives, sisters and aunts waited upon the customers. Tradespeople greatly outnumbered the gentility, and a Creole gentleman would prefer to support his impoverished relatives than have them disgrace the family by engaging in common pursuits. Most families had a fainéant (loafer) or two, whom Papa supported. There was no way, of course, in which a lady could possibly earn money, and so Papa also supported all the spinster tantes and cousines.

Two blocks on Royal Street were given over to commerce, to stores and banks. Tucked in among the bigger buildings were gambling houses, coffeehouses and patisseries, apothecaries, letter-writing shops, and small stores of all kinds. It was a day of specialists, and every type of trade was stretched out on the ground-floor homes of the less well-to-do who lived on the side streets. There were cabinetmakers and silversmiths, printers, undertakers and jewelers. There were many china stores, and stores where religious articles were sold. All the shops had signs that were small and artistic and added to the charm of the streets.

There was a man from the North who visited New Orleans a hundred years ago who wrote a book about his *Southern Travels,* and this is what he saw on Rue Royale:

> Clergymen, priests, friars, nuns, women of all stains:
> Negroes in purple and fine linen and slaves in rags and chains;
> Ships, arks, steamboats, pirates, robbers, alligators;
> Assassins, gamblers, drunkards and cotton speculators;
> Sailors, soldiers, pretty girls and ugly fortune tellers;
> Pimps, imps, shrimps and all sorts of dirty fellows;
> White men with black wives, *et vice-versa* too.
> A progeny of all colors—an infernal motley crew!
> Yellow fever in February—muddy streets all the year;
> Many things to hope for, and a dev'lish sight to fear.

Royal Street is not so very different now, except that there is no yellow fever and there are no slaves, nobody makes steamboats, and there is nothing to fear. For a parallel, I made a list one day, and it could start off just the same: "Clergymen, priests, friars, nuns, women of all stains." Then come the alligators, and also turtles and horned toads, food shops and Mexican marts all in one block. Rothschild's Magnificent Antiques and Sloppy Jim's bar, native perfumes, art stores, and the Hotel Monteleone, a drugstore, a "real lace" shop, a beauty shop, Solari's, fruit stands, a furniture store, a doll shop, a fortuneteller and a sidewalk artist. There is a shop where they make cedar chests, there are restaurants and patios, a big marble court-house, and a shop where exquisite small things are carved from ivory, a silversmith, some decorators, and a printer, shops that sell precious French bric-a-brac, figurines and porcelain clocks, a toy store, an art school, beautiful mansions, and some rooming houses, a grocer, a plumber, and the Cathedral squeezed tight between Pirates' Alley and Père Antoine's Alley, a bakery, a tinsmith, more antique stores, book and print shops, an ironwork gallery, junk shops and a room-ing house for colored people—all on the street floor, in a few blocks of Royal Street, and I won't list the rest because it is getting tiresome. I will only tell you about the Wig and Toupee Shop.

There are two famous wigmaking families in New Orleans, one on Dryades Street and one on Royal Street. The biggest part of their business is making wigs and beards for Carnival. Carnival wigs are all made of human hair. Moths get into hair like they get into fur or wool, so the wigs must be kept in camphor, and aired and combed so they won't get smelly. Before the war, most human hair came from Europe. Before that, it came from China. Where it is coming from now, heaven knows.

To make beards for Carnival Kings, wigmakers import yak hair from Tibet. A yak is a stupid-looking creature between a buffalo and an ox, who chews his cud like a cow, and has long white whiskers. Yak hair is as stiff and strong as sisal and makes a wonderful beard, much better than a man could grow for himself. The dictionary says that a yak, besides his beard, has long hair fringing his shoulders, sides and tail, so that one yak would probably do nicely for several Kings.

Rue Royale was to old New Orleans what Fifth Avenue is to New York, the most elegant of thoroughfares, and the most central. It was half a block to the fencing academies in the Passage de la Bourse, a block to the gaming salons on Rue de Chartres, and a block to the French Opera, where there is nothing now but a vacant lot. The Opera House was built in 1859 from plans by Gallier the Younger, and was burned to the ground in 1919. It must have been very beautiful. For sixty years the French Opera House was the scene of operatic triumphs, and of such dazzling Carnival balls as dimmed the splendor of the Thousand and One Nights. And the night it burned was one of the saddest nights in Vieux Carré history. When they saw the walls of their dear Opera House totter, and heard them fall with a dismal crash, men cried that night. Right at the corner of Bourbon and Toulouse streets, they cried.

It is good to know that there will be a new Opera House, that it will stand on the same corner, and look exactly like the old one. And I hope that the men who cried when the old one burned will have seats for the première in the proscenium boxes of the new Opera House, that they will have beautiful ladies by their sides, in marvelous décolleté with long kid gloves, and that the beautiful ladies will wave feather fans, as they did when they were young, and wear birds of paradise in their hair, that the singers and the musicians and the ballet will measure to all their expectations, and the gentlemen and ladies will be as happy as they were when they heard the opera for the first time in the dear dead days when New Orleans was the greatest opera- and music-loving city in America.

John Galsworthy visited New Orleans when the St. Louis Hotel had fallen into decay, and wrote a piece about it called *That Old-Time Place*. A few years later a hurricane tore the roof off the hotel, and then it was torn down. But let me tell you how it looked when Galsworthy saw it.

There was an old lady who had moved in. People said she had no authority at all. She was one of those Creoles tantes, who had grown old in her brother's house, and her brother was dead, and there was no one to care for her. So she lived alone in the St. Louis Hotel, with the bats and a cat for company. And when visitors stepped over the crumbling threshold, there she was. She was tall and thin, and as gray as a wraith from the past. And she would ask for twenty-five cents, and show the visitors about.

"Now we shall see the slave market," she would say, leading the way.

Galsworthy tells how the water lay in pools on the crumbling marble floor. "And down there came wandering the strangest thing that ever strayed through deserted grandeur—a brown, broken horse, lean, with a sore flank and a head of tremendous age. It stopped and gazed at us, as though we might be going to give it things to eat, then passed on, stumbling over the ruined marbles. For a moment we had thought him a ghost—one of the many. But he was not, since his hoofs sounded. The scrawling clutter of them had died out into silence before we came to that dark, crypt-like chamber whose marble columns were ringed in iron.

"'Here's where they sold them,' the guide said. 'And in here they kept them.'

"We saw before us a sort of vault, stone-built, and low and long. Trying to pierce the darkness we became conscious, as it seemed, of innumerable eyes gazing, not at us, but through the archway where we stood, innumerable white eyeballs gleaming out of blackness. From behind us came a little laugh.

"It floated past through the archway, toward those eyes. Who was that? Who laughed in there? The Old South itself—the incredible, fine, lost soul! That old-time thing of old ideals, blindfolded by its own history! That queer proud blend of simple chivalry and tyranny,

of piety and the abhorrent thing! Who was it laughed there in the
old slave-market—laughed at those white eyeballs glaring from out
of the blackness of their dark cattle pew? What poor departed soul
in this House of Melancholy? But there was no ghost when we
turned to look—only our old guide with her sweet smile."

12

FLOWERY COURTYARDS AND OLD MANSIONS

Most of the houses in the Vieux Carré were built after the beginning of the nineteenth century. This is a good thing to remember, because most people, even architects, imagine that Creole architecture is completely of the eighteenth century. Among the few houses that weathered the last disastrous fire of 1794, were Casa Merieult at 529 Royal Street, and Casa Cavalier, more commonly known as "Patti's Court," at number 631.

Since almost everybody visits Patti's Court, I want to tell you something about Adelina and her New Orleans triumphs. But first let me straighten you out on architectural dates. The 600 block on Royal Street was built almost entirely in 1831, and after that there was very little building in the Vieux Carré. In another ten years the Garden District was flourishing, and a new generation had begun to call the Vieux Carré old-fashioned. Young people talked of lawns and porticoes, and baths with running water. The Americans in their new houses on Jackson Avenue and around Annunciation Square had flush toilets, the young people said, like Queen Victoria's in Buckingham Palace. "Mon Dieu!" their parents said. "What would those Anglo Saxons think up next!"

Patti lived on Royal Street the year she first sang at the French Opera, and the young men of the town adored her, so that they walked up and down Rue Royale all day, hoping for a glimpse of her. They unharnessed the horses from her carriages, and drew her through the streets. They told her she was the most wonderful woman in the world, that she looked like an angel and sang like a mocking-bird. And Patti, who was seventeen years old, thought it was won-derful. One night she stood on the balcony and sang *The Last Rose of Summer,* and the young men talked about that wonderful night until they grew old and died.

The ladies who live in Patti's Court sell pralines, and although I am sure they (the pralines) are very nice, I think you can get the best ones in town at 611 Royal Street, in a shop on the same block where Mrs. Tobin sells antiques and her daughter sells pralines.

The first time Patti sang in New Orleans it was in Odd Fellows' Hall, and she was nine years old. It was an age of child prodigies. Newspapers of the period tell of little boy drummers and little girl dancers. There was a Fat Girl from New Hampshire who sang, danced and played the piano. The advertisements said she could also knit, spin, weave, make a shirt and bake a batch of bread—and the poor child weighed 478 pounds!

Because there were so many young entertainers, nobody paid much attention when Ole Bull, a Norwegian violinist, announced a little girl with big dark eyes. Her name was Adelina Patti, Ole Bull said. She came from Madrid, and she would sing Jenny Lind's *Herdsman's Song,* with the echo. When the audience heard the child, they were enchanted.

No people ever loved music more than the Creoles did, or applauded it more generously. The *Delta* next day declared that Adelina was "every inch the musical prodigy she was represented to be," that her voice had "the boundless flexibility of a finished prima donna." The time would come, predicted the critic, when "she might challenge the world for a peer." And of course the critic was right.

Eight years later la petite Patti paid her second visit to the Crescent City. She was to fulfill a concert engagement. But the prima donnas at the new Opera House had not lived up to expectations, and Patti was persuaded to cancel her proposed concerts, and sing instead at the Opera House. She made her debut on December 19, 1860, in the title role of Lucia di Lammermoor, and created a sensation. Role after role followed, and in each she seemed more wonderful than before.

Twelve years later Patti returned to New Orleans. She was twenty-nine then, and the Creoles loved her as much as when she was seventeen. She sang with "a rope of diamonds around her beautiful throat," in a dress that was "a marvel of loveliness." Its effect, the newspapers said, was of "falling rose petals caught in a drift of snow." She sang magnificently, and was a vision of delight.

Ten years later she was back again. "The slender debutante," pronounced the man on the *Era,* "has mellowed into a rounded diva. The delightful freshness of yesteryear has been replaced with the polish of divinest art."

She sang *Comin' Through The Rye,* and boys who had dragged her carriage through Rue Royale, and were now middle-aged men, brought baskets of flowers to the diva of thirty-nine, and swore they loved her still.

Twenty-two years later she returned once more. It was 1904, and fifty-one years had passed since her first appearance. She was then the Baroness Cederstrom, and she sang again at the French Opera. But the old critics were dead, and the young ones did not understand.

"The audience thought it their duty to applaud that which they had paid $7.70 to hear," wrote the man on the *Times Democrat.* "The performance was worth about $1, over half of which was merited by the violinist, who was young and pretty."

There were eighteen hundred persons in the audience, mostly women eager to see how Patti held up. Gentlemen who could guess stayed away. Of those who went, some had heard Patti when she was nine, and had fallen in love with her when she was seventeen, or twenty-seven, or thirty-nine. They wanted to hear her voice again, to see if time had dealt more gently with her than with them.

She transposed the airs they had loved, to avoid notes she could not take. At the last she sang *Farewell Forever,* and tripped to the edge of the stage, and bowed and smiled and kissed first one hand and then both hands.

It was a miracle, the critics said, that she could sing at all. "It is to be hoped," they added, "that in exposing the ruins of her phenomenal endowments, Madame Patti is not merely mercenary."

* * *

Everybody wanted to get to New Orleans in those days, and in 1851 Lola Montez arrived. Lola was the ex-mistress of the king of Bavaria, who made her a countess. But the king was overthrown, and Lola was dancing again. There were all sorts of stories about her, that she was the daughter of Lord Byron and a Spanish gypsy, that her mother was a washerwoman in Scotland and her father an Indian prince.

She had sung and danced her way around the world, and the Creoles were curious to hear and to see her. But the Yankees were not. She registered at the St. Charles Hotel, and was welcomed by a Creole band whose music was drowned by the boos and catcalls of the Americans.

Lola was twenty-seven, a handsome girl, with fine hard eyes. Everywhere she went she carried a riding whip. She was sick, she said, of love and life, and fascinated by the ennobling melancholy of Catholicism.

"All is changed in my heart. What I loved before, now I hate. I think," said Lola, "that I may become a nun."

The prompter at the theater made an amorous advance that night, and Lola kicked him. To her astonishment, he kicked back. Stagedoor Johnnies attacked the prompter, who happened to be an American, and he retaliated by filing charges of assault against Lola. The case went to trial, and Lola exhibited a bruise high upon her thigh. The Creole judge dismissed the complaint, the Creole crowd applauded. And the poor Yankee prompter was known all the days of his life as "That Man Who Kicked the Countess."

Lola caught the gold fever in New Orleans, and went overland to California. When she returned, she was broke. And nobody wanted to hear her sing or see her dance. But Lola was invincible and a passionate believer in herself. She rented a hall, and charged a dollar admission. For fifteen minutes, ticket holders were privileged to gaze upon her faded beauty, shake her hand, or "converse with the Countess in English, French, German or Spanish."

Lola loved the Vieux Carré with its excitement and its romance. She said it reminded her of many places she had known, of Paris, and Algiers, and of the West Indies. She loved the quiet gardens of the nuns and the tranquillity of the convents. But the joy of living was still too strong, and the courtesan who was to become a convert returned to England, penitent but unconverted. In London she took to pious lecturing, to poverty and to prayer. And when she died, Lola was not a nun. But a Methodist.

* * *

The Vieux Carré has kept its continuity with the past. To walk its narrow streets is to be aware not only of the day's hot sun or sudden rain, but of the sun and rain of other days, when other people walked the same banquettes, seeking shelter of the same balconies. There is an almost mysterious link with the days and the lives that are gone.

I have already told you about Patio Royal, where Paul Morphy lived, about the Haunted House and the Labranche mansion, about Madame John's Legacy, Laffite's, the Napoleon House, and ever so many other places. But I have scattered them through the book, and now I am afraid you are going to miss something. And it worries me. I wish that I could gather them all, and put them in one chapter for you. And that is not the only thing I wish.

I wish I could write another chapter about the restaurants and the bars, and another about Creole food with some of the recipes I have

collected. I have recipes for the best dishes you ever tasted. I have
them from every restaurant in the Vieux Carré, and also from Kolb's
and Manale's. Kolb's, which is on St. Charles Street, specializes in
German dishes. Manale's, on Napoleon Avenue, is one of the best
restaurants in New Orleans. Pascal, who is the owner, pays a bonus
for his oysters and crayfish, and there is no better seafood in town.
One of his specialties is eggplant stuffed with shrimp which his wife
makes at home and brings to the restaurant, and she showed me how
to make it. Besides the wonderful restaurant recipes, I have recipes
from ladies who learned Creole cooking from their mothers and their
Creole grandmothers, who had the recipes from cooks who belonged
to their families before the war.

I have had dinner parties in my New York apartment with shrimps
Rémoulade from Arnaud's and oysters Rockefeller, packed in dry ice
and flown from New Orleans. Once when planes were grounded, and
I had promised my guests shrimps Creole from Lena Richard's and
they didn't come, I boiled some Fulton Market shrimps and made
the sauce myself. It turned out so well that I tried my hand at fancier
things, and now—Roy Alciatore will never in this world believe me—
but I can make oysters Rockefeller that would make Papa Jules turn
in his grave. I can also make a very good gumbo filé to say nothing
of Creole jambalaya, and crayfish bisque. I can make grillades, and
pecan pie, and pralines (Frances Tobin gave me her recipe). I can
make café brûlot, and a mint julep like General Beauregard used to
make. And, boy, can I make a Ramos gin fizz! I had meant to put
all these things in the book. But now there isn't room, so I have decided to write another book about *Creole Food and Drinks*. I have
some nice stories for it about Lafcadio Hearn, who had a restaurant
on Bourbon Street and wrote a cookbook of his own, and about absinthe, which is a fascinating subject. You will probably go to the
Old Absinthe House, or the Absinthe House Bar, for an absinthe
frappé, because practically everyone does. And I think you would be
interested in hearing what I learned about absinthe. But I cannot tell

you now. If you want to know, you will have to buy my next book, and if you like to eat, it will be a lot for your money.

Now I will tell you about Dear Dorothy Dix and Le Petit Salon. Dorothy Dix arrived in New Orleans in 1896 and went to work for the *Picayune,* where she began her *Advice to the Lovelorn* column more than half a century ago, and now it is the oldest and most popular newspaper feature in the world. Dorothy Dix told me about a stenographer who wrote her a letter, after having dinner one night with a new boy friend.

"We had four Martinis," wrote the stenographer, "and wine with dinner, and then we had liqueurs. Did I do wrong?"

"Probably," said Dorothy Dix.

Dorothy Dix is president of Le Petit Salon, a group of New Orleans ladies who meet on Thursdays for tea and culture in the beautiful old house at 620 St. Peter Street that used to be the David mansion, but now it is Le Petit Salon. The ladies bought the house when it was in sad disrepair, and restored it to its former grandeur.

One day they invited me for tea. First there was a lecture, and afterward we drank café au lait and orange pekoe out of eggshell Sèvres, while the crystal pendants on the girandoles tinkled in the breeze that crept in from the patio. And little Dorothy Dix held court in a big palissandre chair, and the ladies all chattered in French.

One of the charming things about Le Petit Salon is the bow-and-arrow ironwork on the balcony. When Mr. David built the house, he sent for the Vieux Carré ironmonger. There were Indians in New Orleans then, and Mr. David thought a railing of bows and arrows might be nice. Would Monsieur undertake the design? "Something symbolic," said Mr. David, thinking of the Choctaws.

"Avec plaisir, monsieur," said the ironmonger, who was a Frenchman with his mind always on love, and away he went. And he crossed the arrows and tied them with a bow, and for the bow he used a lovers' knot!

In some of the iron lace railings the owner's monogram is wrought into the design. You know about the baroness's "AP" on the Pontalba Buildings. Another beautiful monogram is the "LB" for Louisiana Bank over the Royal Street banquette of the Patio Royal, and almost next door there is another one, "DR," on a very old house that is now an antique shop.

The house was built in 1807 by Dominique Rouquette, who came from Bordeaux to import wines, and became very wealthy, as nearly everyone did in New Orleans who had a brain in his head. The Rouquettes had four boys and one girl, and two of the boys became famous. But Adrien was the most famous. He and Dominique Jr. were educated in Paris, where each published his first book of poetry.

Adrien came home and fell in love with an Indian girl named Oushola, which meant "mockingbird." Adrien took the name Chata-Ima, which meant "Like-a-Choctaw," and went to live among the Indians. (I think probably he and Oushola were going to be married.) But Oushola died, and Adrien went back to Paris, where Victor Hugo and Dumas père acclaimed his writings, and he became a great sensation. But all the time he kept thinking of Oushola. He came back to New Orleans and studied for the priesthood, so that he might become a missionary to her people. For a little while he had a parish in the city. But later he was given permission to conduct a mission among the Choctaws. And he lived with the Indians in the forests by the Mississippi until he was an old old man, and then he died.

*   *   *

It was the Mississippi that made and broke New Orleans. First it brought the Creoles money. Its rich earth gave them their crops, indigo, cane, cotton and rice. It brought them commerce, and multiplied their wealth. And when they had become the richest, gayest and most extravagant people in America, the Mississippi ruined them. In the War Between the States, it was the river blockades and the river gunboats that broke New Orleans. Down the Mississippi, when the war was scarce begun, came the armies of occupation. And when the war was over, down came the carpetbaggers. But the worst man who ever came down the Mississippi was Major General Benjamin F. Butler, U.S.A., or anyhow that was what the Creoles thought.

I told you about the inscription on General Jackson's statue that says:

THE UNION MUST

AND

SHALL BE PRESERVED

which seems so strange a legend in a state that not only seceded from the Union, but proclaimed herself a "free and independent nation." It was General Butler who ordered the inscription carved, Butler whom the Creoles called "Beast," because he ordered a New Orleans man hanged for pulling down the Stars and Stripes. The people also called the general "Silver Spoons" Butler because he stole their silver, they said. Of course he really didn't. History tells that he was scrupulously honest, though a very hard man.

The Army of Occupation arrived on a troop transport on May 1, 1862, a year and three weeks after Beauregard ordered the shot fired that began the war. The USS Mississippi anchored at the levee, and out poured fourteen hundred troops followed by General Butler, and Mrs. Butler no less. The Butlers proceeded to the St. Charles Hotel, where the general ordered Parlor P, traditionally reserved for notables. When the manager refused to give him the key, Butler took over the entire hotel. And the general and his wife swaggered up the broad stairs, and moved right into the best bedroom.

The streets swarmed with Union soldiers. The Creoles were away fighting with Beauregard, and since there was not a Confederate soldier in the city the women took up the cudgels. When they passed the Yankees on the streets the women drew their full skirts about them, and turned their heads away.

A few days later, a federal officer died and was buried. As the caisson passed down St. Charles Avenue, a Creole woman laughed, and Butler had her sentenced to two years on Ship Island under Negro guards. Then he issued his famous *Woman Order:*

> As the Officers and Soldiers of the United States have been sub-ject to repeated insults from the women (calling themselves ladies) of New Orleans, . . . it is ordered that hereafter when any female shall, by word, gesture, or movement, insult or show contempt for any Officer or Soldier of the United States, she shall be regarded and held liable to be treated as a woman of the town plying her avo-cation.
>
> By command of Major General Butler.

The mayor of New Orleans protested the Order, and Butler sent him to military prison where he was held for four years, in solitary confinement for six months, with a ball and chain on his leg. Butler also imprisoned a minister who refused to pray for Lincoln.

The next thing Butler did was order all soldiers who had been stonecutters in civilian life to report in Jackson Square. He had writ-ten a sentence which they were to copy on both sides of General Jack-son's statue. It was a toast, Butler said, that President Jackson made at a Jefferson Birthday dinner thirty years before. But it wasn't, ex-actly. What Jackson had said was, "Our Federal Union: It must be preserved." Butler made it a bit stronger, and told the stonecutters to carve the legend in letters that would never fade.

Butler was undoubtedly the most hated man in America. When secession came, he is said to have gone stark mad with rage, not over slavery, which he upheld as a constitutional fixture, but because he believed in the Union, and he could never forgive anyone who didn't. In New Orleans he expelled many of the best families from their homes, ordering that they "walk out into the streets with only the clothes on their backs." The Creoles hated him more than the Geor-gians hated General ("War is hell") Sherman who, by his own ad-mission, did a hundred million dollars' worth of property damage in

Georgia, and the Georgians hated Sherman for two generations and more.

Captain John William De Forest, a New England novelist with the Army of Occupation in New Orleans, wrote gossipy letters to his wife, which were published forty years after his death in a book called *A Volunteer's Adventures*. The Captain told how all the soldiers who could manage it "got drunk as pipers" when the army moved in, and how the officers took the Creoles' "elegant houses with cellars full of choice wines." It was Butler's fault, De Forest said, "for the officers understand that he likes to see it. So they use what they want, and pack up the rest to carry away." De Forest was with a field regiment, but he went into the city to dine one day with a colonel and pass the night with his adjutant, and the next day he wrote his wife:

> The adjutant's house is small, but it is a treasure box. The bedsteads are lofty four-posters, elaborately carved and of solid mahogany. In my bedroom was a bureau encrusted with patterns of gilt enamel set in tortoise shell. Bills found in a secretary proved that the furniture cost more than $15,000. Knickknacks lay about in profusion, music boxes, dress swords, inlaid pistols. Embroidered handkerchiefs worth from $20 to $50 lay tumbled in an armoire. . . . I heard the Lieutenant say, "I think I shall send this thing to my wife." He held in his hand a large tortoise shell fan which I judge must have cost fully $100. I suspect that he had no idea of its value and had never heard of fans worth more than a dollar or two. . . . The cellar is well stocked with old madeira and burgundy, but as there was no champagne, the adjutant plundered two other private wine cellars. He told me that in one day he and his friends drank 46 bottles. . . . The owner of the house was a rich swell of old French colonial stock who is now a Captain in the Rebel army. . . . Meals are exquisite, and no wonder, for the cook is a noted artiste, a handsome quadroon formerly chef in one of the best restaurants.

The invaders lived well, but many Creoles went hungry. Sugar was

$9 a pound, coffee $10 and corn meal $12. This was because New Orleans, having resolved to commit suicide if invaded, had burned her cotton, wrecked her factories, and sunk her ships. When news reached the city that Farragut's fleet was passing the blockade, church bells rang a prearranged signal, and the people broke into the warehouses and took what they could. What they could not take, they spilled on the ground. Gutters flowed with molasses and rum, and sugar lay along the banquettes like drifts of northern snow. Twelve thousand bales of cotton were carted to the levee and set on fire. Tobacco warehouses were burned, and ships and steamers set ablaze. New Orleans, sacked and gutted by her own people, was a sad sight, and that was the beginning of years of poverty and misery.

*   *   *

In April, 1865, Richmond fell. Five days later Lee surrendered, and Beauregard was summoned by Jefferson Davis to Greensboro, North Carolina, to assist in arranging details of surrender. The Great Creole went in a box car. When everything was over, he had $1.15 to get to New Orleans. His soldiers bought a wagon and stocked it with what they could buy. Then the Elegants, headed by Beauregard, peddled tobacco and nails, needles and thread from Greensboro to Atlanta. In Atlanta, Beauregard borrowed money to take a boat from Mobile to New Orleans.

His friends, the Le Carpentiers, had moved from 1113 Chartres Street, and the lady of the house was taking roomers. The general rented a room, and went job hunting. He heard that Napoleon III was looking for a military adviser and suggested a command for himself in the Argentine or Egypt. Nothing came of the idea, and he took over the presidency of a little railroad that ran from New Orleans to Mississippi. Soon the little railroad was gobbled up by a bigger railroad. Then the general lent his name, for $10,000, to the Louisiana Lottery, and with his first check he moved from Chartres Street to 943 Royal Street. The place is dreary now, but it was probably nice then, and I expect the general never returned to the house on Chartres Street, the so-called Beauregard House, where he and I each lived for a month.

The lottery that put the general on his feet was honest, but smelly. The legislature, made up almost entirely of carpetbaggers, granted the backers a 25-year charter, in exchange for an annual contribution of $40,000 to the Charity Hospital. To lend the lottery respectability, Beauregard and General Jubal Early presided at the drawings. For the use of their names they received $10,000 apiece.

The Grand Prize, the first year, was $3,700 on a 25-cent ticket. The next year, tickets were 50 cents, and the Grand Prize jumped to $7,500. After that, drawings were held semiannually. Tickets and prizes went up and up, until the Grand Prize was $600,000, and the tickets cost $40. No one person ever won the entire prize. But a New Orleans barber once held a prize-winning $20 ticket, and was paid $300,000.

When its charter expired, the Lottery Company offered the state $1,250,000 for a renewal. But the lottery was in bad repute then. Reformers said it had a demoralizing effect on the poor, and possessed political power which was being misused. A federal statute was passed prohibiting interstate sale of tickets, and the company moved to Honduras where it remained until 1907, when it was forced out of business by government prosecution of its American agents.

The worst thing that befell New Orleans and the entire South was "reconstruction" after the war at the hands of carpetbaggers, who organized the freed slaves and sent them to the legislature and to Congress. The carpetbaggers got themselves the most lucrative offices, and let the ex-slaves have the inferior ones. Many of the new legislators could not read, and there was a state senator who made speeches declaring that no one who could read or write should be allowed in the legislature. Exploited by unscrupulous whites, black men moved from the cotton fields to Esplanade Avenue, and went to Congress as poor as boll weevils and came back driving horses worth $1,000 a pair. Peace was kept only by the presence of federal troops.

Time goes fast in New Orleans, and the gap between generations was like a gulf between worlds. The Vieux Carré became a slum, and the old mansion where Paul Morphy was born and General Beauregard lived went down and down. At the beginning of the century it was bought by Sicilians who made and sold wines in its spacious rooms.

The Sicilians were honest enough, but one night a group of rough characters dropped in for supper and on the gallery afterward there were the killings I told you about. A year later, a wagon with one side screened with canvas went rumbling up Chartres Street. As it passed the house, a volley of pistol and shotgun shells spattered the walls. The Mafia was striking back. The family usually sat on the front gallery after supper. But that night they luckily sat somewhere else. Police rounded up the would-be assassins, but the winemaking Sicilians had had enough.

The house was deserted for twenty years, and was finally bought for a macaroni factory. A group of civic-minded ladies raised funds and bought it back from the macaroni man. The ladies permitted William Warrington, a noted friend of Vieux Carré bums, to use the ground floor and slave quarters as a flophouse. Warrington had an ancestral castle in England, and $5,000 a year from a sister who lived in London and wanted him to stay in New Orleans. For fifty-three years Mr. Warrington labored with his bums. Some nights there were as many as eighty, packed like shrimps in a can, lying in Monsieur Le Carpentier's old counting room, hopeless and dreamless. In the morning they shuffled into the streets, and at night they returned. When Warrington died they disappeared. Nobody knew where they went, and I guess nobody cared.

13

*P*LAGUES AND MILLIONAIRES   The Creoles' Golden
Age was an exciting, a mad and lovely age. And never was a city
gayer than New Orleans then, with balls and the opera, with gambling and dueling, and Carnival and the theater. Steamboats and
river commerce meant trade and wealth for the Crescent City, and
the Mississippi brought gold to the merchants. There was rich
foreign commerce, and ships came from all over the world to the
great port of New Orleans. Planters reaped rich harvests with sugar
and cotton, and rice and tobacco. On every plantation there were
hundreds of slaves, and everywhere there was money to burn.

The Creoles had imagination, and the sugar millionaires loved
parties. One planter, when his daughter was getting married, sent
to the Orient for a shipment of spiders, and to California for barrels
of gold and silver dust. He released the spiders in the mile-long
avenue of live oaks that led from the River Road to the Big House.
When the spiders had spun miles of filmy web, slaves with bellows
sprayed the webs with gold and silver dust, and the wedding guests,
strolling under the twinkling canopy, said to the bride, "Heaven
suah is shinin' on youah weddin', Sugar."

There was a party for General Beauregard after the first Battle of
Bull Run, when champagne was piped to a fountain in a courtyard
on Royal Street, and all night long it bubbled and flowed in a golden
stream.

Jessie Benton Frémont (daughter of the senator) went to an ante-
bellum party, and wrote a letter home to Missouri, pages on end

about the ladies, the gowns, and the beaux. Jessie described the dinner, and that was two pages more. Then she came to the dessert:

> For dessert we went into another room, large and lofty, and opening wide upon a garden, where the moonlight was making fairy effects on the feathery foliage, and changing the spray of the fountains to showering diamond dust. The table was completely covered with flowers, and all its service was cut crystal and solid gold. The Venetian glass chandelier, with its many wax tapers reflected in prismatic glass, was so wreathed with flowers as to make a subdued and charming light upon the table, which had on it only fruits and ices and fragrant wines.
>
> In a wide circle were young slaves in pure white, each with a great, long-handled fan of peacock's feathers, which they waved gently—fanning the air in the same way as the *punkah-wallahs* of India. Large mirrors lined the room, and repeated this lovely picture of softly brilliant light on flowers and waving peacock plumes, making an endless vista of gardens and fountains. . . . There were sixteen courses, with music and much wine. . . .

"To eat and to drink and to be merry" was the Creoles' motto. For tomorrow they might die, and they wanted to forget it. Plagues swept the city periodically, and a fearful proportion of the people died of cholera and yellow fever. The year after a plague, Mardi Gras was gayer than before, and visitors said there was a strange quality in the air. There was pestilence, they said, and love and laughter after. And always there was death.

Yellow fever first appeared in 1766. Many died, but those who recovered built up an immunity, and there came a time when the Creoles considered its ravages almost a blessing in disguise. When Louisiana was transferred to the United States, the Creoles considered the Americans rude and barbaric, and many were of the hopeful opinion that yellow fever might keep the aliens where they belonged. For the Creoles, despite their distinguished participation

This is the courtyard that Seignouret built.

in the Battle of New Orleans, were very European. "Some of my best friends are Américains," they used to say, "but *really,* mon cher . . . !" And although they were obliged to do business with the Yankees, that was as far as most of them wished to go. Maybe, they said, the plagues would keep the noisy outsiders away.

The Creoles did not know, nobody knew, that their beautiful city was plague-ridden because it was so dirty. The people drank filthy water from the Mississippi, with nothing to purify it but a lump of charcoal in the bottom of the carafe. Rats were everywhere. There were swamps in the city, and sewers in the gutters. When the gutters overflowed, the ladies, with proper delicacy, stayed at home. But the gentlemen and the slaves went sloshing all about. Nobody dreamed the germs that filth could breed, or guessed that the mosquitoes that buzzed day and night carried germs from the gutters into the ballrooms and the Opera House, and under the mosquito bars of all the big Seignouret beds in town.

After it was discovered, in 1905, that yellow fever was caused by the sting of a mosquito, there was never another epidemic in New Orleans.

A vivid account of the worst plagues is given in the *Autobiographical Sketches* of the Rev. Theodore Clapp, a Presbyterian minister who became a Unitarian, and comforted the sick and buried the dead, through thirty-five years of plagues. Dr. Clapp was a New Englander of Puritan stock, who married a Hawes from Boston, and went to New Orleans in 1821 to become pastor of the Presbyterian church. He was brought up in the doctrines of Calvinism, and admitted he should have thought it as unlikely to turn pirate or highwayman as Unitarian. But there came a time when Dr. Clapp no longer believed Death to be the awful consequence of Original Sin, or felt that man's chances of salvation are slim. He believed, instead, in the final happiness and holiness of everybody. When he dared to preach such precepts, his congregation reminded him that Unitarianism was not what he was getting paid for. Please stick to Presbyterianism, they said. Dr. Clapp said he could not, and after a controversy that split the church he was dismissed.

Clapp's Unitarian doctrines were pleasing to a number of his flock. But they had no money for a new church, or to pay the minister a salary. Judah Touro, who was the first and for many years the only Jew in New Orleans, bought the little flock a church, and paid the Christian clergyman out of his own pocket. But before I tell you about Judah Touro, I want to copy some stories about the plague from Dr. Clapp's *Autobiography,* which has been out of print for nearly a hundred years. First, he tells about the cholera epidemic of 1832.

On the morning of the 25th of October, as I was walking home from market, before sunrise, I saw two men lying on the levee in a dying condition. They had been landed from a steamboat which had arrived the night before. Some of the watchmen had gone after a handbarrow or cart, on which they might be removed to the hospital. There was quite a crowd assembled at the spot. An eminent physician rode up in his gig, and gazing a moment, exclaimed in a loud voice, "These men have the Asiatic cholera!" The crowd dispersed in a moment, and ran as if for their lives. I was left alone with the sufferers. They could speak and were in full possession of their reason. They had what I afterwards learned were the usual symptoms of cholera—cramps, convulsions, etc. They complained of a great pressure upon their chests. One of them said it seemed as if a bar of iron was lying across him. Their thirst was intense. They entreated me to procure water.

Dr. Clapp attempted to go on board the steamboat which had put the men ashore. While he was gone, the watchmen arrived with a dray, loaded the sufferers aboard, and trundled them off to the hospital. Dr. Clapp says that he "subsequently learned they were corpses before 11 A.M. the same day."

The weather, he says, was very peculiar:

Everyone felt a strange difficulty of respiration. I never looked upon such a gloomy, appalling sky before or since. Not a breath of wind stirred. It was so dark that in the banks, offices, and private houses, candles or lamps were lighted that day.

Before nightfall the pestilence had spread through several squares. By evening of the second day, it had made its way through every part of the city. During fourteen succeeding days seven thousand deaths were reported. On some days more than five hundred persons died. Newspapers suspended, hotels locked their doors. Stores and banks, even drugstores, closed. A private hospital was found deserted. Physicians, nurses and attendants were all dead, or had run away. Not a living person was to be seen. The wards were filled with bodies which were piled in the yard and burned.

Dr. Clapp tells of the awful scenes in the cemeteries:

> Words cannot describe my sensations when I first beheld the terrible sight of carts driven to the graveyards, and there upturned, and their contents discharged as so many loads of lumber or offal.

Ditches were dug for the dead, and they were buried uncoffined. Gravediggers were paid $5 an hour and some of them fell and died in the holes they dug.

The cholera lasted fourteen days, and disappeared as suddenly as it had come. All one night there was thunder and rain. In the morning the sun shone, and the plague was stayed. The following June it reappeared, and in September yellow fever broke out again. Within twelve months (1832–33) New Orleans had two Asiatic cholera and two yellow fever plagues:

> In almost every house might be seen the sick, the dying, and the dead in the same room. Multitudes began the day in good health, and were corpses before sunset. On a certain evening a gentleman asked me to say a short service over the body of a particular friend. The next morning I performed the same service for him. I went, one Wednesday night, to solemnize the contract of matrimony between a couple of very genteel appearance. The bride was young

and possessed of the most extraordinary beauty. A few hours only had elapsed before I was summoned to perform the last offices over her coffin. She still had on her bridal dress.

Three brothers lived together. I was called to visit one of them at 10 o'clock P.M. He lived but a few minutes after I entered the room. Whilst I was conversing with the survivors, a second brother was taken with cramps. We instantly applied the usual remedies, but without success. At one o'clock in the morning he died. The only surviving brother immediately fell beside the couch of the lifeless ones, and at daylight he died. We laid the corpses side by side.

One family of nine persons supped together in perfect health. At the expiration of twenty-four hours, eight were dead. A boarding house that contained thirteen inmates was absolutely emptied. Nobody was left to mourn.

A thick, dark atmosphere hung over the city like a funeral shroud. All was still. Neither sun, nor moon, nor stars shed their blessed light. Not a breath of air moved. A hunter who lived on the Bayou Saint John assured me that during the cholera he killed no game. Not a bird was seen winging the sky.

The horror was made even worse by the things men did to stop it. They burned tar and pitch on every corner, so that horrid fumes and smoke filled the air. Every day at sunset they fired cannon, which shook the city and frightened the sick to death. The smoke and the noise were supposed to "change the atmosphere and dispense the infection." But the stinking swamps that surrounded the city were no less foul, and filth from the cesspools and gutters washed into the houses on every flood. There was a dreadful smell to yellow fever, but the outside air was believed to be polluted, so the people kept their doors and windows tightly closed. Dr. Clapp assigned his preservation to a miracle:

Let the reader imagine a close room, in which are lying half a dozen bodies in the process of decay, and he may form a faint conception of the physical horrors in which I lived, moved, and had my being continually for two entire weeks.

They called the fever *yellow* because the sufferer's skin turned, first, sulphur yellow and then green. With the fever came excruciating thirst and ravenous hunger. A swallow of water, a taste of food, brought on a horrible, revolting sickness. At the end came madness. It was believed that if the venom could be drawn from the body in the beginning, the patient would recover.

Cupping was a terrible thing. It was usually done on the neck. A bronze gadget was held against the flesh. In the gadget was a spring that released a series of tiny, razorlike blades that twirled savagely, slashing the flesh. As blood gushed from the wound, it was cupped with a glass, and the vacuum drew the scarified tissue up into the cup.

Leeches also were used. The patient's head was shaved, and bloodsuckers placed behind each ear, and over the kidneys, thirty or forty, if they could be found. Usually the sufferer died on his stomach, as the leeches, swollen to monstrous size, sucked his blood.

This is a ghastly thing to be reading about in a book that you bought for a holiday. But the plagues show another side of fabulous New Orleans, and to appreciate the Creole city you should know of the horrors it survived as well as the beautiful things about it.

* * *

One pleasant story of the period is about Julien Poydras who founded the Poydras Female Orphan Asylum for little daughters of yellow fever victims. Monsieur Poydras had a soft spot in his heart for poor girls, and also established a romantic fund for brides. In Brittany, where he came from, it was the custom for a girl's family at the time of her marriage to give cash, or a piece of land and some livestock, to the bridegroom. Julien, when he was very young, fell in love with a girl so poor that her family couldn't give him even a pig. You might think he would have married the girl anyhow. But no, provincial custom ruled against such a thing, and Julien joined the French Navy. And he landed in New Orleans, where he bought himself some pots and pans and went to peddling. With his hawker's box upon his back, he went up and down the Mississippi, selling at plantation homes and Negro cabins, until he had enough money to become a planter. Then he became a merchant and, by and by, he became a poet and a philanthropist. I think he was also a millionaire, but I am not sure. Anyhow he became so rich that he had money enough to set up a fund to provide dowries forever for poor girls in the parish in which he lived.

* * *

The worst plague in New Orleans was the Great Epidemic of 1853. Yellow fever broke out on the first of July. On that day there was incessant rain; and between dawn and dark the people died like flies. The scourge started at the waterfront where immigrants lived in damp and horrid squalor. "Bronze John" they called the fever. Bronze John passed lightly through the Vieux Carré—most of the Creoles who lived there were immune by that time—stalked the length and breadth of Canal Street, and leaped into the Garden District. Then panic seized the town, and people fled in terror. One in ten was destined to die before the summer was over.

Dr. Clapp tells of the high mortality among his parishioners, who were mostly from the North:

> I visited two unacclimated families belonging to my church, who were all down with the plague. In these families were nine persons, but two of them survived. I knew a boarding house from which 45 corpses were borne away in 13 days. A poor lady of my acquaintance kept boarders for a livelihood. Her family consisted of 8 unacclimated gentlemen, intelligent, refined and strictly temperate, who used to meet once a week to enjoy music, cheering conversation and innocent amusements. They passed a certain evening together in health and happiness. In precisely one week five of them were gathered to the tomb.

Fifteen clergymen died that season—two Protestant ministers and 13 Roman Catholic priests. They were strangers to the climate, but could not be frightened from their post of duty. The word *fear* was not in their vocabulary.

Dr. Clapp says that in one epidemic he was the only Protestant clergyman who remained in the city, except for an Episcopal clergyman "who was confined to his house by a lingering consumption and unable to leave his room. So it was," he concludes, "that I had no coadjutors but the Roman Catholic priests." . . . And that brings us up to the remarkable story of the Rev. Peter Thevis who built the Campo Santo of St. Roch and established its cemetery.

Father Thevis was a German priest who came with Father Scheck from the old country. Father Scheck was to be pastor of Holy Trinity Church, and Father Thevis was to be his curate. Hardly had they arrived, when yellow fever broke out. Father Scheck died, and many of his flock. Immigrants had scarcely a chance when Bronze John struck.

In Europe, St. Roch was the patron saint of plague sufferers, and although he had long been beloved throughout Europe, the Creoles seemed scarcely to have heard of him. It was said that when the Black Death roamed the hills of Tuscany, in the fourteenth century, the sign of the cross made by St. Roch healed the stricken. His mere presence had cleansed Cesena, and his prayers saved the Eternal City. But God, in His unscrutable way, had reserved a terrible ordeal for the saint, and after years of labor among the sick, God permitted the plague to attack him. In the delicacy of his charity, Roch dragged himself out of the city of Piacenza and into a forest, where he was found by a dog, who supplied him with bread. He recovered his health, but was falsely accused of being a spy, and died in prison. Devotion to him as a "healer" began almost at once. The governor of Monpellier ordered a chapel erected, in which he was buried beneath the altar. And if you know Paris, you will remember the beautiful church of St. Roch that was built in 1580. Father Thevis had lived in Paris and often worshiped there. Feeling a special veneration for the saint, he begged his intercession for the congregation of the Holy Trinity. Father Thevis promised that if the saint would protect his flock, there should be a shrine erected to him in the Third District, where the Germans lived.

God must have listened. For the parish was miraculously spared, or so it seemed to Father Thevis. "Not one member of the congregation of the Holy Trinity," declared Father Thevis, "died of cholera or yellow fever from that time on." Undertaker Jacob Schoen, who was in charge of all burials at Holy Trinity, supplied a supporting affidavit. Books of his association, according to Mr. Schoen, did not record a single death from pestilence among the congregation of the Holy Trinity.

Father Thevis set about fulfilling his promise. The City Council at first rejected his petition. But the cemetery was finally dedicated, and, brick by brick, the chapel rose. Father Thevis wanted to build it himself, and is said to have laid the marble floor and set the stained-glass windows. In the walls he cut niches for the burial of friends who came, when he was tired, and took the labor from his hands. At the foot of the altar he built his own grave. When the work was finished, he hung an old bell in the belfry. And on a summer Sunday its chimes rang clear and sweet, as Father Thevis led his flock along the then-wooded road from the town to the promised shrine.

But St. Roch was not the only one whose reputation as a healer was enhanced by the plagues. Marie Laveau also was called upon. There were two schools of thought regarding the cures effected by the Voodoo Queen. There were many who believed she was the best yellow fever nurse in town. Others declared she was born with a caul, in the eclipse of the moon, and baptized with the blood of a white pigeon. She rubbed the bodies of the sick, they said, with dust from a murderer's grave, and it was by such magic that she drove Bronze John away. A committee of Creole gentlemen, appointed at a mass meeting, once waited upon Marie and requested her, on behalf of the citizens, to minister to the fever-stricken.

That was the year when most of the priests and doctors died, when grave diggers fled the city, and scavengers went through the streets calling, *"Bring out yo' daid! Bodies! Bodies!"* They collected the bodies and piled them in carts, and threw them in open trenches. Then Creole women dug graves with their own hands and buried their men who had died, in courtyards, that they should not be desecrated by the scavengers.

* * *

That was the year when Judah Touro, the Jewish philanthropist, founded the Touro Infirmary for yellow fever sufferers, and made provision under his will that it should be nonsectarian. Many years later Senator Bilbo, who hated Jews, racked by cancer of the mouth, applied to Touro's Jewish doctors for surgery and care, and was given expert medical help.

In his will Touro ordered that every book, paper and letter among his effects be immediately burned, and it was not until Leon Huhner, after many years' research, published a brief biography, that a later generation learned of the lonely life and unhappy romance of New Orleans' first Jew. Touro led a quiet, unglamorous existence in the most romantic city in America. A bachelor with few friends, he lived with great frugality. When he died, he left half a million dollars to found hospitals, orphanages and almshouses, to encourage libraries, universities, churches, and synagogues. Touro Synagogue on St. Charles Avenue, a handsome Byzantine structure, is proudly shown to visitors. But hardly anybody knows the strange story of the sad old man for whom it was named.

Judah Touro was born in Newport, Rhode Island, the son of a rabbi. He was born on the eve of the Battle of Bunker Hill, and this circumstance afforded him peculiar satisfaction. Fifty years after the battle, Lafayette, visiting in Boston, laid the cornerstone of the famous Bunker Hill Monument. Fifteen years later, with the monument far from completion, the committee announced that its funds were exhausted. Touro heard of the deficit and wrote that he would be happy to furnish the necessary sum ($10,000), upon condition that the gift remain anonymous. He disliked publicity almost as much as he loved money.

Nobody spent a dollar more carefully than Touro, or gave $10,000 more prodigally. Once he sent a clerk to buy him a frock coat. Shortly his friend Nathan dropped in. Nathan said he had bought a similar coat at D. H. Holmes for two dollars less. Touro immediately took off the coat, and ordered his clerk to return it.

"Two dollars is two dollars. And I cannot afford to waste it," said Mr. Touro. "Go to Mr. Holmes, and get me one like Nathan's."

An hour later he wrote a check for $5,000 for the sufferers of the Mobile fire.

Touro was orphaned when he was a small boy, and brought up by an uncle in Boston. In his uncle's home Judah fell in love with his cousin Catherine Hays. In order to separate them, Hays, who disapproved the romance, sent Judah abroad on a business trip. The ship was attacked by privateers, but Judah landed the cargo safely, returned to Boston with the profits of the enterprise, and declared his desire to marry Catherine. Hays discharged his nephew from his employ, and compelled the boy to leave his home. At the same time he sternly forbade his daughter to see her cousin again. Judah decided that New Orleans offered the best opportunity for success, that he would go there and build up a great fortune. Then he would return to Boston and claim his sweetheart.

He left with $100 and traveled by boat to New Orleans. On the voyage he was robbed, and when the ship stopped at Havana he was penniless. He worked in Cuba until he had money enough to continue to New Orleans, and found employment as a clerk. The next year Louisiana was transferred to the United States, and a period of wild speculation followed. Judah worked hard, saved diligently, and opened a little store where he sold Boston codfish, Maine potatoes, and New England rum. From the beginning, he opened his store at sunrise, and kept it open until dark, even after he had his own clipper ships that he sent on voyages around the world. In ten years he is said to have amassed a comfortable fortune. His business relations with New England continued throughout his career. If he kept in touch with Catherine, no one knows. Three weeks before his death he remembered her in his will. Catherine was mortally ill at the time, but Touro did not know that.

When he was seventy-nine and on his deathbed, he talked in delirium of "walking in a beautiful garden with Catherine Hays, my first and only love." Catherine, still a spinster, died in Richmond, Virginia, a few days before Touro died.

The old man's last words were: "When I am dead, carry me back to the place of my birth, and bury me beside my mother."

In accordance with his request, his body was sent to Rhode Island, and buried in the grim old Jewish cemetery that fronts on Touro Street, in the frivolous and fashionable little town of Newport.

* * *

Touro had a friend, another old bachelor, who was a terrific miser. Nobody loved greedyhearted John McDonogh until he died. Then they thought he was wonderful because he left more than fifteen million dollars, and all to charity. Which was really pretty mean of him, because he had a widowed sister living in Baltimore who hadn't a cent to her name. Her name was Jane. And all that Mr. McDonogh left Jane was $6,000, with the admonition that she invest it wisely, practice economy, and live on the interest in her old age. To Jane's children Uncle John left ten acres of land in Maryland, although he owned about four-fifths of all the cultivated land in New Orleans, and enormous tracts in eighteen other states besides. The property, which was worth millions when McDonogh died, is worth billions now. McDonogh desired that it be held in perpetuity and administered for the care and education of children forever. The Supreme Court set the will aside on ground that it was against public policy. Then they struck oil on the land in southern Louisiana, and if McDonogh had left a son, his grandsons might be richer than the Rockefellers. They might, in fact, be the richest men in the world.

People said that McDonogh had an unhappy love affair that blighted his life. But he probably loved power more than he ever loved anybody. He was a deacon in Mr. Clapp's Presbyterian church, and fanatically religious. It was said that he was in love with the Baroness de Pontalba and also with an Ursuline nun, who became a mother superior in New York, and that between them, the ladies made a misogynist of Mr. McDonogh.

The story about the baroness is embellished with fancy rhetoric, and not a word of it is true, because her father, who is supposed to have thwarted the romance, died (as I told you) when the baroness was a baby. Her father, you remember, was Don Andrés, Royal Standard Bearer of the Illustrious Cabildo, Chevalier of the Royal Order of Charles III, and ever so many other things. He was also at that time, which is important to the legend, the richest man in Louisiana, and McDonogh was a young nouveau riche, with no background at all.

McDonogh, according to the story, saw the fair Micaëla praying in the Cathedral, and asked her father for her hand. Outraged at the young man's presumption, Almonester is said to have taken from his wall a painting of St. Jerome praying in the wilderness, which he dispatched to McDonogh with a note:

Go, McDonogh [the note said], and do as this saintly man. For know that it is not given to a plebeian such as thou to marry the daughter of Almonester.

McDonogh is said to have returned the painting, with a note of his own:

> Sire: I return your painting. As for your answer, I swear by the Almightly and Eternal God that the name of McDonogh shall be reared high in this land, when that of Almonester is thought of no more.

McDonogh, with a friend named Shepherd Brown, arrived in New Orleans from Baltimore at about the same time as Judah Touro, and began exploring the uncultivated lands of Louisiana. This was before the Purchase, when Louisiana extended to Canada and was bigger than all the United States put together. McDonogh acquired property, and made fictitious sales at very high prices to Brown, and through Brown to others at still higher prices. McDonogh bought a house on Chartres Street in the bon-ton section of the city, and seems to have been acceptable to Creole society. He owned horses and carriages and a great many slaves.

McDonogh went to the Quadroon balls, and there was a woman by the name of Carmelite Pena, who became his mistress. Carmelite had a daughter, and a son named Francis. When the daughter married, McDonogh gave her a large sum of money, and she went abroad to live. Francis received $100,000 seven years after McDonogh's death. By that time Carmelite was probably dead, or else she was about eighty years old.

McDonogh, when he was young, bought a plantation across the Mississippi, on which he began the construction of a great house. He is said to have fallen in love with Elizabeth Johnson, a girl from Baltimore who was living in the Vieux Carré. It was when New Orleans was giddy and gay, and besides all their beautiful parties and balls, the Creoles loved the most grisly entertainments. Newspapers of the period tell of:

Interesting Exhibitions

Adults $1.   Children 50 cents.

A Strong Attakapas Bull Attacked and Subdued
—by Six of the Strongest Dogs in the country.

Six Bulldogs Against a Canadian Bear.
A Beautiful Tiger Against a Black Bear.

Twelve Dogs Against a Strong and Furious Bull.

If the tiger was not vanquished in his fight with the bear, he was sent against the bulls. Then fireworks were set upon the back of the conqueror, which were "guaranteed to produce a very entertaining finale."

McDonogh went to the fights and the balls and lived like other bachelors of the time, until one amazing day he ordered the immediate sale at auction of his house and furnishings, his slaves and horses, and all that he owned in the city. From the time on, he lived in an unfinished wing of the house he had begun to build in McDonoghville across the Mississippi.

It was said that he had asked for the hand of Elizabeth Johnson, and her father refused his consent because the Johnsons were Catholics, and McDonogh was not. Elizabeth became a nun, and McDonogh became a recluse. When he had business in New Orleans a slave rowed him across the river. Never again was he known to spend a night in the city. He never accepted an invitation and never received a guest.

When he grew old he always wore a tall silk hat shiny with age, and under it he tied his thin white hair in an old-fashioned queue. He was tall and gaunt, and wore a threadbare blue swallowtail coat with gilt buttons, and a high white stock. Rain or shine, he carried a blue umbrella. People said that the old man ate only enough to keep body and soul together, and patched the pantaloons he wore when he was young, to make them last until he should need them no longer.

He hardly talked to anyone, and was severe and niggardly with his slaves as he was with himself. He forced them to work at night and before daylight, to earn their freedom. But when he died, they learned that he had made provision for them to go to the Free Republic of Liberia, with money and provisions for the journey, a Bible apiece, and medicines, tools and seeds to take along with them.

Alone in the bare bedroom of his half-built castle, John McDonogh wrote his will, leaving his entire fortune for the establishment and everlasting support of free schools for the poor children of New Orleans and of Baltimore, which was his native city. The only stipulations he made were that the Bible be read every day, and there be singing lessons in the schools. He wrote on seventy pages of foolscap, and added in a small, neat hand a final paragraph:

I have one little favor to ask, and it shall be my last. I ask that the children of the free schools be permitted, annually, to plant and water a few flowers around my grave.

He ordered a plain funeral at the least possible expense. The undertaker, mindful of cost, dressed him in his tight-fitting, old-fashioned pantaloons and swallowtail coat. They buried the old man on his plantation, and nobody went to the funeral but his slaves. Ten years afterward, in accordance with his request, his remains were taken to Baltimore "to mingle with the dust" of his parents. And at that time pupils in the thirty-five McDonogh Schools in New Orleans began a collection. Contributing pennies, nickels and dimes, they raised a fund to pay for a statue of Mr. McDonogh. Which reminds me of something I want to tell you, because unless you are a Jew, I am sure you don't know it. Most Jews don't know it either.

When Judah Touro died, his Christian friends in New Orleans

wanted to erect a statue in his memory. The City Council adopted the proper resolution, and contributions began to pour in. It was decided to have a group of heroic bronze figures, all representing Charity. A sculptor was commissioned, and work was proceeding, when a Jew who was visiting New Orleans entered vehement protest.

He wrote a letter to the papers saying that for a Jew to even assist in such a movement would be a most impious thing, because a statue would be a direct violation of one of the Ten Commandments, the one that forbids the making of any graven image. It was contrary to Jewish law, to Jewish tradition, and reprehensible in every way, he said. There was a long and bitter controversy. The matter was finally put before a council of European rabbis. And the rabbis decided that the Jews of New Orleans could not erect a statue to Judah Touro, either alone or with their Christian friends. They could if they wished, the rabbis said, erect a shaft. But nobody wanted just a shaft. That, in case you ever wondered, is why there are no statues of Jews anywhere.

For McDonogh's statue the children raised $7,000 and a sculptor made a monument of bronze and granite, with a bust of Mc-Donogh on a pedestal, and a little boy and girl standing on tiptoes to give him flowers. The monument is in City Square, opposite City Hall. In the center of the square is a statue of Henry Clay, whose daughter married a Creole. Behind the Clay monument is a statue of Benjamin Franklin, which was given to New Orleans by an old gentleman from Chicago. It is an exact copy of one in Lincoln Park, which the old gentleman admired, and he gave it to New Orleans on his ninetieth birthday.

On the First Friday of every May, known now as *McDonogh Day,* thousands of school children, marching two by two, place flowers about the statue of McDonogh, fulfilling the "one little favor" that he asked. It is a beautiful ceremony and might make one believe, to see it, that McDonogh was not a miser at all, but a great humanitarian. The children gather under the magnolias, with their lilies and roses, and oleanders and bunches of gardenias. The magnolias are in bloom on McDonogh Day, and the square is fragrant with the sweetness of their great white blossoms. Around the children stand a wall of people, fathers, with hat in hand and a baby on one arm, mothers, both hands busy with little ones, and all begin to sing when the children start their *Ode to McDonogh*:

McDonogh! Let the trumpets blow,
    And with fair garlands twine his brow,
Extol him with strong voices now,
    Praise to him, all praise to him!
Now eager hands our offerings bring,
    Now youthful hearts our praises sing,
Until in heaven the echoes ring,
    Praise to him, all praise to him!

14

LIVES AND TIMES OF THE QUADROONS

Nowhere in the world was there ever a group of women so beautiful, so notorious and so terribly hated as the Quadroons of New Orleans. Even today white women hate their memory.

"You Northerners glorify the Quadroons," remarked a New Orleans lady. "I have lived in the South all my life, and I know more about colored people than you do. There are no beautiful colored women."

That, of course, is a matter of opinion. The most beautiful woman I ever saw was the colored wife of a Negro diplomat from Haiti, a pale girl with skin like gardenias. I met her at a reception at the President's Palace in Port-au-Prince. Her eyes were the color of Haitian bluebells, which is that shade of delphinium which is a cross between clear blue and purple. Her mouth was a pomegranate cut in halves, and the wings of her blue-black hair were the wings of a Congo thrush. Her maiden name was Dumas, and she was descended from the great Dumas, père and fils. The first Dumas was the son of a French marquis and a colored woman from Santo Domingo. Some of Dumas's descendants are white and some are black.

It is very complicated, this color business. You might, you know, have a touch of the tarbrush yourself. It would be possible—and you might never know it.

The French colonial government at the end of the eighteenth century registered in Santo Domingo some sixty combinations of white with Negro blood and gave a name to each. A Quateron, for example, was thirty-two to fifty-seven parts black and seventy-one to ninety-six parts white—the result of twenty possible combinations, among which was the mating of white and Marabout. A Marabout was approximately eighty-eight parts black to forty-four parts white. In Louisiana, the term Quadroon was erroneously used to cover a multitude of combinations.

The life of a Creole Quadroon was romantic and appalling and, in some ways, peculiarly pleasant. But of course everybody did not see it that way. There were women among the Quadroons congenitally fitted for the existence they led who made the most of it, and undoubtedly enjoyed it.

There were white women, Harriet Martineau, for example, and Harriet Beecher Stowe who also made the most of it, and as genuinely deplored it.

Miss Martineau was an English lady with hound-dog instincts who crossed the ocean to see what America was like, and raced home with several thousand horror-stricken notes on what she found. She published a two-volume report and made a large sum of money. The lives and loves of the Quadroons shocked Miss Martineau more than anything she encountered in two years in America, although she was nearly, or supposed she was nearly, hanged in Ohio, on her way to New Orleans.

A Duke of Saxe-Weimar-Eisenach, on the other hand, was most favorably impressed by the Quadroons. He visited New Orleans in 1825 and attended a Quadroon Ball where he danced with the girls, and met their mothers. The duke, who was a brother-in-law of William IV (the uncle of Queen Victoria) said the Quadroons were "the most beautiful women in the world." If Victoria heard that, she probably washed her hands of the duke.

Lafcadio Hearn said the same thing and so did a number of other travelers, as well, of course, as many native New Orleanians. It is true, however, that the gentlemen considered the Quadroons and their place in society from an entirely subjective angle, while Miss

Martineau considered them more objectively, and from an intensely moral point of view. Miss Martineau later became an infidel. But during her American tour (1834-1836) she was a devout church-woman and consorted entirely with Unitarian abolitionists.

The Quadroons lived in small houses on or near Rampart Street and were supported by well-known Creole gentlemen. They lived in eminent respectability and brought up their children piously, and often sent them abroad to be educated. Although their homes were traditionally unimpressive, they had slaves, excellent cooks, maids to dress their hair, and boys to "make messages." Making messages meant running errands, fetching fruits and wines from the French Market, matching silks and threads on Royal Street, and flying on swift black feet to the pâtisserie for petits fours when Missieu was coming for tea. Some of the Quadroons who were cherished by the richest, most honorable and most important men in town were said to have quantities of jewels, and money in the bank.

But if a Quadroon walked down Rampart Street in a bright silk dress, or with plumes in her hat, or went to market with a diamond ring on her finger, any white woman could have her whipped like a slave. For a trifling charge, whippings were administered in the cala-bozo. Naturally when the white woman's husband heard about it there was hell to pay, and this may have been one reason why the law was seldom evoked. Another reason was that the Quadroons were irreproachably circumspect. In the daytime they wore simple cotton gowns. At night they wore décolleté silks and satins, and sex hovered about them like a tropical mist. If their demeanor did not reassure the white women, there was very little that could be done about it.

First official recognition of the Quadroons was made by the Span-ish Governor Miro who passed an ordinance in 1788 that is a most extraordinary document. The directory of that year shows fifteen hundred "unmarried women of color, all free, living in little houses near the ramparts." Governor Miro's ordinance made it an offense for these femmes de couleur to walk abroad in silk, jewels, or plumes. The only head covering they might wear was a madras kerchief known as a tignon, twisted about the head and knotted on top. West Indies women wear such turbans today.

French planters in Santo Domingo had long ago taken the handsomest slaves for their mistresses. The planters were usually aristocrats. The slaves came from widely varied tribes in Africa. Many of them came from what is now French Senegal, and they were a handsome people with silky black hair and straight fine features. Gold Coast Negroes were black and ferocious. Those from French Dahomey were the color of tobacco and a gentle lot. By a process of selective breeding, the French (and to a lesser degree the Spanish) had produced in Santo Domingo an exotically lovely type of woman with straight lithe figures, small hands and feet and exquisitely chiseled features. They were known as "Les Sirènes." During the slave uprisings in Santo Domingo, the planters fled to Louisiana bringing their mistresses and children with them. It was the daughters of these women and their daughters' daughters who came to be called Quadroons. This was a misnomer, since a Quadroon is a person having one-fourth Negro and three-fourths white blood. Many of the Quadroons had only one sixty-fourth Negro blood.

The Sirènes practiced voodoo and taught it to their daughters, in order to hold, or sometimes to get rid of, their lovers. They were a wild and magnificent lot.

Marie Laveau, the celebrated Voodoo Queen, was the daughter of a Sirène. Marie died in 1881 when she was ninety-eight, and is buried in St. Louis Cemetery Number One, and I will tell you more about her later. A man who knew Marie's daughter told me that the daughter claimed descent from the noblest family in France, and that she looked it.

"She carried herself like a queen. She had snow-white hair, as fine," he said, "as a baby's, and a long regal nose. I always believed," he said, "that she had noble blood in her."

Marie was a girl of fifteen when the Duc d'Orléans visited New Orleans with his brothers. She was famous then as a beautiful young sorceress, and the de Marignys took the princes around to see her. Her mother was dead and Marie was on her own, brewing love potions and peddling gris-gris. She made amulets to keep the princes safe from harm, and told the duke that he would be king of France. And of course he was, but nobody believed her.

In Marie's last years she lived in a little old house on St. Anne Street, and beside her bed there was a golden candelabra which she said had been given to her by the king. When Marie died her daughters placed the candelabra at the foot of her coffin, with blessed candles in it.

There were laws in the colony prohibiting marriage between white men and colored women, and the only way white fathers of colored children could protect their children from becoming slaves was to set the mothers free. Sons were sometimes sent to France where there was no prejudice against their origin. Sometimes they were placed on land in the back of the state where they usually prospered, became planters and often made fortunes. Many of those who went to France became distinguished musicians, poets or dramatists. More than a hundred years ago there was published in America an anthology of Negro verse from the published writings of seventeen poets of New Orleans. One of these poets, Michel Seligny, founded a school for rich colored children on St. Philip Street.

Life was pleasant enough when the children were small and living at home with their beautiful mothers. But as they grew older the colored boys had a bad time of it. When white men visited their sisters, it was accepted etiquette for the brothers to efface themselves. If they "knew their place," as white folk put it, they were never present when their betters trod the primrose path.

Many colored men married the former mistresses of white men. They often had their children educated in France, and many of them became wealthy and had slaves of their own. White men sometimes

sent their discarded mistresses into the country, comfortably endowed with means to pursue the pleasant Creole custom of enjoy-
ing life. The women took their children with them, married colored
men and had more children. And so it happened that half-brothers
and sisters sometimes varied in color from almost white to very
dark.

There is a true story about a white man from the North who went
to Pointe Coupée where he met a Quadroon, ex of Rampart Street.
He fell in love with her and wanted to marry her. But as marriages
between white and colored persons were forbidden, the white man
opened a vein in his arm with a penknife, pricked the girl's finger
and squeezed a drop of her blood into his vein. Then he swore that
he had Negro blood in him, and the marriage took place. On the
record they both signed as Negroes. This is the plot that Edna Ferber
used in *Show Boat,* and it is probably where she got the idea.

The Orleans Theatre was about the only place where white
women could keep an eye on their husbands. Since it was impossible for Creole gentlemen to attend their Quadroon sweethearts
at the play, colored men were permitted to escort their mothers and
sisters. Performances began at six in the evening and lasted until
two or three o'clock the next morning. The second tier, reserved
exclusively for colored people, billowed with the taffeta crinolines of
the Quadroons and gleamed with their jewels. And after the white
wives grew tired and faded-looking, the Quadroons went on
sparkling.

"The white ladies," wrote the young Duke of Saxe-Weimar,
"maintain the most violent aversion toward the Quadroons." And
then the duke went on to tell of "flitting back and forth with many
other gentlemen" from a Carnival Ball to a Quadroon Ball, leaving
the white ladies—bredouilles (wallflowers), he called them—to
"make a tapestry against the walls." Anyone could guess how the
bredouilles felt.

There was an Englishman, James Silk Buckingham, who visited

New Orleans a little later, and wrote a piece for the London *Times* and sent it home to be published.

The Quadroons with their lovely countenances resembled, according to Mr. Buckingham, the highest order of Hindu women. They had dark liquid eyes, lips of coral, and teeth of pearl. Their long raven locks were soft and glossy. They had sylphlike figures, beautifully formed limbs, and exquisite gaits. They practiced subtle and amusing coquetries, and they had the most adorable manners.

Mr. Buckingham's propaganda, along with the duke's, helped maintain the "violent aversion." The duke, by the way, was entertained in New Orleans by Colonel Grymes, the ex-district attorney who defended Jean Laffite. I do not know that Grymes had a Quadroon sweetheart. Quadroon mothers were extremely particular about the alliances their daughters made, but before Grymes lost his fortune he would probably have been considered a fine catch.

Pirates, proverbially bad husbands, were said to be good lovers. But I don't know about Jean either. There were no gossip columnists in those days and New Orleans papers, through all the years, never once mentioned the Quadroon Balls.

A New York reporter did a series for his paper called *Southern Travels*. In the course of his investigations he attended a ball at the French Opera House and reported that there were very few men there and too many women. The ladies, he said, were dull, fat, and badly rouged. The next night he went to a Quadroon Ball.

"The Quadroons," he reported, "conducted themselves with equal propriety and modesty. Moreover, they were beautiful to look upon. They were gracefully gowned, their smiles came and went with their talk, and they captivated all who were present." No wonder the white ladies felt as they did!

Most of the young Creoles had mistresses. If they did not, it was a reflection upon their virility. Abstinence was no virtue, and a handsome mistress was as much a mark of social distinction as the possession of fine horses and carriages. This being so, the Quadroons inevitably got most of the nicest young men first, and sometimes kept them longest.

Lafcadio Hearn, when he was on the *Item,* was taken to a Quadroon Ball by John Augustin, dramatic and music critic of the *Times-Democrat* and beau sabreur among journalists. Augustin, a Creole aristocrat and an extraordinarily handsome man, was an authority on the punctilious code of the duel and much in demand as a second. Lafcadio Hearn was five feet three. He weighed less than a hundred pounds, he had only one eye and he was as shabby as Augustin was elegant. Because of Hearn's shyness, Augustin steered his little friend to a quiet corner behind the potted palms. But Hearn, who was usually painfully bashful, became astonishingly animated and disappeared among the beautiful girls. And at three o'clock in the morning, Augustin, who had to work the next day, went home by himself.

In New Orleans Hearn fell in love with a Quadroon. But because he was penniless and could never have supported a woman, it is quite unlikely that he met his amoretto at the ball. She was probably an older woman, a discarded mistress. Hearn was twenty-seven and as poor as could be.

I have suffered the tortures of a thousand damned souls [he wrote to a friend]. I became passionately in love before I knew it; and then!—It required all the reason and all the strength I could summon to save myself; but it took me months to do it—she came to me in dreams and made me feel her shadowy caresses. Don't think I am exaggerating. You have no idea of the strange fascination possessed by these *serpent women.* At last the dreams became vaguer and have finally vanished. Yet as I write I do not dare to state that I am cured. For I know that another kiss, even another look, would plunge me into a depth of ruin which no earthly power could save me from. And the temptation is always before me. You do not understand me, perhaps! You think I am writing folly and madness! But you could never understand unless you lived in this accursed city. Still I love it so much. I love New Orleans!

The Quadroons were not in any sense prostitutes. They were courtesans, impossible to any other time or place than eighteenth-century New Orleans. Many of them were as tenderly and carefully brought up as any white girl, and until they secured a "protector" they were just as virtuous. They attended the colored annex of the Mount Carmel Convent School. If they did not learn much more than to sing a pretty song and sew a fine seam, neither did the white girls who were taught by the Ursulines. Creole women never read much. They were accomplished in music, which they all loved, and in embroidery, which most of them disliked. The nuns also taught them painting and drawing.

But it was the home work that counted. When it came to love, the colored girls' mothers had forgotten more than the white girls' mothers ever knew. Most of the Quadroons were beautiful. Their dispositions were naturally sweet and submissive. They accepted life as they found it, and did not try to change it.

L'amour (or what passed for it) was what they were born for, and their mothers before them. It was what they lived for and their mothers schemed for. When they achieved it they were happy. And if, when they lost it, they were sad, and their sadness was heart-shattering, that too was what they were born for.

It has been said that only a harlot can be a harlot. That the virtuous woman resists because there is no temptation. And it isn't only her heart that keeps her pure, but her nerves—and her stomach. Custom may also have something to do with it, and the result of habit.

In Creole times well-born white women were always virtuous. And gentlemen were incurable romanticists—eternally seeking love and more love—and yet more love. The gentlemen wanted it kept at fever heat, and the woman wasn't born who could go on satisfying them. And that is why they had Quadroons on Rampart Street, wives on some other streets, and slaves on the plantations—if they had plantations.

It wasn't that the gentlemen were so extraordinarily virile. But because they were everlastingly romantic.

Their virility, as a matter of fact, gave them considerable concern. To sustain it, they ate dozens of raw oysters, which were considered (and still are considered in New Orleans) a great aphrodisiac. They also took a stimulant made from Spanish flies, dried and powdered and made into a potion. They drank a great deal of champagne and much absinthe. But there was nothing, they said, like oysters, and this curious contention has some basis in fact—curious, I mean, because it sounded so silly until along came a scientist recently and said it was true.

The gentlemen's romantic proclivities were their everlasting concern, and there was no place for romance like a Quadroon Ball. The balls originated at the end of the seventeenth century while Louisiana belonged to Spain. They lasted for nearly a hundred years, degenerating after the War Between the States into shabby, ill-mannered affairs with no resemblance to their ancient elegance and decorum.

The first ball, a sort of coming-out party sponsored by Quadroon mothers to introduce their daughters to white men, was called Bal de Cordon Bleu, and it was by this name that the balls were always known among the Creoles. After the Americans came to town they were more generally called Quadroon Balls.

In Paris, before the war, I took a course at Cordon Bleu and learned how to cook with wines and how to make pastries. When I heard the name in New Orleans, and it didn't mean cooking school, I went to the encyclopedia. And I learned that the term (Blue Ribbon) was first used in France to designate certain sixteenth-century gentlemen who entertained with great munificence. In appreciation of their parties, they were knighted by Henry III, and they wore the white cross of their knighthood on a field of blue.

Later the name (Cordon Bleu) became associated with cooks who prepared banquets for the Blue Ribbon Knights. Later still it became the name of a cooking school in Paris. L'Ecole du Cordon Bleu was originally for professional chefs. By and by, it was for Frenchwomen who wanted to learn—not so much to cook—as to set a fine table. When I went, it was for everybody. The instructors did not use spoons or cups for measuring, but only weights. It was very confusing to a girl who didn't know what it was all about. So was the first Bal de Cordon Bleu in New Orleans. But with customary amatory candor, the gentlemen asked a few questions, and soon found out. Les Mères were seeking lovers for their daughters. *Voilà!*

Adjoining the Orleans Theatre was a ballroom, Salle d'Orléans, which is now the mother house of the Colored Sisters of the Holy Family. This was the building that the enterprising mamas hired for their daughters' "debuts."

The sweet-natured nuns graciously showed me through their convent, and I expect they would show you, too. But I hope you will not bother them when they are busy with their classes. If you do, you should leave an offering for their orphans. The nuns are naturally a bit self-conscious when visitors want to talk about the Quadroons. But I asked questions like an Inquiring Reporter, and they were very courteous.

Some historians think that the Quadroon Balls were not held in the Orleans Ballroom, but in a building on Chartres Street that has since been destroyed. Stanley Arthur says they were always held on Chartres Street and never on Orleans Street. But André La Fargue and the nuns say they were held in the convent, and I had rather believe Mr. La Fargue and the nuns, because it makes such a picturesque story. Besides, the nuns should know because they have the old records that tell about business transactions and rentals before they bought the building.

There was a duel in the Orleans ballroom long ago, when a wild young man named Lebeau resented the attentions showered upon his lady by another wild young man, named Tomás. Monsieur Lebeau challenged Dr. Tomás to a duel right then and there. They chose their seconds on the spot, and fought with colichemardes, a particularly nasty sword with three sides and all of them grooved. Tomás fell badly wounded. A physician who was among the guests, Dr. Tricou, stanched the flow of blood and saved his life. But there is still a stain like a dark pool on the shining floor. And nothing will take it out. For more than fifty years, ever since they bought the place, the nuns have scrubbed and scrubbed, saying prayers upon their knees for the wild young men who danced and loved and fought, and for the beautiful girls they fought over.

One of the nuns showed me the stain, but she did not want to talk about it. When the Holy Family took over the Salle d'Orléans, the ballroom was purified and the garden blessed. And every morning and every night, at Holy Mass and benediction, the sisters pray for the souls of the Quadroons and for the remission of their sins.

*　　*　　*

There is something wanton and languidly beautiful about Creole gardens. In the daytime they are heady with exotic blossoms and heavy odors, and at night they have a dreamlike quality that is almost too beautiful to bear. But the garden of the Holy Family is different, and just what a convent garden should be. It is trim and neat, and small and very dear. And it smells more like frankincense and myrrh than other gardens do. When I saw the garden, it was bathed in benevolent sunshine, and there were flowers blooming in it that I had not seen before, tidy little four-o'clocks that would seem more at home in New England, sweet alyssum, and old-fashioned candytuft. On the flagstones were pots of fragrant rosemary which, as everyone knows, is "for remembrance." Women tend it, so their lovers who are far, far away will not forget them. But the nuns tend it because they like its aromatic scent.

In the old days, Quadroon belles came tripping down the gallery stairs to the garden where slaves served absinthe frappés, while the fiddles up above played *Dansez Calinda!* and the drums beat *Badoum! Badoum!* There were orange trees in the courtyard then, and in the trees were cages of mockingbirds and lovebirds. There were parrots in the patio, and monkeys that chattered in the moonlight.

On the ground floor were gambling rooms where candles fluttered in shimmering girandoles, and their prismatic crystal drops trembled and tinkled in the breath of night. On the floor above was the ballroom, famous for its cypress floor, the best for dancing in all the pleasure-loving town. There is a sign on the door now that says, *Silence, my Soul, God dwells here.* There are 104 cells in the ballroom, and where the golden concubines once danced the nuns now sleep on pallets hard as boards.

There are two statues in the convent with vigil lights burning before them, one of the pale Mother of Sorrows, and one of the Blessed Martin, who was a colored boy from Peru. Martin's mother, a Quadroon from Panama, was mistress of a Spanish nobleman in Lima. Her son turned out dark, as the Negroes say, and his father hated him. Martin was a humble Negro, who may one day be a saint.

"His mother's sins were forgiven her," the nuns told me, "because she loved much." Their morality was all sympathy, just what morality should be.

In telling of Martin's mother, the nuns spoke of that other woman who was taken in the very act of sin and brought to Christ. The people showed Christ the woman's sentence written in the law, and asked what was to be done with her. Christ wrote with His finger on the ground, as though He did not hear them. When they pressed again for an answer, He looked up and said, "Let him who is without sin cast the first stone at her."

When we were in the courtyard I had wanted to talk about the

Quadroons. Sister Gilbert, stooping to touch a pansy face, wrote with her finger among the walking iris, and I had thought she did not hear me.

*   *   *

October was the beginning of the Creoles' social season and there were Quadroon balls, as there were white balls, nearly every night until Ash Wednesday. The hostesses were always free women of color who had been the mistresses of white men, and the girls they brought out were always the illegitimate daughters of white men.

The purpose of the balls was to display the youth and beauty of the girls in order to find rich protectors for them. Guests without exception were white men. No white woman would have dreamed of attending. No man of questionable color would have dared set foot inside the door. It was a frank and elegant sex mart where Creole bluebloods chose their mistresses with taste and decorum.

The patrons for each ball sat on a dais carpeted in crimson beneath a winged fan called a punka, that was suspended from the ceiling, and kept in motion by a slave child who pulled at the string that descended from the wings. Around the room sat the rest of the chaperons, all in evening gowns, and fanning themselves with palmetto fans. Every girl's mother was there and stayed until the end, her mother or her guardian. Girls from plantations, in town for the social season, were placed under the strict surveillance of a friend of the family. Until a "protector" was found for them, free girls of color were as discreet as nuns.

It was all very correct, with formal presentations and graceful exchange of compliments. The gentlemen paid their respects to the patrons on the dais, and strangers sought to be introduced.

"Permit me, madame, to present my friend—Monsieur So-and-so, of Such-and-such Plantation."

"Ah, monsieur—I remember, I think, your father. A very great gentleman, monsieur." Piquant situations were handled with Creole tact.

There was an admission charge of two dollars, which was more than the sum charged at any other public dance. From all accounts, the balls were gay and lavish and well worth the price.

"Colored" girls were all shades of brown, and some were white. There were lascivious beauties with dusky skins and sooty lashes, who rubbed pomade on their chestnut hair to keep it flat, and there were girls whose blue-black hair was straight as an Indian's. Many of them were almost as beautiful as 'Tite Poulette. 'Tite Poulette, according to George W. Cable, was the fairest young woman in New Orleans. Her mother was Zalli who lived in Madame John's house. I told you about her before.

" 'Tite Poulette," wrote Cable, "was tall, straight, lithe, her great black eyes made tender by their sweeping lashes, her form all grace, her carriage a wonder of simple dignity."

Although marriages between white and colored persons were forbidden, there were agreements that were considered respectable in colored circles, and were acceptable in the male world of the Creoles. When a man saw a girl to whom he was attracted he asked to meet her, and they danced together. If his attentions displeased her, she could decline the next dance. If he invited her to the garden for an absinthe, she could plead a headache. Chaperons were there to save the girls embarrassment.

Quadroon mothers objected to unwise connections for their daughters as strenuously as white mothers might oppose an unwise marriage. It has been said that the Quadroons bartered their girls into concubinage, and sold them like slaves. They did, I think, the best they could for them. There were, to be sure, financial arrangements, but there was nothing shocking or unusual about that. Among the whites there were mariages de convenance, and dowries were always the accepted thing. White girls often had less choice in picking a husband than Quadroons did in choosing a lover. Often, of course, there were love affairs. Mariages de la main gauche, the colored people called them, or left-handed marriages.

When a definite arrangement was reached, a girl was spoken of as placée. Her status was a sort of honorable betrothal, and her immediate future was secure. It was customary for the man to buy a small house on or near Rue de Rampart, and present it to the girl. Until the house was completed, he never visited her alone. It was understood that he should support her during such time as they might be together, and make an additional settlement when they separated. If children were born of the affair, there was no question about their support. A Creole gentleman always provided for his sons and daughters. This was the accepted thing, and there were seldom scandals. Arrangements were oftenest made when the man was a youth, and the girl was about sixteen. Although the affairs usually terminated with marriage, there were many aristocratic Creoles who maintained two households to the day they died.

Girls never deserted a "protector" or betrayed him. Sometimes, when their lovers left them, the Quadroons committed suicide. Many remained "widows" and often removed to the country. The majority probably made other connections. Sometimes they married colored men. But it is doubtful if any colored man ever knew a beautiful, high-class Quadroon until a white man was through with her. Quadroons who remained in New Orleans after they were deserted often became hairdressers or dressmakers. Among them were the best yellow fever nurses in the city. Some turned their little houses into lodgings for white bachelors, and the bachelors reported that there was always an altar in madame's bedroom before which she knelt and begged the good God to send kind protectors for her beautiful daughters. Little sins of the body never interfered with the piety of the Creoles, white or colored.

*　　*　　*

Harriet Martineau spent ten days in New Orleans and talked with numbers of white women. When she returned to England she quoted the ladies as feeling pretty bitter about the Quadroons. This was shortly after the Lalaurie scandal, on which Miss Martineau also commented. She had heard, she said, that Madame Lalaurie was "very pleasant to whites."

Miss Martineau was one of the first travel book writers. For her trips she designed a wardrobe suitable for ships and coaches. There was a "black silk cape which no lady should go to sea without, and a well-wadded hood." For the rest, she wore "clothes too bad to be spoiled, and gloves at all times." She was deaf, and wore a trumpet which apparently exerted magic. It is difficult to imagine exchanging confidences through a trumpet, but Miss Martineau says she gained "many a pleasant tête-à-tête in the Crescent City."

She carried two contrivances to every Creole dinner party, one of which she attached to her ear. The other, with an extra long tube, she tossed to a guest at the opposite end of the table. When his talk bored or annoyed her, or when she felt she could do better herself— and this, they said, was very often—she would snatch back her trumpet.

When the Creole ladies talked about the Quadroons, they all told Miss Martineau that it was other ladies' husbands who kept colored women. Their own husbands, they assured her, would not do such a thing.

In her book, *Society In America,* Miss Martineau wrote:

The girls are highly educated and are, probably, as beautiful and accomplished a set of women as can be found. Every young man early selects one, and establishes her in one of those pretty and peculiar houses, whole rows of which may be seen in the ramparts. The connection now and then lasts for life; usually for a few years. In the latter case, when the time comes for the gentleman to take a wife, the dreadful news reaches his partner either by letter, or by the newspaper which announces the marriage. The quadroon women are rarely known to form a second connection. Many commit suicide, more die broken-hearted. Some men continue the connection after marriage. Each quadroon woman believes that her partner will prove an exception to the rule of desertion. Every white lady believes that her husband has been an exception to the rule of seduction.

Plugging along with her ear trumpet, Miss Martineau accompanied her host to the Slave Market in New Orleans, and watched him buy two "young yellow girls" from Mr. Le Carpentier, the double-tongued auctioneer of the Vieux Carré. Miss Martineau hated slavery with all her heart, and kept a great notebook of case histories. When she was in Washington, the Madisons had invited her to stay at the White House, and there was a story that she kept Dolly up all night debating the subject. The Madisons owned Pauline, the slave girl who was afterward hanged in New Orleans.

If Miss Martineau had thought of it, she probably could have written an antislavery novel as good as *Uncle Tom's Cabin,* because she had all sorts of firsthand information. Harriet Beecher Stowe, when she wrote her bestseller, had never visited the South. All that Mrs. Stowe knew about slavery was abolitionists' propaganda, and her characters were fictional. Miss Martineau, sticking to facts, verified the true story of a gentleman from New Hampshire who bought a plantation in Louisiana.

"In the custom of the time, he borrowed money," she explained, "paid a light interest, cleared off his debt year by year as the crops were sold, and finally owned the place." He had a Quadroon mistress, "a beautiful, well-educated woman," with whom he lived for twenty years, but neglected to free. The couple had three daughters who, at the time of their parents' death, were fifteen, sixteen and seventeen. When their parents died, an uncle from New Hampshire went to Louisiana to settle the estate. Enchanted with the beauty of his nieces, he determined to take them to New England and "introduce them into that society for which they were so well fitted." But their father had died insolvent, and there were financial matters to be attended. The uncle prepared an inventory of the estate and delivered it to the creditors, who complained that he had not in-

cluded the three girls. Shocked and horrified, the uncle offered all
he had to redeem them. It was not enough to satisfy the creditors,
and the three beautiful daughters, according to Miss Martineau,
"were sold in the slave market to the highest of bidders for the
vilest of purposes."

Although she hated slavery, there were many things about the
Creole city that charmed Miss Martineau. And one thing was the
bathing habits of her hosts.

"In private homes," she explained, "baths are a rarity. But the
Creoles, who are the most satisfactory of hosts and hostesses, have
a tub of fresh cold water with soap and towels brought to every
bedroom both night and morning."

Miss Martineau spent two weeks in New Orleans. While she was
in town a number of duels took place. The Creoles dueled over almost everything. But especially they dueled over the Quadroons.
Visitors to New Orleans are almost always taken to City Park to
see the famous Dueling Oaks. When Miss Martineau saw them,
City Park was a part of the Allard Plantation, and its oak grove had
long been the favored spot for duels. The trees were big even then,
and their far-flung branches were draped with Spanish moss. The
owner of the plantation, Louis Allard, was a gentleman who wrote
poetry. After he lost his fortune and was obliged to sell the plantation, Monsieur Allard was permitted to live on the place until his
death. And he was buried at the spot where he used to sit and write
his verses (next to where the Art Museum is now). It was also the
spot where the duels were fought, sometimes ten or twelve of
them in a week.

The Creoles always fought with swords. They believed that the
Americans had degraded the honorable art of dueling by fighting
with pistols. If a man could not defend his honor with a sword, he
was not, they felt, quite a gentleman. Because they loved sword-
play, the Creoles challenged over nothing, and killed for trifles.

Fencing is still a popular sport in New Orleans and exhibition tournaments are frequently staged. The Mardi Gras Duello is held on Mardi Gras Day in St. Anthony's Close, behind the St. Louis Cathedral where many duels were fought in the days of the Quadroon balls. The close was very handy to the Salle d'Orléans and sometimes men went directly from the ballroom, to kill or get killed in the little garden below. Then the ball broke up, and the girls went home crying. And the next day the white women said that those dreadful Quadroon balls were a disgrace to the whole town, and something should be done to stop them.

Causes for challenges were often ridiculous. If a man asked a girl to dance and her escort refused his permission, that might be cause for a duel. If a man should tread on a lady's train, that also might be cause.

The fiery young men drank quantities of absinthe. They had a great deal of money and a great deal of leisure. And since they thought more of honneur and of amour than of anything else in the world, they spent a great deal of time defending them.

Challenges did not mean that the gentlemen had to kill each other. Their seconds often met to discuss the quarrel, and sometimes arrived at a settlement "both amicable and honorable." On other occasions it was enough merely to draw blood. Many duels, however, were fought to the death. There was a terrific pride involved. One could not duel with a social inferior, or with a man who had struck another man. Striking a blow automatically debarred a man from the "privilege of the duello." When that happened, a Creole might as well leave town and hope to be forgotten, because the ignominy of being refused a duel was a terrible thing to live down.

When challenges were formally issued there was considerable ceremony to be observed. The young gentlemen went in their barouches, rattling in the dawn's early light, over the cobblestones to the Allard Plantation on Bayou St. John. Each party brought his own surgeon and seconds. The seconds decided whether their principal might go on, if he was wounded.

Once in a while, but not very often, women went too, and men have died in their sweetheart's arms under the moss-hung oaks. The sweethearts were always Quadroons, because no nice white girl could manage to get out of the house at that time in the morning. Sometimes, pour le sport, girls from the better bordellos were taken along, and after the duel, the man who won had a party attended by the girls and the fencing masters. And everyone drank champagne and toasted the victor, while the other poor fellow went home to die. Or sometimes he was so wounded he was crippled for life.

There was a planter named Faustin St.-Amand who quarreled with an American slave dealer from Kentucky. The Kentuckian slapped the Creole's face. Only blood could wipe out a dishonor like that. But of course the American could not fence, so there was nothing for it but pistols. It was agreed that they would stand beside an open grave, back to back, less than six feet apart. And each with a loaded pistol, cocked, in his right hand. At the word, both were to wheel and fire. Faustin St.-Amand was the faster, and the man from Kentucky fell into the open grave.

The Americans passed laws against dueling, but nobody paid any attention to them. Finally it was decided that duelists should be disfranchised. But nearly all the leading citizens, finding themselves disfranchised, protested so violently that the law was repealed. Arrests were occasionally made for dueling and trials were held. Jury verdicts were always "Not guilty," and the packed courtrooms cheered them. For nearly two hundred years New Orleans dueled until, in the 1890's, the sport petered out. The last challenger was a newspaperman, an editorial writer on the *Picayune,* who challenged an editorial writer on the *Times-Democrat.* But friends talked them out of it.

Fencing masters were never persons of social importance, but they were more like prizefighters. They dressed well and had money. And they were idolized by Creole youths as movie and radio stars are idolized today. They had lithe, beautiful bodies, and were great favorites with the girls in bordellos, who threw themselves at the heads of the handsome, dashing fencing masters.

The academies were in Exchange Alley, which runs from Canal Street to Conti, between Royal Street and Bourbon. The fencing masters lived in Conti Street in houses that are still standing, where they gave fabulous parties for their pupils. Stag parties, we would call them today. Girls from the bordellos sat in tubs of champagne, and everybody drank and sang, and there was a wonderful banquet.

It was a legend that the masters were greatly successful in love affairs, because to cross words with them meant certain death. Sometimes they fought with each other. And that of course was the end of one of them. Monsieur Reynard, one of the greatest maîtres d'armes, fenced with his rival Booneval and killed him, and then Reynard inherited Bonneval's pupils and prestige.

One of the most famous fencing masters was Bastile Croquère, a Quadroon who was the handsomest man in New Orleans. Croquère was famous among other things for his collection of cameos, rings and breastpins. He even wore bracelets. Many of the masters affected effeminate manners, dressing like dandies, and carrying perfumed handkerchiefs up their sleeves. Croquère wore high-colored coats, very tight at the waist, with roll-collared waistcoats of magnificent brocade, embroidered by a Quadroon dressmaker who would not sew for anyone else, not even the richest white men in town. Men of the period wore snug trousers strapped under their feet. The tighter the trousers the dandier the dandy. Croquère's trousers were so tight they fit him like his own skin.

The fencing masters were graceful as dancers. Most of them were tall, with shining black hair, and many of them had mustaches and side whiskers. There was Señor Pépé Llulla, who owned a grave-yard all his own, St. Vincent de Paul, where he sleeps to this day. When Llulla bought the place, it was known as the Louisa Street Cemetery, and rumor had it that he meant to fill the ground with the graves of his victims. Llulla fought not only with swords, but with pistols, and he was probably the most skilled all-round duelist in the world.

Gilbert Rosière was quite as good with swords, and more of a gentleman. But Pépé Llulla was the more picturesque. Pépé used to put eggs on the head of his small son, and crack the shells at thirty paces with a bullet.

Gilbert Rosière came from France to practice law in New Orleans. But he fell in with the masters, and took up fencing instead. In one week Rosière fought seven duels, all under the oaks in City Park. And I don't know how many men he killed. For all his killings, Rosière was remarkably tenderhearted. After he became quite old, and maybe he was getting childish, he went to the opera and heard his favorite song so beautifully rendered that tears ran down his cheeks. An unmannerly young man laughed to see the great Rosière crying.

"If I weep," exclaimed the master, "I can also fight!" and at dawn the youth learned a memorable lesson in manners.

Rosière did not quite kill him, but wounded the rude boy badly —and that was also under the oaks. To commemorate the thousands of duels beneath Les Chênes d'Allard, there are matches during Spring Fiesta called the Dueling Oaks Encounter fought, as in days of old, under the live oaks of the old sugar plantation. If you should go to see them, look for General Beauregard on his little horse at the entrance to City Park. Then visit the rose gardens and listen to the mockingbirds, and you may have an adventure like Emily Dickinson's—you remember a bird came down the walk. He did not know she saw; he bit an angleworm in halves, and ate the fellow raw. Once I saw two mockingbirds having a tug of war with an angleworm. The worm didn't break, but just stretched until one of the birds dropped him, and the other one flew away with him. City Park is a wonderful place for mockingbirds, but Audubon Park is even better.

There are all sorts of birds in Audubon Park, native birds and foreign ones, including a number of storks standing around on one leg. The foreign birds are in a big flight cage. There is a monkey island, and a zoo with camels and sacred cows. There are bears and seals and alligators. And there is Mr. Audubon (on a granite pedestal) standing behind a tree with a notebook and a pencil in his hand, looking so intent and interested you might think he had never seen a bird before.

15

DEATH LOOKS DOWN Almost everybody has heard
about the cemeteries of New Orleans, those strange walled cities of
the dead, where the rich sleep in little white houses, and the poor
sleep in ovens. It is a macabre way to be buried, and nearly all
visitors want to see the famous tombs that are above the ground.

Metairie Cemetery is one of the show places of the city, with
lagoons bordered by motor drives with stately palms, and weeping
willows hung with Spanish moss. Metairie is where Josie Arlington
was buried, the rich madam from the Red Light District who
picked herself a red granite tomb, and paid $17,000 for it. I'll tell
you later about Josie and that tomb, but first I want to tell you
about the ancient little cemeteries near the Vieux Carré.

St. Louis Number One borders the old Red Light District, and is
across from Lulu White's Mahogany Hall, which was once a
Quadroon bordello, and now belongs to the Jazz Foundation of
America. St. Louis Number Two is next to St. Louis Number One.
St. Louis Number Three is on Esplanade Avenue, which was once
the aristocratic avenue of the Creoles where wild young men dueled
under the live oaks on Bayou St. John.

The little streets of St. Louis Number One are stark and treeless,
and lined with the small whitewashed houses of the dead. The
walls of the cemetery are white, and ranged with tombs into which
the poor were thrust in "ovens" (holes) in the walls, like cells in a
honeycomb. Closed tight in the ovens, the dead send up grass and
flowers that bloom on top of the walls.

Beneath a blinding sun or under the moon the cemeteries seem from a distance like wastes and drifts of northern snow, still and quiet as death, and full of whiteness and peace.

"One story says the statue is of Josie herself."

On closer acquaintance they are tumbledown places with a rather cheerful air, busy with the little businesses of birds and crabs and dragonflies and bees. The shared sepulchers seem cozy and domestic. The cemeteries are filled with the small sounds that insects make, and the struggles of plants in a graveyard. They burgeon with the life that springs from death. Weeds tumble from tombs, and ivy grips the crumbling vaults. Ferns sink their roots in dust within the walls, and buttercups bloom in the chinks that time has made. Everywhere there is a tiny hustle and bustle. And sometimes there is music, for the homes of the dead are, strangely enough, the homes of many mockingbirds. The mockingbirds sing while priests mumble litanies, and lizards, slithering through decaying tombs, feast their ugly souls.

> Kill ol' lizard on the grave
> Ain't no charm your life can save.

It is bad luck to kill a lizard, but extremely good luck to have one cross your hand, and when people decorate their graves on All Saint's Day they stand for hours with their hands against the tombs, waiting for a lizard to crawl over them. A graveyard lizard crossing a person's hand can bring luck for a year.

All the old cemeteries are still used. Ovens in the wall tombs, just big enough to hold a body, can be either bought or rented. If they are rented, it is usually for a year and a day, which costs eight dollars. If no further payment is forthcoming, the remains are removed and burned. Even family ovens are used again and again. Each has a hole in the back through which the bones may be pushed, to make way for a new coffin.

An English girl who visited New Orleans in 1839 wrote to her parents about the cemeteries and the Mardi Gras balls, and apparently sent a copy of her letter to the *Picayune* because a part of it appeared in the paper.

"The Creoles," she said, "bake their dead in ovens as we do our brown Johns for breakfast! During Carnival there were OVER A THOUSAND balls, and how many funerals I do not know. The social affairs surpass in magnificence anything you might imagine. There was a street parade in which the King rode on a horse richly caparisoned, attended by knights and cavaliers, and surrounded by gentlemen of the first respectability dressed in female attire, riding in superbly ornamented carriages. The Creoles take great pains to make a fine show. But when Death comes they will put the King in an oven, and bake him like a slave."

The English girl had not been around. There were poor tombs and rich tombs, and many that were big and costly. In St. Louis

Number One, the late Governor Claiborne erected two pretentious monuments, one for each of his girl-wives. Eliza, the first wife, was buried in the Protestant section, and Clarice, the second wife, in the Catholic section. Both died at twenty, Eliza, with her three-year-old daughter, of yellow fever, and Clarice when her baby was born. Then the governor married Sophronia, the girl who wore glasses whose portrait is in the Cabildo.

In all the cemeteries are magnificent and ornate tombs, with recesses where private Masses are celebrated, and statuary that cost a fortune. The dead in a cemetery are like the living. Families who lived in fine houses are provided with fine tombs and modern conveniences. And the poor, as in life, have humbler lodgings where vines creep, and wild flowers flourish. The rich are surrounded by grassy plots, with settees and chairs, and are supplied by their heirs with cut flowers in amethyst vases.

But the vases, which are cut glass of the Victorian period, do not belong only to the rich. On most of the tombs, even on the ovens, there is a shelf for flowers. The vases, before they got to be antiques, when they were in fact brand-new, cost only a dollar or so, so that almost everybody bought them for the cemetery. Whatever may be said of Victorian bric-a-brac, its cut glass was certainly durable. When the vases were new they were colorless. They still are on a gray day. But time and the sun have done a lovely thing to the old glass. Now it shades from lavender to purple, and every facet is a twinkly tiny gem that throws a pendant of violet light to dance in the sun on whitewashed walls, and shimmer on the shining sepulchers.

The first time I saw the vases I thought of the purple window-panes on Beacon Hill in Boston. Some people think that only *Mayflower* descendants can have purple windows in their houses. But the truth is that in the early nineteenth century a shipment of glass arrived from England for some new houses in Boston. It was ordinary window glass and was put in as usual. But as the years went by a gradual chemical reaction transformed the colorless panes into a miracle of violet, of pure light and loveliness.

Perhaps New Orleans cemetery vases were made in England at the time that Boston's windowpanes were made. Or maybe the semitropical sun will turn to violet any colorless glass that is exposed to its direct rays. But I do not think so, or there would be purple glass singing in the sunshine, in southern cemeteries everywhere.

A pair of opulent purple vases was shown at a recent New York Antique Show against a piece of crimson brocade, and they gleamed in the bright light with the radiant splendor of unnamed jewels. At $75 apiece they sold before you could say St. Louis Number One. And the next time I go to New Orleans I should like to be a ghoul. But of course I won't, because I understand that it is a federal offense to take so much as a daisy out of a cemetery. Even if I replaced the old purple things with some nice new ones of that cement that is so popular nowadays, it would still be a federal offense. Or anyhow that is what the sexton told me.

Since purple is my favorite color, especially the shade that is used in stained-glass windows, I looked up its ecclesiastical symbolism, and now I think I may change—to red maybe, or blue. Red is for love, and blue is for wisdom, and they are both comparatively uncomplicated. But purple is all mixed up. Purple symbolizes the union of love with pain, and is also associated with repentance and passion, suffering, humility and truth. When Christ is represented as the Man of Sorrows, He is shown in violet. Angels wear violet when they call men to penance, or to share in the sorrows of the Lord.

In olden times virgin recluses wore violet veils. Benedictine monks also wore violet. But now they wear black, which is for mourning, and monks and nuns wear black for the sins of the world.

The Creoles were great people for mourning. In the old days, they were always in mourning for someone or other, and middle-aged people wore black most of the time. They had a saying: "Si un chat mourrait dans la famille, tout le monde portrait de deuil." (If a cat should die in the family, everyone would be in mourning.)

When a death occurred, every post in the Vieux Carré carried the news on a black-bordered poster, telling who had died and when, and when the funeral would be. And every tante and cousine draped herself in black for a year.

The houses of the dead in New Orleans cemeteries sometimes have wrought-iron balconies, and doors on hinges. Out front are white iron chairs where mourners can sit and visit, and think of those who lie within.

There was a man who interred his only daughter in St. Louis Number One. For a long time after her death the grieving father went every day to the cemetery and sat, as people do, on a pretty little chair at the door of the tomb, with his rosary between his fingers and his thoughts on the dead. Then one day he unscrewed the marble door of the tomb and gazed upon the crumbling casket. When he went away he put the marble back. The next day he unscrewed it again and crawled inside, closing the door after him. His wife, who knew it was his custom to visit the cemetery, went that night to fetch him home. She saw the door of the tomb ajar, and found him there. After he crawled inside, he had swallowed a vial of poison.

The reason that the tombs in the old cemeteries are above ground is that in the early days the colonists were forever striking water when they dug even twelve inches down. New Orleans was known as the "Wet Grave" because of difficulties in burying the dead. An English traveler visiting the city in 1832 described the gruesome burial of a friend:

"The coffin was sunk three or four feet by having holes bored in it, and two black men stood on it until it filled up with water, and reached the bottom of the moist tomb.

"Some people," continued the Englishman, "are particular, and dislike this immersion after death; and therefore, those who can afford it have a sort of brick oven built on the surface of the ground, and the coffin hermetically sealed within."

In the old cemeteries are countless graves of brave and foolish boys who fought for love and died for honor's sake. "Mort sur le champ d'honneur," it says on their tombs, and "Pour garder intact le nom de famille."

On going to the duels when they bade their Creole girls good-bye, the brave young men murmured those lines about, "I could not love thee, dear, so much, lov'd I not honour more," which seems a nasty thing to say to a girl, particularly when men dueled over such things as slurs on the Mississippi River and reflections upon the manner in which they knotted their cravats. But they were young. Life was brief, and they adored it. And everybody admires men who die for what they believe in.

Near graves where "lightfoot lads are laid" is the tomb of Marie Laveau, the Voodoo Queen. Heaven knows the duels that woman had a finger in! The tomb is a three-tiered affair that says on it *Family of the Widow Paris*. The Widow Paris was Marie, and the epitaph is that of a daughter whose name was also Marie. Not everybody believes the tomb is that of the Voodoo Queen. There is another tomb that is said to be hers in St. Louis Cemetery Number Two, marked with red crosses which are a symbol of voodooism. There should be no doubt about Marie Laveau's last resting place, because she had a huge funeral (I read about it in the *Daily Picayune* of June 17, 1881) and you would think that people would know where she is buried.

There are chinks in one tomb, and flowerpots on the other, in which people—mostly colored people—deposit coins to pay Marie's spirit for answering their prayers. On St. John's Eve they scoop up goofer dust from the top of the tomb to use for obeah. Goofer dust is earth from a grave, and all goofer dust has a certain potency. But if it comes from the grave of a Voodoo Queen it is naturally more efficacious than dust from an ordinary grave.

Marie was the daughter of Charles Laveau, a wealthy white planter who was a member of the legislature, and a Quadroon named Marguerite Henry, the daughter of a Sirène from Santo Domingo. She was married, at the ripe old age of thirty-six, to a free man of color, a carpenter named Jacques Paris, and received as a part of her dowry a house on a Rampart Street, from her white father. Paris died, Marie became a hairdresser, and took a lover named Glapion. After which she had fifteen children and became a leader among the voodoos.

The slaves brought voodoo to New Orleans, and many of the Creoles were almost as afraid of it as the Africans. After the slaves were baptized into the faith of their masters, they worshiped the Virgin along with the Serpent, and added new symbols, statues of saints and blessed candles, to the symbols they had brought from Africa. They also mixed medals and scapulars and holy water with the entrails of toads and the claws of lizards, and voodoo became more exciting and potent than before.

Ceremonies took place on Bayou St. John and Lake Pontchartrain, with the traditional snake of the zombis, the black cat, roosters, and a little white goat. They killed the goat and drank his warm blood. They also drank a great deal of rum, and between one thing and another the ceremonies were pretty exciting.

Marie Laveau sold love philters and gris-gris to kill or to cure. She also placed and removed curses, even for white folk. Everyone knew how Marie got herself a new house on St. Anne Street. A young Creole of good family was arrested, charged with murder, and his father, with more faith in voodoo than in lawyers, solicited Marie's help. She waited until the trial began, and put three hot peppers in her mouth, and knelt all night at the altar rail in the Cathedral. Then she went to the Cabildo, and somehow put those three little peppers under the judge's bench. The evidence was against the young man, but the judge acquitted him, and his father gave Marie the house on St. Anne Street.

Everybody in New Orleans knew Marie, because early in her career she had taken charge of Congo Square where the slaves had their Sunday afternoon dances. Country blacks came to town on Sundays with their masters' and their own produce for the French Market. They began selling at dawn and in the afternoon, when they were through, they went to Congo Square to meet their friends and celebrate. Marie was always there, in a crimson tignon with gold hoops in her ears, her white skirts swishing around her, and her beautiful head held high. It was said that white ladies who knew of Marie's powers bought amulets from her for tremendous prices through their servants.

During the last decade of her life Marie became very businesslike. She had cards printed with her name and address, describing herself as a healer. Her minimum charge to white clients was ten dollars. Matters of importance she handled on a contingency basis. A well-known politician who aspired to become a judge solicited Marie's help, and is said to have kept her on a secret payroll from the time he went to the bench until he died.

It was on love potions that Marie cleaned up. She practically guaranteed them and they were considered, by those who could afford them, cheap at any price. If you doubt the power of love potions, let me remind you of what happened to Tristram and Isolde. Isolde was to drink a love potion with King Mark to whom she was betrothed. A servant divided it instead between her and Tristram, and no sooner did they taste it than they fell in love.

Lucullus, the old bon vivant, spent a fortune on love philters, and had great success with the ladies. He finally died, however, from the effects of a potion that did not agree with him. Through the ages, in all countries and times, people have bought love potions, drunk them, and believed in them.

There is no doubt that Marie promoted many affaires d'amour, legal and otherwise. Her fame spread from the Vieux Carré until she was famous throughout the city, and became a tourist *must,* like the restaurants and the French Opera. The secret of her power, colored people said, was drinking black cat's blood. But the white people said she took after her daddy, who was a legislator.

In the Cabildo is a copy of a painting by George Catlin that may be Marie. But nobody is quite sure about it. Catlin, who painted mostly Indians, visited New Orleans during the height of Marie's success, and was attracted to her, in her bright tignon and gold ear hoops. He asked her to sit for him but she declined, and he is said to have done the portrait from memory after he left the city. There is a story that Father Divine, when he heard about it, offered $5,000 for the portrait, to hang in Harlem's Heaven.

I had a maid from Harlem, a sweet, fat woman about sixty years old who had lost all her teeth. When she smiled she looked like a middle-aged baby. I wanted her to buy some store teeth, but she said she would rather give her money to Father, because, she explained, before she became an Angel, she was bad, *bad*. "And now, miss," she said, "I'se a Virgin! Peace, it's wonderful."

After Marie Laveau died, there was a succession of lesser Queens, and there were a few Kings. Henry C. Castellanos, a New Orleans writer who published a book about the city in 1895, wrote of a voodoo orgy, of which "the most degrading and infamous feature was the presence of a large number of ladies (?) moving in the highest walks of society, rich and hitherto supposed respectable."

Police once seized a Queen with her cohorts, black and white, all frothing at the mouth and dancing in a wild debauch about a bloody little goat. Their names were kept out of the papers. But the next day a white man committed suicide, and people said that his wife was arrested the night before.

It is possible today to buy love, health and happiness from a number of colored practitioners, and also from a well-known white druggist. Mister Jimmy, the white man, has made a small fortune with vodoo. Colored people buy his gris-gris over the counter, and he conducts an enormous mail-order business.

Mister Jimmy mixed me a gris-gris of love powder and sacred sand, dragon's blood and controlling powder, a few get-together drops, and a dash of black cat oil. He mixed them in a mortar, and tied them in a little chamois bag. It should, he said, bring me a rich husband within three months. But that was over a year ago, and I am afraid it isn't going to work.

* * *

The persistent infiltration of water from the Mississippi was New Orleans' biggest problem from the days of colonization until the early 1900's. For two hundred years the Vieux Carré, and all the low ground surrounding it, was likely to be flooded almost any time. Newer parts of the city, built on higher ground, were safer. But after spring showers, it was often necessary to use boats on Canal Street. In 1850 the Levee Board offered a $2,500 prize for the best plan to drain the city. But nothing came of it for another fifty years. New Orleans has often been compared to a saucer floating in water. The edges, or levees, keep the water out. But when rain water falls in the saucer—that is, in the city—it has to be pumped out. Now there are big pipes that flow into bigger pipes, and the bigger pipes flow into big canals. The water does not exactly flow, but is sucked or pushed along by the biggest pumps in the world. Before this modern drainage system was introduced, the old cemeteries were always getting flooded. And in 1872 it was decided to convert Metairie Race Track into a cemetery where people could be buried in the ground, or on top of it, whichever they preferred.

There is a legend that a man who wanted to join the Metairie Track Club was refused admission, and he was so furious that he swore he would make a cemetery of the place. Metairie was a fashionable and very exclusive racing club in those days. There is a painting in the Cabildo of forty-four well-known New Orleanians assembled at the track, all looking prosperous and happy, and never dreaming that pretty soon a social climber was going to be as good as his word, and make a graveyard of their beautiful track. Maybe it is not true, but that is the story. The race track got into financial difficulties and was taken over by the stockholders of the cemetery. The course where the horses ran became the main drive, fine roads were laid, and artificial lakes were dug. The whole thing was landscaped to make a beautiful cemetery for the richest people in New Orleans when they were dead.

Probably you never thought about it, but public parks are, in a way, cemeteries, embellished with sculpture and shrubbery, but minus the dead. The word *cemetery* comes from the Greek, meaning *lie down*. But not *lie down dead*. Before there were parks in America, people used to visit cemeteries to smell the flowers, lie down on the grass, and have a good time for themselves. And that is where all those iron chairs came from—the kind you see in penthouses and on country terraces.

When Laurel Hill Cemetery in Philadelphia and Mount Auburn in Cambridge were new, tickets of admission were distributed by owners of family plots to friends who "longed for a breath of sweet cemetery air." In the beginning, Mount Auburn was a botanical garden. Then it became a combination garden and cemetery.

People used to plan a nice long Sunday in the cemetery, the way we plan a weekend in the country, and, naturally, they wanted something to sit on. And that was when the cast-iron manufacturers thought up the armchairs and settees, and tables on which to spread a cemetery luncheon.

There is a New Orleans foundry that has the molds from which the first cemetery furniture was made, and now the old molds have been dusted off and are being used again. Nobody in New Orleans pretends that the furniture is old, but in New York the same pieces are often called "antiques" and are sold at outrageous prices. New

York dealers just dirty them up, and then you have to paint them again. And that is the only difference. The antique stores call them "old-fashioned garden furniture," because maybe they think it would sound grim to call them "cemetery furniture." Or maybe they just don't know.

I have a chair that I bought on Royal Street that has grapes on it, and I had a purple velvet cushion with torquoise bows made for it. It is pretty dizzy but I like it, and I use it at my dressing table. I have a friend who bought its little twin on Madison Avenue, and she paid three times as much for it.

* * *

If I were you, I should spend a few hours visiting Metairie Cemetery, because it is beautiful, and very interesting with its mockingbird choirs, and tons and tons of fashionable bronze and marble that cost millions of dollars. Speaking of mockingbirds reminds me that I read recently of a South American bird that is said to be the only bird in the world that sings in the rain. Right in Metairie Cemetery I have heard mockingbirds singing in the rain.

Some people who read my books think I talk too much about cemeteries. It is morbid, they say. But it isn't, really. Beautiful cemeteries make me think of what Shelley said when he visited Keats's grave in Rome: "It might make one in love with death, to think that one should be buried in so sweet a place." But I hate death. I just like peaceful places.

The tombs in which visitors are most interested are the Moriarity Monument and the tomb of Josie Arlington. The Moriarity Monument stands at the entrance of the cemetery, and marks the last resting place of a man named Moriarity, a man and his wife. There are various stories about it. One story is that Mr. Moriarity was mean to his wife, and when she died he was sorry and determined to do the right thing. Better late than never, said Mr. Moriarity, and ordered a sculptor to carve the "Four Graces" for her monument.

"But there are only three Graces," said the sculptor. "There's Faith, there's Hope, and there's Charity," he said.

"Then make a Grace of Mrs. Moriarity," said the widower, "and let not the cost stop you."

I met an old friend of Mr. Moriarity's who told me a different story. "Daniel Moriarity," he said, "married a woman who had a vegetable stall in the French Market. Mary Farrell was her name, and it was Mary Farrell who gave him his start. He bought a small grocery and sold liquor in it, as was the custom of the times. 'Bad Liquor Dan' they called him for a joke. He resented the name, and so did she. They made money, and she died when she was young. 'I'll give her a fine monument,' said Dan, 'for she was all that a wife could be. A fine, big monument, but none too good for her,' he said, 'and when people see it, they will ask, "Who is this man Moriarity?" 'Twill please Mary,' he said."

The "Four Graces" were too heavy for horses to drag, and a railroad track was laid from the main line to the cemetery. The shaft cost Mr. Moriarity $85,000. When it was in place, he went to California where he lived for his health, for thirty-six years. And when he died, he came home to sleep with Mary.

There was a period when young men were possessed with the idea of being sculptors, and New Orleans, inordinately rich at the time, acquired more than her share of their offerings. At every turn in Metairie, marble angels mourn and marble willows weep. But it was not only in the cemeteries that the young men showed their wares. There was a plague of palatial bric-a-brac in every Creole parlor.

Small busts of the departed—suitable for mantels—could be bought for $25 a head, and were widely distributed among friends. For a $1,000 and up many Creole gentlemen had portrait busts made of their wives and daughters. They were life size, and sometimes monstrously larger. Some of the ladies went to Rome and sat

for Canova, who did the celebrated nude of Pauline Bonaparte re-
clining on her couch. But the Creole ladies, of course, were fully
dressed.

After the Battle of New Orleans, the demand for monuments
and memorials got under way, and sculpture flourished in America
almost as it did in Greece in the days of Pericles. When Monsieur
Daguerre invented his daguerreotype, hundreds of young men had
to throw away their mallets and chisels, and go back to farming
and the hills. It was backwoods boys who had made the best sculptors. There was, for example, Hiram Powers, whose *Greek Slave* set
off much indignant headshaking in the 1840's. At a Congressional
ball in Washington, Powers showed his *Slave Girl,* a slender nude
with manacled wrists and ankles. Modest Washington was outraged. But when Mr. W. W. Corcoran pronounced the statue
beautiful, everybody who had said it was terrible changed his mind
and said it was magnificent. Mr. Corcoran was the man who bought
The Battle of New Orleans for the Cabildo.

James Robb, a New Orleans banker and planter, commissioned
Powers to make a duplicate of the *Slave* for his Italian Renaissance
home on Washington Avenue. But Mr. Robb suffered financial re-
verses, and hardly had a chance to enjoy the statue before he had a
nervous breakdown and had to sell the house. The house belongs
now to the Baptist Bible Institute, and the rooms are still beautifully
rococo. But the Baptists sent the *Slave* away. It was not the Creoles
who objected to her, but New Englanders. She brought the blush
of shame, they said, to the cheek of modesty.

A New Orleanian named Richard Henry Wilde met Powers in Italy at a time when Powers was working on a statue of Benjamin Franklin, which he hoped to persuade Congress to buy. Wilde became professor of law in the University of Louisiana, and raised money among the Creoles to send Powers a down payment to secure the unfinished Franklin. It was agreed that the remainder should be paid when the statue was completed, and Powers promised to finish it as soon as he could. Meantime the Civil War came along, Wilde died, and Powers became famous. He also became forgetful. Twenty-five years later the contract was dug up, and Powers was reminded that he owed New Orleans one Benj. Franklin. Another two years passed, and when the statue arrived, the city had no money to pay the freight charges. While the money was being raised, times were hard, and the statue was offered for sale. Eventually Franklin was set up in Lafayette Square. Years later it was noticed that the marble was being damaged by exposure, and the statue was moved to the Public Library at Lee Circle. People who know about such things say that it is the handsomest and finest piece of statuary in New Orleans, and maybe you would like to see it.

The statues in Metairie are nothing, compared with Hiram Powers's Benjamin Franklin. Yet a thousand people, ten thousand probably, would rather see the Virgin on Josie Arlington's tomb, knocking at the door with her armful of lilies, than see the famous statesman in the Public Library, pensively stroking his chin, in his three-cornered hat and his swallowtail coat.

Josie Arlington's real name was Mary Deubler. She was born in New Orleans of German parents, just before the Civil War. When she was about seventeen years old, she fell in love with a cheap "sporting man" named Philip Lobrano, and was his mistress for ten years, during which time she lived in various brothels in the Red Light District.

There is one story that says the statue on the tomb is of Josie herself, that the night she met Lobrano she stayed out too late, and her father, a stern and terribly righteous old man, locked her out of the house, and wouldn't let her in, though she knocked and pleaded. So she went away with Lobrano, because she had nowhere else to go. And Lobrano put her in the Red Light District.

After ten years, during which she established a reputation for being one of the toughest girls in the district, Josie opened a place of her own. On the profits of the establishment she supported Lobrano, who lived in the house, and several members of his family.

On All Saints' Eve in 1890 when decent people were decorating their graves, there was a terrific fight in Josie's house, in which Josie and all her girls were involved. Lobrano shot Josie's brother, and was tried twice for it. Josie stuck to him through both trials. But after he was acquitted, she broke with him. Then she dismissed her quarrelsome girls, and announced that she would fill her house with gracious, amiable ladies, who would be at home only to gentlemen of taste and refinement.

When Storyville was established, she opened the Arlington and there she acquired her reputation as the snootiest madame in America. In another ten years she had amassed a considerable fortune, with part of which she built a $35,000 house on Esplanade Avenue. In the house on Esplanade she established her convent-bred niece, who is said never to have guessed what Aunt Josie did with her time.

There was a fire in the Arlington, and Josie, having narrowly escaped death, was so frightened that she began to prepare for the end. She took to meditating on her sins and talking about hell-fire and damnation, and it put a damper on the girls. Business fell off, and Josie was persuaded to lease her place and retire to her beautiful new house. In 1911 she bought the plot in Metairie, for which she paid $2,000. And on it she erected a $15,000 tomb of red marble, with a bronze woman knocking on a bronze door.

There is another story that says Josie never permitted a virgin to enter any house she ever ran, and when she ordered the tomb, she had the statue placed there to symbolize her principle.

Three years after it was completed, Josie died in her fiftieth year, and was buried the next day. There were three well-known men at the funeral, Tom Anderson, the "Mayor of Storyville," Judge Richard Otero, who managed her business affairs, and John T. Brady, her great and good friend. Mr. Brady soon married the convent-bred niece.

A few months later the city installed a traffic light in the street beside the cemetery, which shone on the tomb and created the illusion of a red light above the door. Crowds gathered every night to see the spectacle, and it was one of the sights of the city until the red light was replaced by a white one.

In 1924 the Bradys had Josie's bones placed in a receiving vault, and sold the tomb to Mr. J. A. Morales, for his nine-year-old Catherine. The Virgin was moved aside, and the bronze doors opened to admit Catherine's little white coffin. Soon another Morales child died, a little girl named Rita, and the Virgin was moved again and the doors opened for Rita to join her sister Catherine in the great marble tomb that belonged to Josie Arlington.

* * *

The oldest Protestant cemetery in New Orleans is the Girod Cemetery, and although it is probably the saddest place in town, it is interesting in its dreary way. There is an English feeling about it, a terrific desolation, and a sort of melancholy beauty. Ancient rosebushes bloom pink against snow-white tombs and old honeysuckle, faintly fragrant, clings to crumbling walls. There is a big tomb that belonged to a big family, the Palfreys, dead and gone these hundred years and more, and this is what it says:

> Together may we sleep,
> Together may we rise,
> And sing our everlasting songs
> Together in the skies
> **One household still!**

There were Creole Benevolent Associations, composed of young people who had social affairs to raise money with which to buy big vaults in which they might be together after they died. It seems strange to think of young people doing anything so grim as buying a plot in a cemetery and building a tomb big enough to hold every one of them when they were dead, boys in one tomb and girls in another, "many a rose-lipt maiden and many a lightfoot lad." One of the rose-lipt maidens whose name is graved on a communal tomb had the strange name of Ophelia Breedlove. Now the tombs are falling to pieces, and you may think when you see them of what Emily Dickinson wrote:

> This quiet dust was Gentlemen and Ladies,
>   And Lads and Girls,
> Was laughter and ability and sighing,
>   And frocks and curls.

*   *   *

James Caldwell was an English actor who came to New Orleans in 1817 and played in the Creole city's first English-speaking plays. The plays were so well received that Mr. Caldwell was encouraged to build a theater in which only English plays would be produced. He built the American Theatre, and imported a "gas machine" from England to illuminate it. It was the first gas in New Orleans. The venture was a tremendous success, and then Mr. Caldwell built another theater, the first St. Charles Theatre. The chandelier, which weighed two tons, had 250 of the new gas burners and 25,000 prismatic crystal pendants. Nowhere in America was there a theater so beautiful. It opened with *School for Scandal,* and one of the actresses was Jane Placide, with whom Caldwell was madly in love.

Mrs. Caldwell, piously outraged, refused to give her husband a divorce. There was a good deal of a scandal, and Jane, who was young and beautiful and terribly in love, died of a broken heart.

Caldwell canceled performances as a tribute to her memory, and ordered for his sweetheart's tomb a graven verse as evidence of his enduring love. You can imagine the talk there was when people went to the cemetery and saw for themselves what it said:

> There's not an hour
>   of day, or dreaming night but I am
>   with thee;
> There's not a breeze but whispers
>   of thy name,
> And not a flower that sleeps
>   beneath the moon
> But its fragrance tells a tale
>   of thee.

And if Mrs. Caldwell repented too late her hard heart, not all her Piety or Wit could cancel half a Line, nor all her Tears wash out a Word of it.

*   *   *

New Orleans had three perennial bachelors who were philanthropists, each in his own queer way. One of them, John Fink, is buried in Girod. The other two, John McDonogh and Judah Touro, are in Baltimore and Newport, and I have told you about them already. There is nothing to tell about Mr. Fink. Except that once he asked a girl to marry him, and the girl turned him down. It would seem that she was kind about it, and tried to be gentle.

"I want to work out my own destiny, John," she said.

Fink waited until he was about to die and then he left his fortune to found a home for widows, to tell the lady off—the Fink Asylum on Camp Street. Under the terms of his will, the directors cannot accept a woman who has not been married.

"Let every old maid work out her own destiny," wrote Mr. Fink in a mean, firm hand.

*   *   *

The strangest cemetery in New Orleans is St. Roch's Campo Santo, or Holy Place, with its queer little chapel and picturesque shrine. There are somber tombs in the graveyard and a cheerful sundial. But the graveyard itself is not particularly interesting, only its Old World chapel with the figures in it of St. Roch and his faithful dog, and the little old woman in the brown dress. Nobody knows who the woman is, or where she came from. St. Roch was good to her, that is all they know. Maybe he cured her of a painful disease. Perhaps she was a spinster and he found her a husband, or barren and he sent her a child. To show her gratitude for whatever it was St. Roch did for her, the woman had a life-size statue made of herself, a plain sweet thing, and sent it to the little Gothic chapel, to stand among the votive offerings that the faithful bring to the shrine of St. Roch.

The shrine is famous for healing. On its walls hang plaster hearts and hands and feet and limbs and lungs, and even stomachs of plaster. There are also crutches and trusses and surgical appliances of all sorts. And there are hundreds of little marble plaques, heart-shaped, square and oval, on which is printed one word in gold letters: *Thanks.* The replicas of limbs and organs testify to cures. And if it all sounds mysterious, it is really very simple. If a person is suffering from, let us say, an affliction of the heart, he prays to St. Roch to beg God for relief from the pain. If the saint successfully intercedes, and God is pleased to cure the suppliant, he orders a replica of his heart to hang in the shrine, and also a plaque that says *Thanks* on it. The plaques are polite little thank-you notes, inscribed with golden words of gratitude.

Almost everything in the shrine came from an old store on Royal Street where religious articles are sold, and black candles such as are used for voodoo. A woman came into the store one day that I was there to order a candle as tall and as heavy as her son. People make strange promises to the saints, and have trouble sometimes fulfilling them. But the proprietor is used to this, and helps them all he can.

The woman said that her son, Tom, got mixed up with a bad girl, and he was worrying the heart out of her. She had prayed to St. Roch to put a stop to the affair, and St. Roch had handled the matter in his own way. Within the week, Tom up and joined the Marines, bade the girl good-bye and was off to China. With the fighting and all that was going on, she'd never have an easy moment, his mother said, and she couldn't help wishing that the saint had separated the two of them in some other way. But a promise was a promise, and she had promised St. Roch a candle as tall and as heavy as Tom. Five feet eleven inches tall, she said, and it should weigh 178 pounds.

The man in the store said they could make a candle that tall, but not that heavy.

"But it's the spirit," he said, "that counts."

The woman shook her head. "It's my word," she said, "I'm thinking about, and I promised the saint what he should have."

"It would be very expensive," said the man.

"Make no mind of the cost," she told him, "but do as I say now. Make it six feet for good measure, and a good 178 pounds, for Tom is a fine big boy, and I'd not be cheating the saint," she said.

"And when it's made, will you come and get it?" asked the man.

"I'll ask Father will he bless it," she said, "and I'll take it myself to St. Roch."

16

$\mathcal{S}$TREET OF DREAMS

TO THE LADIES OF THE STREET OF DREAMS

From courtyards all down Royal Street
    Ghosts drift in the wind with the jasmine sweet,
And I seem to hear, as the soft wind swells,
    Like tinkling of tiny swaying bells,
The girandoles, crystal chandeliers,
    With the fluttering candleflames of years,
And I dream of a shimmering yesterday,
    Tonight as I pass along the way. . . .
It was round me today, as I chose to wander
    Through shops with the rose-carved palissandre.
Enchanted—a pale blue canopy
    And fluted (in French, a *ciel de lit*),
On a bed of violet ebony—
    A crystal bell with a wax bouquet,
An armoire built by Seignouret,
    Flowered in petit point slender chairs,
And figurines posing in charming pairs. . . .
    While near was a portrait in golden frame,
With proud dark eyes and a prouder name,
    A lovely face of the *bonnes familles,*
And the golden Creole legacy.
    Were they yours—oh girl in the picture there—
Camellias lighting your dark, dark hair,

Rose-lipped, white-shouldered? I looked at you,
And the years rolled back as I wished them to. . . .

*   *   *

Royal Street is lined with antique shops filled with the loveliest (and some of the costliest) antiques you ever saw, bric-a-brac and portraits and fabled swords of kings, porcelains and brûlot bowls and shining glass that sings. The shops sparkle with solid silver and gleam with burnished woods, and some of the shops have big beds a hundred years old, made from chinaberry trees, with canopies called ciels de lits. The most elaborate canopies are of pale-blue silk that were made for Creole brides to dream under, with a sunburst in the middle all tufted and shirred, and a Cupid in every corner. They are very old now and faded and frayed, but the aura of romance clings to them still.

Down the length of Royal Street, Time strews his lovely things. And it doesn't make any difference if you are a collector or a millionaire, or a girl with a few dollars to spend, you are almost sure to see something irresistible. What I love most I have never bought because they cost so much, girandoles and candelabra with crystal drops, and chandeliers with pendants that dance in the sun. Their tiny tinklings come and go like chimings from an ancient music box, and I go and look at them and think, Wouldn't it be nice to be rich!

In Royal Street, the Vieux Carré
    Are all the things I want some day—
Fragile Sèvres—pink and gold,
    Tea set of glimmering silver. Old
Wine glasses, amber, for Tokay.
    A small snuff box of cloisonné—
Limoges plates with golden crests,
    To set before proud dinner guests—
A crystal chandelier alight,

An Aubusson that's creamy white,
With wreaths of roses palely wrought,
Twined with the sweet forget-me-not—
In Royal Street, the Vieux Carré,
Are all the things I want some day—

It is pleasant, wandering down Royal Street, to imagine that everything in the antique stores came from the Vieux Carré and from Creole families of the long ago. But the truth is that most of the old things came from far away. This does not make them less lovely of course, and it is a story in itself.

A few of the portraits in the antique shops and some of the heavy furniture are eighteenth-century Creole, and there are odds and ends of hundreds of dinner services that were used by the Creoles, and handed down for generations. Every old-time respectable householder had a service for twenty-four, and there were plantation people who had service for a thousand, with glass and silver to match. Whole families often went visiting and stayed for a week or a month. It was not unusual to feed fifty at a time, and Creoles had prodigious appetites. There were innumerable courses, and a dinner might end with a dozen desserts. Since it would have been a disgrace to run short of dishes, it is reasonable to suppose that some of the old china is still around.

In the shops are lovable, winsome little things that the Creoles brought home from abroad. Every Creole parlor had a whatnot, and the shelves were cluttered with bric-a-brac, little figurines, china from Sèvres, Chantilly patch boxes, and porcelain flowers from Vincennes.

It was Madame Pompadour who launched the vogue for porcelain flowers. For her small Château at Bellevue the king's mistress ordered a huge glass house, and filled it with little flowers from the factory at Vincennes. They were so natural that Louis XV, when he went to call, tried to pick a crocus, and he was so enchanted that he placed an order with the factory for 800,000 livres worth of porcelain flowers. That was twenty-five times as much as the Ursulines' convent cost, and when the Creoles heard about it they were pretty indignant because Louis was always sending word about how broke he was, and how his subjects must economize.

The Creoles traveled in Europe long before the days of "Grand Tours" and spent fortunes on objets d'art. They bought so much stuff that probably some of it is still around. But most of the antiques on Royal Street were not bought by the Creoles, and they did not come from old New Orleans homes.

Lulu White had a cut-glass chandelier for which she paid $200. When she put in gas she sold it to Old Man Hawkins, who had a shop where the Monteleone Hotel is now. When the Red Light District closed many of the madams sold their mirrors and whatever else they could to the dealers on Royal Street. And wouldn't some respectable matrons be surprised if they knew where the Victorian pieces came from they picked up in the Vieux Carré!

New Orleans' antique business began in the days that followed the War Between the States. It began with old-clothes-and-bottles men, secondhand stores and pawnbrokers, all patronized by old families who needed money desperately. Armand Hawkins, who had a loan office on Canal Street, moved to the Vieux Carré to be nearer his victims, and opened a secondhand store. It was an auspicious move for Hawkins and because of it, Royal Street is now one of the great antique centers of the country.

When he had done what business he could with the Creoles, Hawkins went afield. He boasted that he "emptied" plantations as far north as Natchez, west to San Antonio, and east to Biloxi. In 1894 he broadcast a flier announcing that, since 1876, he had won gold medals at all expositions for his incomparable collection of Creole Antiques. He called his shop "The Only Gold Medal Antique House in America" and "The Oldest Antique House in the South." Carl W. Dreppard, well-known authority on antiques, says of Hawkins that he was "unwashed, unbelievably shabby and yet rakishly devil-may-care," and that he sold with the combined techniques of a midway barker and the persuasive gentleness of a 57th Street art gallery salesman.

In the course of his travels Hawkins overbought on dueling swords, and had a dozen that were exactly alike. He also had a painting of Napoleon that nobody wanted. He hired a local artist to paint one of the dueling swords on Napoleon, and when a rich stranger came to town, Hawkins exhibited portrait and sword. He did not wish to sell the sword, he said, since it added to the value of his portrait. Finally, of course, he was persuaded to sacrifice his precious relic—and for a mere $1,200! At discreet intervals, thereafter, he disposed of the rest of the swords.

During Hawkins's day, three of the great present-day dealers opened stores, Waldhorn, Keil and Feldman. Mr. Feldman began with a horse and wagon, buying feathers. Where Feldman bought feathers, he found old furniture. It had fallen apart in the damp climate and people could neither repair or replace it, so Mr. Feldman opened a little repair shop. In the course of his labors, a customer persuaded Feldman to buy a pair of unsigned paintings for $100. To his surprise, for Mr. Feldman in those days knew no more about art than the next fellow, the paintings turned out to be worth $100,000. And if you don't believe it you can ask him, for he told me the story himself.

Until recently there was considerable late Hepplewhite and Sheraton in the antique stores, and it is interesting to know where the pieces came from. After the Purchase in 1803, many English immigrants and some Pennsylvania Dutch traveled down the Mississippi on flatboats. There were also Germans and Irish. They brought the best of their furniture with them. Many had Sheraton and Hepplewhite and some, maybe, had Chippendale. They settled along the banks and bayous, bought a few slaves, and pretty soon they were planters. They prospered and many of them became enormously rich. During the war they lost their plantations, and numbers of them moved into New Orleans where they disposed of their furniture to junkmen, or lost it to Pawnbroker Hawkins. In the course of time, most of the plantation furniture was acquired by the antique dealers.

Before the last of it was sold, some of the dealers had excellent reproductions made. Local furniture makers copy all the antique brotherhood, from Chippendale to Phyfe. There are professional wood-agers in the Vieux Carré, worm-holers, wood-crackers and fly-speckers, who can make new furniture look at least two hundred years old. New Orleans dealers do not sell artificially aged pieces as antiques, but reproductions are often aged to suit their period.

There was a worm-holer who went to work on a new frame to match one of a broken pair. When he finished, it looked more ancient than the old frame, and the worms who had lived for a century in their own little holes moved over from the violetwood frame to the new one, into the cozy holes that were made with an icepick.

In 1905 dealers whose original Creole stock was nearly exhausted began buying abroad. Except during the wars, they have been buying abroad ever since. Mr. Feldman, for one, has made eighty-two trips to Europe.

There are still old people in the Vieux Carré, living on memories and pennies, who take their treasures to the stores to be sold on commission. Dealers used to charge ten per cent, but now the dealers charge twenty per cent. And some of the old people are down to their last teacups.

There was one lady, a Creole aristocrat, who died recently in an Old Ladies' Home. Before she entered the home, she called upon another Creole lady who has a shop on Royal Street, and left with her a pair of hurricane shades.

"When I die," the old lady said, "I want a nice funeral with a solemn High Mass, and flowers for my bier. Do you think, ma chère, that you could arrange it for the price my shades will bring?"

"Certainement," said the antique dealer, "and an anniversary requiem, as well, and also a bunch of chrysanthemums on All Souls' Day. But you must not talk of dying, madame!"

"No," said the old lady. "But I wanted to be sure, ma chère."

She left her shades and went away, and in a week she was dead. The antique dealer sold the shades for $150 to a movie star, who knew the story and quibbled about the price. And I would tell you her name, but I promised I wouldn't.

The same old lady sold unsigned portraits of her in-laws for $150 apiece, and lived on the proceeds for months. The portraits of the in-laws, who were French, were bought by a German refugee in search of ancestors. The portraits of her parents, which were signed by Vanderlyn and worth a fortune, the old lady proudly bequeathed to the Cabildo.

Nouveaux riches, according to the dealers, often acquire synthetic ancestors. It is not, however, a new custom. There was once a madam in the Red Light District who called herself Minnie Haha, and said she was descended from the heroine of Longfellow's poem. In Minnie Haha's parlor were portraits neatly labeled "Mr. and Mrs. Hiawatha, Ancestors of Minnie Haha." Minnie was a light colored woman with a touch of Choctaw. But her "ancestors" were pure-blooded Creoles.

There are thousands of crystal chandeliers for sale on Royal Street, most of which came from châteaux and castles in France. In the old days dealers bought the chandeliers from old houses in the Vieux Carré and from plantations. They also bought them from the St. Louis Hotel. After there were no more for sale in New Orleans the dealers started buying abroad.

Before the War Between the States, there was one oil well in the United States. Now there are about a million. Other cities took to oil lamps before New Orleans did, because in the South there were such beautiful candelabra that it seemed almost wicked to discard them. But in 1870 Mr. D. H. Holmes, the most enterprising merchant of the South, advertised a sale of brand-new oil lamps. Nearly everybody who could afford it bought one. The people used the lamps in the parlor, and found them good for reading. And that was when the dealers began picking up crystal candelabra for a dollar or two.

Furniture in Creole days was dark and massive. Everything was big, the rooms, the chairs, the armoires, and especially the beds. I must tell you about the beds. The handsomest of them were made on Rue Royale by Seignouret and Mallard. They were like the bed George Moore wrote about (I think it was in *Evelyn Innes*): "Wide as a battlefield, deep as a hay mow." Mallard's beds, which were the biggest (eight to nine feet long and almost as wide), were also the fanciest, carved with garlands of flowers and festoons of fruit. And they had birds too, although birds on a bed are generally considered unlucky. Seignouret's pieces were more restrained and often had no trimming at all, only a big S carved at the top. Both men worked in mahogany and in rosewood, which the Creoles called palissandre or violet ebony. It was said of the big beds that the tradition of southern hospitality originated with them. "Always room for one more," people said.

If you are interested in Creole antiques, you will want to know something of Seignouret and Mallard. Their names are scarcely known except to collectors, but in nineteenth-century New Orleans they were as popular as Duncan Phyfe was in New York.

Seignouret was a wine merchant from Bordeaux who built himself a fine mansion at 520 Royal Street, and besides conducting his wine business set himself up as a cabinetmaker. He hired numbers of freed men who were skilled artisans, and established them off his pleasant patio in the courtyard that is now called the Brulatour Court. Brulatour was another wine merchant, who rented the mansion from Madame Seignouret after her husband's death. Everything was falling apart when Mr. Irby bought the place and made it beautiful again, the same Mr. Irby who did so much to restore the Quarter, and then shot himself at the undertaker's.

Prudent Mallard came from Sèvres to work with Duncan Phyfe; but New York was bad for Mallard's asthma, and he journeyed to New Orleans where he opened a workshop at 305 Royal Street. Mallard was especially noted for his duchesse table, an ornately carved dressing table, with a marble top that was sweet and cool to the touch.

Seignouret's specialty was armoires ten feet high with mirrors on their double doors, "one for the master and one for the dame."

Beds were always four-posted because of the necessity for mosquito nets, which were attached to the tester. At the foot of the big bed in the master's bedroom of every Creole home was an accouchement couch, which was as indispensable a part of a bride's bedroom suite as her dressing table. Creole women never had physicians when they had babies. They had colored midwives, who were called accoucheuses, and during labor the women were lifted from their vast four-posters to the narrow couches, to make things easier for the midwife. Sarah Bernhardt kept a casket in her bedroom, for the restraining influence it exerted. But the accouchement couches didn't work that way. Creole ladies all had enormous families.

The nuns slept in small four-posters with square posts and no carving that were made of fruitwood. They were the only beds in town that were not dark and big and shining. After a hundred and fifty years, they were replaced by iron cots. The chaste little four-posters were gobbled up by an antique dealer, who bought them from a junkman, who bought them from the nuns.

Prudent Mallard married a Spanish Creole, and went to live in the famous "skyscraper" three blocks from his workshop, only it wasn't a skyscraper then. The fourth story was built some years later by an old-clothes-and-bottles man, who added seven rooms to the top and made a terraced garden on the roof, which was certainly doing well for a junkman. That is the sort of thing that is always happening in New Orleans.

The Creoles think it was the War Between the States that finished them. But the gentle Creole culture was doomed from the time of the Louisiana Purchase, when aggressive newcomers came to New Orleans, with more energy than the Creoles and less distaste for work. It was the Anglo-Saxons and the Jews who doomed the Creoles. The war was only another catastrophe. And when it was over, for better or for worse, the leisured ways of Creole days were over.

*   *   *

There was a gentleman named Monsieur Dafau who made ciels de lits for the beds of Messrs. Seignouret and Mallard. Monsieur Dafau used the most exquisite fabrics, sheer silks from China, fine lawns and shimmering satins. For brides he always used Madonna blue silk, trimmed with a flounce of deep Valencienne. If you ever see a perfectly beautiful old canopy you can be almost sure that it was Monsieur Dafau's handiwork.

Monsieur belonged to a Creole club called Le Comite des Bon Amis, and upon an occasion, monsieur procured for his colleagues a keg of Barbados rum. The Good Friends said it smelled strange. They had a drink or two, and then they'd had enough. Monsieur was chagrined. If there was anything wrong with the rum, there might be something in the keg, he said. He found an ax, and split the keg open. And there, sitting upright with his hands clasped around his knees, and in the most perfect state of preservation, was a little old man with long white whiskers. Poor Monsieur Dafau had a nervous breakdown, and never made another ciel de lit.

17

THE RED LIGHT DISTRICT

In Basin Street, in Basin Street,
   The night wind's soft and indiscreet,
Murmuring in whispers still a name,
   An address of unhallowed fame,
Of gilt and crimson, careless laughter,
   Champagne and roses swirling after,
"Bright wraiths slip down the dark," it sighs,
   "With laughing lips and flashing eyes,
With lacy skirts and crimson shoes."
   Murmurs the night wind—"These are whose?
From Josie's place? Or Lulu White's?
   Or Countess Willie's?" . . . Moonlight nights,
In Basin Street, in Basin Street,
   The night wind's soft, and indiscreet. . . .

Prostitution began in New Orleans when the king sent over a shipload of "correction girls" to make his subjects happy. There were eighty-eight of them, all from La Salpetrière, a house of correction in Paris. They arrived on March 4, 1721, in custody of three nuns and a midwife nicknamed Madame Sans-Regret. Six weeks later Bienville reported to the Duc d'Orléans, "Nineteen have married. Ten have died." Then there were fifty-nine.

Marie, Toinette and Suzy,
   Julie, petite Lucette,
All found a house in Royal Street,
   With Madame Sans-Regret.

And that was the way it began.

A hundred years later the Americans promoted the Creoles' cabarets into a gaudy Red Light District with magnificent houses and fantastic madams. Jazz was born in a brothel and swept the world from Basin Street, and the extravagant bordellos, with their bewigged madams and legends of butlers in scarlet uniforms, of diamonds and octoroons and beautiful girls made New Orleans' Red Light District the most famous in the country.

Legalized prostitution ended with the first World War and now it is a part of history. Its beginnings are in the old records, and its ending in the memory of many living "girls" and madams. To find out what I could about the district I talked with a police officer, an ex-madam and a social worker who were all on North Basin Street the night the district closed. The madam had a party to which she invited the police. The social worker did not go to the party, but she looked in at the open door. In line of duty, she was around making notes.

"As I passed Mahogany Hall, Lulu White came out of the house," she said, "with her red wig on and a champagne glass in her hand. People said Lulu had more diamonds than any decent woman in town. But that was probably an exaggeration. The next time I saw Lulu, she was frying chicken in the saloon on the corner. Her wig looked frowzy and she was putting on weight."

Mahogany Hall, the house where Lulu kept her famous octoroons, where the crystal chandelier hung in the parlor, is headquarters now for the National Jazz Foundation, and the saloon where Lulu fried chicken is Teen Town, a recreation center for young people. Lulu was arrested after the district closed for selling liquor to a soldier. She was found guilty and sentenced to a federal penitentiary for a year and a day. It takes a presidential pardon to get out of a federal penitentiary. But Lulu got one, signed by President Wilson, who was in Paris at the time for the Peace Conference. Lulu said it

"*Mahogany Hall belonged to Lulu White, a colored woman who had a red wig and more diamonds than anyone else in town.*"

cost her $50,000, and maybe it did. She had sold most of her diamonds. But she still owned Mahogany Hall.

A man pretending to be a movie producer went to Lulu when she was running a little speakeasy and told her that Hollywood wanted to make a movie of her life as the Black Queen of Storyville. Lulu sold Mahogany Hall for $6,000, bought herself a wardrobe and flew to California. A few weeks later, broke and bitter, she returned to New Orleans on a bus. Then she took to drink.

"She got terribly fat," continued the social worker, "and at one time she weighed almost three hundred pounds. Then she became sick, and applied for a free bed at Charity Hospital. They say she had on her famous diamond garters when she was admitted, that she had kept them to the last so she wouldn't be buried in a pauper's grave. But I don't believe it. Lulu was panhandling toward the end."

In French days, houses were called cabarets, and they weren't just brothels, but convenient, cozy places, which, in the beginning, sold everything from red beans to love. Dramshops, gambling dens, groceries and houses of prostitution were all under one roof. The most celebrated was Maison Coquet on Royal Street which advertised in forthright Latin fashion on lampposts and public buildings. "With the Express Permission," it said on the circulars, "of the Honorable Civil Governor."

Until the Americans made a racket of prostitution, there was nothing blatantly sordid about sin in New Orleans. In the days of early river commerce, there was the Swamp, where there was a murder practically every night. But the Creoles never went to the Swamp. It was exclusively for river men and their strumpets. During the first half of the nineteenth century, the cafés and gambling houses, the theaters and brothels operated happily side by side.

Among the more fashionable bordellos was Odette Crusol's on Toulouse Street, for which Odette imported blonde girls from Antwerp who wore gowns from Paris, and dined with the customers at small tables under crystal chandeliers, as in a restaurant. Tradition says that Odette had a liveried butler, and one of the finest sets of Sèvres in New Orleans.

The first houses were in the commercial district of French Town and were so discreetly operated as to be inconspicuous. With the advent of politicians from the North, the houses were exploited into something resembling a district and swindling was established. By the time the Americans wrested control of the city from the Creoles the Red Light District was a profitable source of graft, and famous throughout the country.

Walt Whitman visited New Orleans when he was twenty-seven and got himself a job on the *Crescent*. That gave Walt a front seat at every public show and a chance to get earfuls and eyefuls in a hundred giddy arcana. He is said to have fallen in love with a girl in the district. He wrote his first verse in New Orleans and much of it appeared later in *Leaves of Grass*.

When *Leaves* was published, Whitman sent copies to two New England poets whom he admired. Whittier threw his in the fire. But Emerson sat down and wrote Whitman a marvelous letter beginning, "I salute you at the beginning of a great career." In the book was the poem Whitman wrote "To a Common Prostitute":

> Be composed—be at ease with me. I
>   am Walt Whitman liberal and lusty as nature,
> Not till the sun excludes you do I exclude you,
> Not till the waters refuse to glisten for you
>   and the leaves to rustle for you, do my
>   words refuse to glisten and rustle for you.
> My girl, I appoint you with an appointment, and
>   I charge that you make preparations to
>   be waiting to meet me,
> And I charge that you be patient and perfect
>   till I come.
> Till then I salute you with a significant
>   look that you do not forget me.

After the War Between the States, when the Vieux Carré deteriorated and many of the old families moved away, the prostitutes took over. Various attempts were made to get them out, but the politicians who controlled the Fourth Ward were more powerful than the reformers. And the French Quarter became a heaven for whores. Old-time residents finally secured an ordinance that required prostitutes to vacate the ground floors of all houses on Burgundy, Bienville, Dauphine, St. Louis and Conti streets. The order shifted only crib girls and sidewalk strumpets. Parlor houses continued to operate without restraint.

Cribs were one-story unpainted shacks with nothing in them but a bed, a chair and a washbasin. They rented for a dollar a day, and were the last refuge of destitute, derelict prostitutes. The girls stood at the open doors calling, "Come on in, honey. Venez ici, honey. Won't cost you nothing to just talk with me. How about it, honey?" Many of the crib "girls" were old women.

In the nineties a new minister, the Rev. E. A. Clay, came to town to become pastor of the German Methodist Church. Someone told him that there were girls as young as fourteen in the houses and the minister preached a sermon on the district that some people still remember.

"In our fair city are five hundred slaughterhouses of darkness and despair!" thundered Mr. Clay. "These reeking pestholes are inhabited by fifteen hundred angels of death and damnation. Foul hags in palatial palaces of gilt imperil the virtue of every innocent girl! And what, dearly beloved, can we do about it?"

After services a group of parishioners promised to do what they could, and the Methodists organized to fight the politicians and the district. Various measures were proposed to establish some sort of control, and women's clubs took up the cudgels. When the Creole ladies heard about the American ladies holding a meeting and discussing the matter in public, the Creoles were shocked at their indelicacy. There were two things the Creole ladies had always known about, but seldom mentioned. One was Quadroons and the other was prostitutes.

Finally Alderman Sidney Story went abroad at his own expense to study the methods by which prostitution was regulated in Europe. When he returned, he secured legislation to set aside certain streets where bordellos, although not actually legalized, might operate without police interference. This meant that hundreds of prostitutes were forced to move from residential and business sections into the restricted district. Rental and property values in the proposed area promptly doubled, and the indignant prostitutes retaliated by christening the district Storyville.

There were thirty-eight blocks occupied solely by houses, restaurants, cabarets, saloons and cribs, all devoted to vice, and making a nice thing of it. Within a few years, Storyville was the principal tourist attraction of New Orleans. Conducted tours began with a drink at the Arlington Annex, the bar owned by Tom Anderson, the "King of the Tenderloin." Later I am going to tell you about the famous "Ball of the Two Well Known Gentlemen" which Mr. Anderson gave during Mardi Gras for the girls of the district.

Anderson published the "Blue Book," an illustrated Directory and Gentleman's Guide to the Sporting District, tastily bound in pale blue with harp and flowers on the cover, which listed the name and address of every registered prostitute, white and colored, in the business. There were nearly five hundred white girls and about half as many who were colored. White and colored Madams bought space from Mr. Anderson to advertise their houses and their girls. There was nothing salacious about the "Blue Book." It was painfully "genteel" and as "refined" as could be.

"To know the right from the wrong, peruse this little book carefully," advised the editor. "Read all the 'ads,' and learn the best places to spend your time and money."

Preceding the alphabetical directory, "An Authoritative Guide to the Queer Zone," was a Preface headed with the high-minded motto of the Order of the Garter, "Honi soit qui mal y pense" (Evil be to him who evil thinks).

"Anyone," proclaimed the editor, "who knows today from yesterday will tell you that the Blue Book is the right book for the right people. New Orleans needs this Directory because New Orleans is the only place in America where there is a district set aside by law for its fast women. This wise law puts the stranger on a safe and proper path. It protects the stranger in our midst from 'hold-ups' and other games usually practiced upon those who are not 'in the know.' The law keeps streetwalkers from thronging the thoroughfares of our fair city, and regulates the women so they may live by themselves. Storyville is bounded on the north by Iberville Street and on the south by St. Louis Street."

The Blue Book carried full-page liquor and jewelry advertisements, and illustrated advertisements of the various houses. There was Josie Arlington's brownstone mansion with a minaret on the roof that gave it the look of a mosque, with a slender tower surrounded by a balcony. From such a balcony Mohammedans summon the faithful to prayer, and Josie's maidens promenaded in the moonlight.

"Nowhere in this country," said the Blue Book, "will you find a more complete and thorough sporting house than the Arlington. It is a palace fit for a king. Within its walls will be found the work of great artists from Europe and America. Absolutely and unquestionably Josie's is the most decorative and costly sporting palace in the world."

There was a photograph of Emma Johnson's Studio, with a "Warning!" printed beneath. "Everybody," it said, "must be of some importance, otherwise he cannot gain admittance to the Studio."

There was also a photograph of Lulu White's Mahogany Hall, with its fabulous fish bowl out front. The fish bowl was of cement, a huge thing that looked like an amplifier. Colored flood lights, playing all night, changed the water from blue to crimson, to purple and to green. Sometimes it was a golden pool, sometimes it was silver. And sometimes it was all colors of the rainbow. Lulu's fish bowl was the brightest thing on Basin Street, and the most amazing sight in town.

"If you want to make the rounds of all the live places, call up Cooke's taxis," advised the Blue Book, "and let Cooke's drivers tell you where to go."

Tom Anderson advertised his famous annex on the front page of the Blue Book, and his cabaret on the back cover. Mr. Anderson had a Darky Orchestra to render all the latest musical selections, and private dining rooms for the Fair Sex. His café, he said, was "noted the States over for being the best conducted café in America," and his cabaret was "The Real Thing." There was "Excellent Entertainment at Tom's from 9 p.m. to ?"

Storyville madams, according to the Blue Book, were "elegant and beautiful women capable of cleverly entertaining the most fastidious gentlemen." Their girls were "always neat and natty and jolly good fun." There was one house called Cairo where the girls were advertised as Egyptians, and the madam, an old Roman with a hawk nose, was said to be an Arabian, "a dusky beauty known as Snooks." Snooks, a good fellow to all who came in contact with her, regarded the word "Fun" as it should be, and not as a money-making word.

Several of the houses had ballrooms, "with orchestras ever in attendance, as well as talented singers and dancers." The grandeur of the mansions was "beyond the poor power of pen to describe," and "words failed to do justice to the hospitality of the madams or the beauty of their young ladies."

There was Chiquita, the Spanish Dove whose motto was "Let's all live and enjoy life while we can." Chiquita had a "coterie of lovely friends, ladies of high class and culture," who helped her entertain in a Chateau that was "without doubt the finest equipped in the Tenderloin." . . . "What more could a person expect? Just think of it! Pretty women, wine, and song!"

Harriet was "the idol of society and club boys." Harriet needed but little introduction, as she was known to "the elite from New York to California both for her brains and beauty." Her mansion was handsomely furnished with the best that money could procure and she was "winsome, witty and lovely." In those days men were supposed to abhor "brainy women," but Harriet brazenly advertised her "brains."

There was the "Parisian Queen of America," "The Dutch Landlady," and a lady "commonly called Grace by all who knew her, a woman of very rare attainments who came of good old English stock from across the water."

Then there was Countess Willie Piazza, who had the French Studio, two doors from Lulu White's. The countess was also a colored woman, and her girls, like Lulu's, octoroons. Willie had been to Paris to have her face enameled, her hair dekinked, and the drawl ironed out of her speech. Willie had a music box in her mattress and a room that was all mirrors. She and Lulu White both ran five-dollar houses. They had elegant carriages with twin bays in which they drove to the race track with their girls. Lulu would put on her red wig and all her diamonds, and Willie would hold her little pug dog in her lap, the girls would tip their lace parasols over their picture hats, and away they would go, with their liveried coachmen up front, and everybody at the track looking at them. A councilman once urged a law to prohibit the madams from driving through the streets with their girls. He said their blatant show of prosperity was a temptation to the tender young maidens of the city. But nothing came of his proposal.

The *Blue Book* had this to say of Countess Willie's house: "It is one place you can't afford to miss. The Countess has made it a study to make everyone jovial who visits her house. If you have the blues, the Countess and her girls can cure them, for she has without doubt the most handsome and intelligent octoroons in the United States. If there is anything new in the singing or dancing line that you would like to see, telephone the Countess and her girls will oblige."

Tom Anderson also published a little red book called *Hello!* that listed the telephone number of every girl in the district.

"Storyville was a business enterprise," an ex-madam told me. "To be a prostitute was a serious business, not a vice. Most of the girls drank in moderation, and that saved them from degradation. Liquor is bad for a woman's looks, and looks were important in our business. A prostitute never had to be beautiful, but the successful ones took good care of themselves. Some of the girls became excellent wives. There was one, the doll in the teacup type, who married the son of a socially prominent and wealthy family in New Orleans. She eloped with him one night, like a girl in boarding school, out a window and down a rope of sheets at Josie Arlington's. The Storyville *Sunday Sun* wrote it up, and there was a big scandal. His family disowned him, and for some time refused to see him or his wife. But after a while things smoothed over. The couple still live in New Orleans. She is one of the prettiest women in the city, and her husband is just as crazy about her as ever."

Some of the madams and a good many of the girls had pimps, she said, whom they supported and sometimes loved quite madly. The pimps, she said, would come around after the house closed, and take the girls' money away from them, and if there wasn't enough to satisfy them, they would sometimes beat a girl.

"I never could see it," she said, "loving a pimp. But I reckon it's the maternal instinct. Women like to feel that someone needs them. They like to make a pimp happy, the way they'd like to buy toys for a child.

"Women like violent men. That's natural. I can see falling for a tough guy," she said. "But not getting beaten up. I can't see that."

A physician told me that he once asked a Madam why she kept

a pimp named Tony. Tony was a small-time gambler with well-oiled hair and small feet who wore patent leather shoes with high heels, and fifteen-dollar neckties that he charged to the Madam.

"When the night's over and I go to my room and Tony's there waiting, it does something for me, Doc," she said. "All night I been selling flesh, and maybe it was a tough night. Other women's flesh —maybe my own—and there's Tony in his blue silk pajamas, the silk pajamas I paid for, waiting for me and I look at him comfortable on my pink sheets, waiting there. And I know there's one thing on God's green earth lower than a whore. That's what that dirty little bastard does for me, Doc."

Girls in the houses were charged a weekly board and lodging fee, and the madams deducted a percentage of their earnings. Before she got a house of her own, the ex-madam told me that she earned a hundred dollars some days. Because she never had a pimp, she saved most of it. She saved $30,000 while she was in Storyville. When the district closed, she went to New York and got a job as saleswoman in a department store.

"I hated it," she said. "I wanted to get back to New Orleans. This town has been good to me, and I love it."

So back she went, and opened a house of assignation.

"I attracted a nice class of trade," she said. "You meet some fine people in this business."

"Do you like the business?" I asked her.

"It gets in your blood," she said, "and you don't want to quit. It's not being a nymph, or a tramp, or anything like that. It's just liking the life, the action and comradeship—excitement—money. A girl keeps her head up, and minds her own business. She hasn't got 'prostitute' written all over her. It's not bad, the way people think."

* * *

There was a minister once who lived in Louisiana who thought it was very bad indeed. He thought about it so much that he determined to raise funds to build a Rescue Home for Fallen Women. But before he started his campaign, he thought he should find out what life in the "dens of infamy" was like. Imagining was not enough. He must see for himself. So he secured a leave of absence in order to investigate.

The minister visited the various houses in Storyville, and in one of them he met a girl who told him her life story. Perhaps he fell in love with her. He wrote a novel called *Soiled Doves* with a subtitle: *The Romance of a Minister and a Courtesan*. The book was published anonymously. Shortly after publication, the minister regretted his indiscretion, and attempted to buy up the edition. He secured all but a few copies, and burned them. The copies he could not buy are now worth a good deal of money.

At Josie Arlington's, the minister met the King of the Tenderloin.

"He was a handsome fellow, though his face was hard. He was about thirty-five, with an evil and sensual gleam in his black eye. A big six-carat diamond adorned his cravat, and his watch was encrusted with emeralds."

"Soiled doves" in the five-dollar houses ranged in age, the minister said, from fourteen to twenty. Most of them had been seduced by that "lecherous, bestial love which leads to the pit of hell."

"The reader may feel," he apologized, "an unwarranted coarseness in my treatment of the subject, but as coarse expressions portray essential characters, I feel that I am justified. I shall write plainly of vice, without the use of veneer or euphemism."

He told of the seduction of the "pure maiden" who was the heroine of his novel. She was a seamstress with a little sister to support. Her name was Elaine, and she was "a golden-haired gem of purest ray serene." Her little sister was run over by a milk wagon, and taken to the Poydras Female Asylum.

Elaine, in "desperate financial straits," went to the apartment of a man who was her father's friend, "a well known gentleman of North Rampart Street."

"Why yes, Girlie, I'll lend you the money," said the well known gentleman, "provided you will remain in this apartment tonight."

The poor girl fell in a dead faint at his feet. He picked her up and laid her on a couch.

"You beast! You viper!" she cried. "I will die first! Have pity, oh have pity on a pure, defenseless girl."

But soon, swaying with fear and loathing, she changed her mind. "I submit," she said. "You win."

Elaine was thinking of her dear little sister in Julien Poydras' foundling home. But the poor girl's sacrifice was in vain, for her sister had died.

Elaine did not claim, as many girls in houses did, that she had been "deceived by some man." She confessed, the minister said, that she had "sold herself into sin."

"But the best man alive," he added stanchly, "doesn't deserve the worst woman on earth." And Elaine was good enough for the minister.

He bought her a feather boa, a black broadcloth skirt and a peeka-boo shirtwaist. Elaine did not drink or smoke. But the minister checked on prices on the wine list. Beer that sold in other places for six cents cost twenty-five cents in Elaine's bon-ton house. And champagne was ten dollars a quart which was high in those days.

The landlady had become a rich woman. In her front parlor was a mantel of black onyx, framed in silver and inlaid with twenty-dollar gold pieces. Elaine said that in her bedroom the madam had a wash bowl and pitcher of gold plate that she kept in a safe.

The six girls in the house had "private apartments, each done in a different color scheme." They had dinner at six o'clock and a "light repast in the wee sma' hours." Sometimes they went with their pimps or "money men" to Antoine's or Arnaud's, and ate in one of the private dining rooms. When business was light, they went "hopping," calling around from one house in the district to another. At the theaters, they always had boxes. Colored hairdressers did their hair. In the house, daytimes, they wore wrappers, and at night evening gowns. On the street they looked trim and smart.

One evening when the minister was visiting Elaine, the madam announced that a friend of Tom Anderson's had bought the house for the night. That was the night the minister told Elaine he loved her, and that he wanted to take her away.

But Elaine apparently was not interested.

*   *   *

During the first World War, the secretary of war issued an order forbidding prostitution within five miles of an army cantonment, and the secretary of the navy issued a similar order with respect to ports. The mayor of New Orleans hurried to Washington to protest. Storyville, explained the mayor, was a model establishment and a necessary adjunct to a seaport the size of New Orleans. The government was adamant. If the Red Light District was not closed, said the secretary of the navy, the city would be put out of bounds for army and navy. This would have been an unsupportable blow to civic pride and a tremendous loss to business interests. There was nothing to do but comply. The mayor issued a statement, and returned to New Orleans to order the district closed.

"Our city government," said the mayor, "believes that the situation can be administered more easily and satisfactorily by confining prostitution within a prescribed area. Our experience has taught us that the reasons for this are unanswerable, but the Navy Department has decided otherwise."

In October the girls were ordered to vacate by midnight on November 12. The exodus began before that. But on the night of the 12th there were farewell parties.

"There was dirges and jazz," the police officer said. "It reminded me somewhat of the funerals of the colored madams. When a colored woman in the district died, she was piped to the grave by a brass band that played funeral marches on the way to the cemetery, and jazz on the way back, and that was the way it was that last night. The brass would be slow and sobbing. Then all of a sudden it would start screeching.

"Most of the houses had a professor that played the piano. The girls would take up collections for him, and the customers would buy him drinks. Those professors sure could tickle the ivories. For dances the madams had orchestras, mostly jazz orchestras, though they liked sweet music too. The night the district closed there was a brass band playing funeral music. But at midnight the band played *Basin Street Blues,* and *Don't Shimmy While I'm Gone.* Louis Armstrong was around then, with that cornet of his. Louis had an orchestra which formed a part of the second line at marches, funerals and Mardi Gras parades. He learned to play the bugle and cornet at the Waifs' Home. Daytimes he worked at odd jobs, and nights he went around Storyville with his choral group playing for peanuts. Louis was the King of Jazz then just like he is now, only nobody knew how good he was but the girls in the district. Some of the girls and the madams cried when Louis and his boys played the blues that night."

The police officer shook his head reflectively. "Them was the good old days," he said. "And that night," he added sadly, "was not only the end of Storyville. It was what you might call the end of an era."

The social worker took up the story. "The next day," she said, "members of the women's clubs and the churches held a meeting, and appointed a committee to help the ex-inmates of the district. And would you believe it?—not one of those prostitutes ever applied."

18

*M*ARDI GRAS

Mardi Gras in New Orleans is mad and wonderful and the greatest free show on earth, and it is strange that visitors know so little about it. People expecting to attend Carnival balls often arrive in town with beautiful costumes, especially people from Hollywood, and when they learn that tickets cannot be bought for love or money some of them get angry. Visitors may watch Carnival parades, wear dominoes, and dance in the streets. But they have about as much chance of going to one of the exclusive balls as the camel had of going through the eye of a needle.

During Mardi Gras the hotels are filled to overflowing and people sleep on cots in the corridors, in fire stations and bars, in the press room at City Hall, on pool tables and park benches. And some of them sleep in railroad cars as far away as Baton Rouge and Biloxi. Mardi Gras is attended by about five hundred thousand persons and hardly anybody, except the natives, has an idea of what it is all about. That is why I am going to tell you what every visitor should know, and something about the fantastic behind-the-scenes business that makes Mardi Gras the exciting and marvelous thing it is.

During Mardi Gras there are parades and balls every night. Over each parade there reigns a masked King in silk and gilt and velvet, with a jeweled crown and a gleaming scepter. The Kings wear ermine robes with tremendous trains and sit on high thrones, and they are attended by mounted Dukes in shining armor and Knights in velvet doublets with satin waistcoats and beautiful wigs.

After every parade there is a ball and over each ball there reigns a Queen. The Queens wear the most gorgeous gowns that ever were seen, embroidered with sequins and pearls, or recklessly studded with rhinestones. Often a Queen's gown costs thousands of dollars, and sometimes her father goes bankrupt after the ball. The Queens are attended by Maids in white, with plumes in their hair and roses in their arms.

Each King gives his Queen a magnificent gift, like a diamond-and-platinum watch or jade earrings or a diamond bracelet. Some Kings have given their Queens engagement rings—but only, of course, if they were going to marry them. And there was once a Duke who bought a pair of diamond bracelets to give to his sweetheart, who was another man's wife. At the end of the maskers' first dance he slipped one over her wrist. During the next dance they quarreled, and then the Duke gave the other one to a poor little Cinderella who was attending the ball with her rich cousins. Cinderella thought, naturally, that the bracelet was paste. But she fell in love with the Duke anyway, and he fell in love with her— and this is absolutely true, although it sounds like a fairy tale. The woman who received the first bracelet told her husband it was a piece of costume jewelry that she picked up at Maison Blanche (the big department store).

"It's just junk," she told him. "But it sparkles like the real thing. It's the way it catches the light," she said.

Then Cinderella's engagement was announced. And when the story of the bracelets got around, that woman was so embarrassed she left town.

At Mardi Gras balls the men wear masks. Most of them make splendid cavaliers, but some have spindly legs and some of them have stomachs that stick out in their handsome doublets, and then of course everyone recognizes them. Women never wear masks.

Before the dancing begins the Queen, on her father's arm, is escorted to the throne where she is received by the King and seated

on his right hand. There is a tableau and a grand march, then the King and Queen dance with their Court while the band plays the Carnival song, *If Ever I Cease to Love*. After that come the call-outs, when girls are called by name from the crowded auditorium to dance with the maskers. A girl dances once following each call-out with the masker who issued the call-out. During the evening she may have twenty call-outs, one for every dance. Every man she dances with gives her a gift from the satin sack that swings from his shoulder. They are no tawdry little gifts that the maskers give, but keepsakes to treasure. At one ball there were gold lapel pins that were copies of the old street lights in the Vieux Carré, with rubies to simulate the flame. Sometimes the favors are jeweled compacts in Carnival colors, sometimes they are necklaces or bracelets of purple and green and gold. When the girls return to their seats and open their packages it is like Merry Christmas, except once there was a girl who received divorce papers from a masked Duke.

On Mardi Gras, which is Shrove Tuesday and the last day of Carnival, there are two parades and two balls. In the afternoon

Rex, the only unmasked King of Carnival, rides through the town with his Knights and Dukes. The Queen of Carnival, surrounded by her Maids, sits on the balcony of the Boston Club (which is on Canal Street, in the middle of the city). As he rides past the club, Rex toasts his young Queen and the crowds cheer as the Queen smiles gravely down.

In the evening, Comus's Queen awaits her King in the stands of the Louisiana Club (which is on St. Charles Avenue), and Comus riding by drinks her health as he passes, from a goblet made of gold.

On Mardi Gras night Rex and his Queen dance with their Court at a ball in the Municipal Auditorium. At midnight Rex takes his Queen to call upon Comus and his Queen, who are also having a ball in another hall of the Auditorium. Comus, the oldest of Carnival Kings, is the God of Joy and Mirth. Instead of a crown, Comus wears white plumes and, by tradition, he toasts his subjects instead of waving his scepter as other kings do. When Rex and his Queen arrive, Comus drinks their health from his golden goblet, and Rex waves his jeweled scepter. Then the Monarchs withdraw, and their two Courts dance—the Lords and the Ladies all together, and that is the official end of Mardi Gras. But it is not really the end because afterward both Queens have a breakfast, each for her King and Court, and everybody drinks champagne until it is time to take off their crowns and go to Mass.

* * *

Mark Twain was a tourist and he loved New Orleans. But he made fun of Mardi Gras. He called it "rigmarole" and "girly-girly romance," and said it was commercial.

What Mark Twain said, and didn't know, about Mardi Gras set the Mistick Krewe of Comus back on its heels, and annoyed the Knights of Momus. The Clemenses (Mark Twain and his wife) had been guests at both balls, and Mark Twain wrote his maligning little piece for the papers after he had accepted Creole hospitality. People were annoyed, but nobody did anything about it because if there was anything the Creole disliked it was publicity. Mardi Gras in those days was for New Orleanians, with street dances for hoi polloi and balls for the aristocracy. Mardi Gras was romantic because the Creoles were romantic. It was not for nothing that men called New Orleans "The City That Care Forgot."

The Creoles always loved a rapturous rigmarole. They made Mardi Gras as joyous and exuberant as possible, and their balls as unashamedly romantic as a midsummer night's dream. If Mark Twain didn't like them, that was his misfortune. People came from the North to see the parades and the dancing in the streets. But unless the guests were very distinguished, they were hardly ever invited to a Carnival ball. You can be sure that if Mark Twain's Creole hosts had known he was going to write a piece for the papers, they would never have invited him—*nevaire!*

Mardi Gras is not, as most visitors imagine, a calculated tourist attraction. It is the culmination of New Orleans' social season which begins on January 5, the Eve of Epiphany, and ends on Shrove Tuesday, the day before Lent. The entire season is called Carnival. Mardi Gras is a period of about a week that precedes Ash Wednesday.

Epiphany is the holy day that commemorates the manifestation of Christ to the Magi. The Magi were the wisemen of the Medes and Persians who, traveling from afar to find their newborn King, followed the star to Bethlehem. "They traveled by night and they slept by day, for their guide was a wonderful, beautiful star." But it was a very long way, and they didn't get there until the twelfth night after the Baby was born. The Church celebrates Twelfth Night with fasting and prayer. But in New Orleans the Twelfth Night Revelers open the social season with a big ball. Ash Wednesday being a movable feast, occurring sometimes in February and sometimes in March, the season can last for almost two months, which has been long enough to wear out some quite durable debutantes.

Civic organizations exploit Mardi Gras and do it in a great big wonderful way. But Carnival is New Orleans' social season and, except for the parades and promiscuous masking, Mardi Gras is a more or less private affair. The city builds the grandstands and twines the lampposts and public buildings with Carnival bunting. The Young Men's Business Club, which planted the Azalea Trail, coaxes the azaleas into bloom. The mayor invites a number of distinguished guests to sit with him in the grandstand in front of City Hall from which he reviews the parades, and serves champagne to the Kings. The mayor also answers requests from persons who offer fabulous sums for ball tickets. Tickets, he tells them, are not for sale.

In 1887 two tickets for the Comus ball were stolen, and the Krewe offered $1,000 apiece for their return. The offer ran in the newspapers and was posted around town. The reward was not claimed, and the tickets were not used.

Carnival is run by secret societies known as Krewes, with memberships of some hundred to three hundred men. New Orleans society has always been dictated by men, and in the beginning the Krewes were composed entirely of men from the best families. Today there are newer Krewes made up of racial and nationality groups. Every Krewe has its own Carnival ball, but comparatively few have parades. Between Twelfth Night and Mardi Gras there are more than fifty elaborate masked balls, but less than a dozen of them are given by socially elect Krewes. To cover the costs of their social affairs, members pay staggering dues.

For its Carnival ball each Krewe chooses a Queen, and a King to lead the Krewe parade and to reign with the Queen at the ball. Only members of the Krewe may ride on the floats, or mask for the balls. Guests at the balls must wear formal clothes, décolleté for the ladies and tails for the gentlemen.

The Rex Organization elects the King of Carnival. Outsiders gossip and say that Rex pays ten thousand dollars for his honor. But Rex is a man above buying honors, and to be King of Carnival is an honor beyond price. Rex must be a gentleman of means, because being King is a costly business. Besides his royal trappings, there is the Queen's gift to buy and all the regal entertaining he must do. Kings buy pecks of caviare and cases of vintage champagne, and they give banquets fit for the gods.

For a long time there were only the Rex Organization, the Mistick Krewe of Comus, the Twelfth Night Revelers and the Knights of Momus and these are still the crème de la crème of Carnival groups.

Momus is a mocking spirit who was banished from Olympus, and his Krewe was born fourth of the great orders.

The Revelers are one of the most exclusive Carnival organizations. If a girl dances at Twelfth Night she is socially acceptable and included on future guest lists. The Revelers choose their Queen at a ceremony that goes back to an Epiphany Eve in 1870 when the "Bean King" cut a frosted cake at the ball and distributed slices to the ladies. In several of the slices there were silver beans and in one slice there was a gold bean. The King said that the girl who had the gold bean should be Queen of the ball, and those who had silver beans should be her Maids. Now the cake is papier-mâché and in it are small white boxes like the little boxes that wedding cake comes in. Masked "cooks" distribute the boxes among the girls. In each box is a slice of cake. In some of the slices are silver beans, and in one slice is a gold bean. Selection is supposedly left to chance, and it is true that the girls themselves do not know what is in the boxes. But I think that the King and his Knights know.

Proteus is God of the Briny Deep, and he rides through the town in a pink seashell on the day before Shrove Tuesday.

Carnival pictures in magazines or on the screen are usually street scenes, or else they were taken at balls less exclusive than those I have mentioned. It is said that a national weekly after much pulling of strings arranged for an exclusive picture story. The Krewe Captain gave permission for photographs to be taken of the Queen and her Court. The girls, chaperoned by their mothers, assembled at the Auditorium and while the photographer set up his lights, his assistant placed the group. Everything was progressing nicely until the assistant, his mind on cheesecake, addressed the Queen. If a photographer at Buckingham asked Elizabeth to sit on the King's lap the Court would have been no less appalled, and after that the posing didn't go so well. The man from New York had asked the Queen to cross her knees!

* * *

About two hundred years ago there was a pope who was so shocked by the sins of European Carnival that he offered a plenary indulgence to whoever would leave their play and take part in the Veneration of the Blessed Sacrament. During Shrovetide nuns in New Orleans called Poor Clares pray for everyone who goes to Carnival. They begin on Sunday and pray until Ash Wednesday. Pious ladies seeking indulgences sign up for half-hour shifts, so the Blessed Sacrament is never deserted. The nuns and the ladies pray in the nuns' cold chapel, kneeling before Christ on a wooden cross.

After the balls, revelers traditionally go to the French Market for coffee and doughnuts. Afterward, in the old days, they went home and to bed because the next morning nearly everyone in New Orleans went to Mass, and the priest put penitential ashes on their foreheads because it was Ash Wednesday.

"Dust thou art," said the priest as he smeared the ashes. "And unto dust thou must return," he said, making the sign of the cross with his thumb—and that was the end of Carnival.

19

"IF EVER I CEASE TO LOVE"

In 1872 his Imperial Highness Alexis Romanoff Alexandrovitch, brother of the czar, set out to see the world. First he went to Boston, where the Brahmins did him honor. Whittier and Longfellow and Oliver Wendell Holmes wrote poems to him, President Eliot received him at Harvard, and Mr. Bancroft entertained him at the Athenaeum. The *Atlantic Monthly* had a party for him attended by its lady contributors who all believed in Temperance, so there wasn't any wine. Then there was a banquet at the Parker House with a great deal of oratory and an ode by James Russell Lowell, and the duke was exceedingly bored because the Bostonians he met were all so highminded.

As soon as possible he took a train to New Orleans which, even in Petrograd, was known as "The City That Care Forgot." Being only one brother removed from the throne of All the Russias, the duke traveled with an enormous retinue, so he rented a whole floor at the St. Charles Hotel, and there he was as happy as could be.

It was Carnival time when he reached the city, and in honor of his Imperial Highness, Rex had a daylight parade, the first in Mardi Gras history. Rex ordered a towering throne erected in front of City Hall for his Highness to sit upon and scores of floats built for the parade, the floats to be drawn by white mules, and the mules to be led by black men in red turbans. For himself Rex bought a royal purple robe, loaded with rhinestones and a sparkling crown as green as the sea. He also bought a pure-white horse and had the horse's tail dyed purple, which was a custom with the shah of Persia whose snowy charges all had tails of regal purple.

Then Rex ordered a band for every street corner, and told the musicians to play *If Ever I Cease To Love,* a song the duke was known to admire. The bands were to play it in march time during the parade, and after the parade they were to play it for street dancing. It was the hit song from a burlesque called *Bluebeard* in which Lydia Thompson was playing Walleck's Theatre in New York.

Lydia was blonde and very pretty, and when Alexis was in New York she taught him the words he went around humming: "In a house, in a square, in a quadrant, in a street, in a lane, in a road. Turn to the left on the right hand, you see there my true love's abode. I go there a-courting, and cooing to my love like a dove; and swearing on my bended knee, if ever I cease to love, May sheep-heads grow on apple trees, if ever I cease to love . . ."

Lydia came to New Orleans for Mardi Gras, and everywhere the duke went the orchestras played her song. Before he left town the duke sent to Tiffany's for a bracelet for Lydia, of amethysts, emeralds and topaz. Carnival colors were purple, green and gold, and he thought that a bracelet in the same colors would be a nice little souvenir. Lydia thought so too. The duke said that every time she wore it, she would think about New Orleans. But Lydia knew she would think about how much it cost, and that would be even better.

The song had many choruses like:

> May the fish get legs,
> And the cows lay eggs,
> If ever I cease to love.

The newspapers said that Alexis clapped so hard he split his white kid gloves when he heard the one about:

May the Grand Duke Alexis
Ride a buffalo in Texas,
If ever I cease to love.

It was played over and over again the night of the ball, and it has been the Carnival song ever since.

Carnival that year was such a success that the legislature at its next session decreed that Mardi Gras should be a legal holiday, and people might mask from sunrise to sunset on every Shrove Tuesday. Carnival colors were established by edict, and that was also the year that Rex adopted his flag.

Carnival's torchlight parades start a week before Shrove Tuesday when the Krewe of Cynthius parades through the town. The following night the Krewe of Babylon parades, and the next night Momus, and the next night Hermes. On Saturday the children parade, with dazzling floats and a King whose name is Nor (derived from the initials of *New Orleans Romance*). Nor has a Queen, and the children have a Court and bands and a ball like the grownups. Venus and her Krewe parade on Sunday afternoon, and Proteus and his Krewe on Monday night. Each parade is so wonderful that spectators are sure there will never be another like it, and then on Shrove Tuesday come the grandest and the most beautiful of all, Rex in the daytime and Comus at night.

For many years Carnival floats were made in France, because nobody in America could make towers and moats and fairyland castles beautiful enough to please the Krewe captains. But now they are made in Dens on Calliope Street that were once cotton warehouses. When the Krewes ran out of warehouses Cynthius built a Den that cost $50,000, and the way that Krewes spend money, that was only a drop in the bucket. Cynthius, a recently organized Krewe, spent another $50,000 on its first parade, and nobody knows how much the members spent on their ball, or the King for his royal robes and gifts, the dinners he gave and the champagne he bought. Many Kings spend $10,000, but Cynthius is said to have spent more than was ever spent before.

Carnival floats, about twenty for each parade, are built on carts twenty-four feet long and nine feet wide. Their papier-mâché figures (humans and animals) are grotesque in order to achieve an illusion of hugeness, so that each float gives the impression of a great stage. From the time the figures take shape, the floats are shrouded in sheets so that nobody can see them until the day that they lumber like prehistoric monsters out of their dens for Mardi Gras. Then the living actors take their places, the Krewe members in their gorgeous costumes that nobody (not even their wives) has ever seen, and the floats line up for the parade.

Every Krewe has an artist next in importance to its Captain, who plans the floats and the costumes for the maskers. He also plans the tableaux for the ball, the elaborate invitations and dance programs, and the beautiful souvenirs. When one Mardi Gras is over, he starts planning for the next one unless, as sometimes happens, he has a nervous breakdown and then he has to take a rest.

Themes for the parades and balls have a historical, a legendary, or a mythological basis, such as Famous Treaties, Shakespeare's plays or Aesop's fables, tales from the Arabian Nights or from the Bible, immortal love stories or epic poems. To give you an idea of how it is done, I will tell about the "Great Gifts of History" that the Krewe of Comus presented one year. There was Moses on a float receiving God's gift of the Tablets and the Trojans on another float, discovering Ulysses' gift horse. There was Prince Charming bringing life to the Sleeping Beauty, Faust offering his soul to Mephistopheles, and there was a magic horse that was given to an ancient King of Persia. The horse could fly if anyone pressed a button concealed beneath his mane. The king's son pressed the button and away flew the horse, with the prince upon his back. When he was far from home the prince found the second button, and when he pressed it the horse came down on the roof of a palace in which there dwelt a beautiful princess. The prince and the princess eloped on the magic horse, and the horse flew back to the palace of the king. . . . *That* is the sort of story Mardi Gras can tell on a float!

Actors on the floats are all men, except in the Krewe of Venus, who is the Queen of Love and goddess of springtime and flowers. Venus and her nymphs look divine in their flowery bowers where roses and lilies and violets grow, and purple dragonflies dart through the sun. Over their heads bluebirds and parakeets nest in a magic world where cuckatoos wing their bright way and butterflies dance on the air. The most beautiful thing about Venus's floats are the fragile, moving things, the quivering devices that glow with pure color and shimmer with gold and silver leaf and tremble with star dust.

Next to the mayor's grandstand is a grandstand for orphans, and when Venus and her Krewe pass City Hall they throw about ten times as many favors to the orphans as they do to the mayor and his distinguished guests in their tall silk hats.

New Orleans has more orphans, in orphanages, than most cities because other cities place their orphans in private homes, but New Orleans keeps them in institutions. The orphans have a grandstand of their own for Mardi Gras parades where five hundred happy children watch the floats go by.

On each float are sacks filled with thousands and *thousands* of favors that cost THOUSANDS of dollars, and the children all cry, "Please, mister, throw me a favor!"

A long-ago Krewe began the custom when members, tossing trinkets into the crowd, singled out their favorites. Most of the favors cost about a dime, although there is a sad old legend about a diamond ring that was tossed from a King's float, and caught by the wrong girl. One year a visitor caught a string of twisted pearls that surely were intended for someone back of her. She advertised and no one answered so, naturally, she kept them. But when she had them appraised they were not worth as much as she hoped. I myself once caught a lovely jade-green bracelet and if it hasn't any value, it's fun to think it has.

As the parades pass, thousands of children keep crying for favors. When I heard them, I remembered that poem about "He who gives a child a treat makes joy-bells ring in heaven's street," and I knew the joy-bells in heaven were ringing like mad. But for all that Venus and her Krewe are so gorgeous and so generous, there are many people in New Orleans who think that it is scandalous for women to take part in the parades.

In Creole society, girls were schooled in self-effacement and it was unthinkable that a lady should exhibit her charms on a float. Women's parts in tableaux were traditionally played by men and women's costumes were designed for the maskers. That is the way it was in the beginning, and always will be with the old-time Krewes.

* * *

There was another time when a Mardi Gras affair scandalized the Creoles and that was in the days of Tom Anderson, who gave a Carnival ball for the prostitutes. Mr. Anderson had prospered in the Red Light District and, as a token of his appreciation to the saloon-men, the gamblers and the brothelkeepers, he decided to give a ball for the girls and their guests. Admission as for all Carnival balls was by invitation. The invitations were from Mr. Anderson and his friend Frank Lamothe, and the first Mardi Gras ball of Storyville was called "The Ball of the Two Well-Known Gentlemen."

It was in Odd Fellows Hall, which was decorated for the occasion with Carnival colors. The madams and the girls bought new dresses and the gamblers bought champagne. And Mr. Anderson bought orchids for everyone. He had hundreds of balloons of purple and green and gold, and favors and gifts for all the girls.

Mr. Anderson had a little white, waxed mustache and looked

rather like a banker. He always wore a white flower in his button-hole, and kept his pants pressed like a boulevardier.

There was a grand march to that good old Carnival song, *If Ever I Cease to Love,* with the balloons bobbing and everybody singing, "She can sing, she can play on the piano, she can jump, she can dance, she can run. For she's a wonderful girlie; she's all of them rolled into one. I adore her beauty, she's like an angel dropped from above. May the fish get legs and the cows lay eggs, if ever I cease to love. May all dogs wag their tails in front, if ever I cease to love:

> If ever I cease to love—if ever I cease to love
> May the moon be turn'd to green cream cheese,
> If ever I cease to love.

Everybody had such a good time at the ball that the Two Well-Known Gentlemen promised to make it an annual event. They did too, even after Mr. Anderson gave up liquor and swearing. The next year he and Mr. Lamothe were joined by Claude Anderson and they gave two balls, one on the Saturday before Mardi Gras and one on Mardi Gras, both in Odd Fellows Hall and attended by every madam and girl in Storyville, except Lulu White and Countess Willie Piazza and their girls, who were all colored.

Lulu cleared the double parlors of Mahogany Hall, and she and the countess had a party of their own.

During Mardi Gras hundreds of guests from out of town trooped to Storyville to see the plush and velvet parlors, and watch the dancing in the cabarets. They bought the girls champagne and liqueurs, and Storyville awoke when the Garden District went to bed.

New Orleans in those days was a city of such rigid propriety that even prostitutes conformed (in public) to Creole codes of conduct. They did not, for instance, go to saloons, or smoke on the street, or stand up at a bar—not usually, they didn't. But during Mardi Gras they masked and did as they pleased, and the spirit of Carnival was so contagious that other women did the same. On Mardi Gras many girls from the right side of the tracks—masked, of course—sipped cocktails in Tom Anderson's Annex, next door to Lulu White's Mahogany Hall. Girls from the district, also masked, crossed Canal Street, to rub shoulders with the respectable bourgeoisie, and cheer the chaste Queen of Carnival. And that is how the Sazerac Bar, which is exclusively for men every other day in the year, came to mix drinks for ladies on Mardi Gras, when lots of people don't know who is who—and nobody cares.

* * *

Sazeracs are served in handsome glasses, double the size of an old-fashioned glass, and there are ten times more of them stolen on Shrove Tuesday than on the rest of the 365 days—which is a nice commentary on my fair sex, the old magpies.

The first Sazerac was invented about a hundred years ago by a man who died unhonored and unsung because, as often happens with inspired creations, the invention was practically an accident. It was during a long-ago Mardi Gras that this gentlemen, having had too much to drink, went to a café with his friends for a pickup. Everybody in those days knew that absinthe—a favorite drink with the Creoles—was good for a hangover. But these gentlemen had been drinking absinthe, and decided to switch. Another favorite drink of the Creoles was brandy—eau de vie, they called it—and the best of all brandies was a cognac made in Limoges by the firm of Sazerac-de-Forge et fils.

The gentleman with the worst hangover asked for a glass of Sazerac brandy with a dash of absinthe. Almost at once he felt better, so he asked for another. Then his friends tried it, and presently they began to experiment—a dash of bitters, a soupçon of sugar, and a bit of lemon peel.

"A Sazerac, monsieur!" cried the gentlemen. "To your very good health, monsieur," they said to their host.

They ordered the same for everyone who was in the café, and everyone thought it was wonderful. The drink became immediately popular and since it was made with Sazerac brandy, it was called a Sazerac. It is strange the way the name has persisted, because for many years a Sazerac has been made, not with brandy at all, but with rye. Mr. Stanley Arthur, who has written a book on New Orleans drinks, says the bartenders substituted whisky because the Americans preferred "red likker." Sazeracs, the best and most renowned of New Orleans cocktails, are sold all over town. But nowhere are they so good as at the Sazerac Bar on Carondelet Street where the sacred portals are opened on Mardi Gras, and nearly every woman in town goes to see what the place looks like. It is just a good bar, handsome in a masculine sort of way, with some very nice murals and no nonsense about it. But the Sazeracs that are mixed there are like none you will ever have anywhere else, though you may buy the best of all possible rye (which I have done many times), and follow directions with care (as I have also done). And still they are not the same.

Carrie Nation once visited New Orleans and scared Joe Duarte, the diminutive barman, out of ten years' growth. It was during Carnival, and Mrs. Nation arrived on a train from the North, with a bunch of pansies on her bonnet and her hatchet tucked under her shawl. She went straight to the Sazerac Bar and handed Temperance leaflets to the astonished customers. Someone telephoned the police and they came and got her, but before she left she told Mr. Duarte it was no place for a nice lad like him to be working. Sometimes, on Mardi Gras, Mr. Duarte thinks she was right.

* * *

Mardi Gras is the day when people dance in the streets . . . and ring bells, and blow horns . . . when harlequins join hands to play ring-around-a-rosy with policemen . . . and perfect strangers kiss girls in dominoes . . . when one man is King, and every man's a lover . . . when everyone is happy, and no one is sad . . . when orphans get presents . . . and pretty girls get diamonds . . . when Zulu rides in a chariot . . . and Kings toast Queens, from ruby-rimmed goblets of gold.

Everybody gets up early on Mardi Gras. The streets have a gala air, and the lampposts wear masks. The white fronts of the buildings are hung with colored bulbs that will flower at night in lights of purple and green and gold. Azaleas open their elaborately fashioned little blossoms, and bloom up and down Canal Street under the lampposts with the funny faces. In the shimmering air is an enchanted feeling as though strange things were about to happen. And presently they do happen, and they keep on happening all through the day and the night, until the sun comes up Ash Wednesday morning.

The first thing that happens is his Royal Highness King Zulu, Negro King of the Carnival, who arrives at eight o'clock sharp on a fishing lugger. Zulu comes, they say, from darkest Africa where he rules a band of head hunters. Accompanied by witch doctors bearing gin and coconuts, he comes to claim his Queen. His subjects, clothed in Mardi Gras raiment, meet the Royal Barge at the shore and the retinue transfers to the floats that await them.

Surrounded by fearsome Bushmen brandishing spears, Zulu is assisted to his throne. The Bushmen are daubed with war paint, and so is Zulu. On his head he wears a crown made from a gasoline tin gilded to catch the shining sun. Sometimes he carries a broomstick for a scepter, topped with cock feathers, sometimes a banana stalk, or a loaf of Italian bread. He wears black tights, a patchwork vest, and a grass skirt. But over his motley attire he trails an ermine robe, and under that moth-eaten mantle Zulu is a proud and happy man. A stuffed owl perched in a banana tree symbolizes Zulu's omnipotent wisdom and a woolly lamb, depicting his innocence, straddles a diaphanous cloud of cotton batting.

Following the royal float, warriors and medicine men ride in palmetto jungles where papier-mâché beasts roam, serpents slither through the bush and grass-green snakes sway from moss-hung trees.

Zulu's Queen awaits her Lord on the balcony of the Gertrude Geddes Willis Funeral Home, where thousands have gathered to see her Majesty. The King's floats wind through the streets, followed by black and white. Many of the Negroes are masked. Most of the women are Baby Dolls, with blonde wigs and white faces. Many of the men are Indians with feathered headdresses and tomahawks. Zulu stops often at bars and restaurants to quench his thirst, and sometimes to make a speech.

"This business of everybody toasting the Queen I has abolished," was once the royal proclamation as the floats approached the undertaking establishment where the Queen sat dying of thirst. "From henceforth on out, I personally will do all the toasting! We has had entirely too much intoxication from the court," proclaimed Zulu, teetering on his throne, "and I decrees it has got to stop. When the occasion arises I personally means to drink the Queen's she-self toast."

"Shucks!" said the Queen, when her subjects brought the tidings. "Me, I'm a real Queen. Don't nobody let that Zulu forget it!"

At last the jungle-shrouded chariot drawn by white mules reaches the Funeral Home, and all is forgiven as her Highness smiles down from the balcony. The King gallantly raising a rented silver goblet toasts his Queen with real champagne.

Zulu's extravaganza is a witty travesty of the white folks' Mardi Gras. On his rattrap float, trailing clouds of tarnished glory, he mocks the white parades and in his mangy robe, he mocks their Kings. His hilarious floats burlesque all the gaudy show of the white Krewes. His horned medicine men imitate their Dukes, and the Big Shot of Africa caricatures their Captains.

But there are two things in Zulu's Mardi Gras that are real. And one is his band, and one is his Queen. The band plays Dixie-land rhythm. And the Queen wears a true satin gown and a rhinestone crown. The gown has a beautiful sweeping train. The crown is as bright as the morning. And the Queen has a party in the undertaking parlor with champagne and sandwiches, and that is real too.

Zulu stays on the streets all day, tossing coconuts and favors to his subjects. All day there is dancing in the streets, and at night there is a Zulu Ball in the Japanese Tea Garden at St. Philip and North Liberty streets, with palm fronds and coconuts for tropical atmosphere, with beer and chitlins for the people and champagne for the King. The King buys the coconuts, but the Zulu Aid and Pleasure Club buys the champagne.

Zulu is the sideshow of Mardi Gras. But Rex is the big show. Rex parades at midday. First come the motorcycle policemen. Then the mounted police, four abreast. The horns of the motorcycles and the pounding of the horses' hoofs make a terrifying and exciting sound as passage is made for the King. His masked Captain rides ahead on a prancing horse with a velvet cape streaming behind him, crimson in the sun, and white plumes on his helmet. Then come the Captain's aides and the King's Dukes, masked and mounted.

After the prancing horsemen comes Rex, King of Carnival and Lord of Misrule. His throne room is drawn by a tandem of mules, and the King, gracious and very grand, sits on a towering throne. His magnificent mantle cascades down its shining steps and page boys hold its flowing train. As the crowds cheer, Rex raises his jeweled scepter and bows and smiles upon his subjects.

Then come the bands, and after the bands come the floats drawn by mules garbed in white, and led by Negroes also in white, with red turbans on their heads. Some of the floats are emerald green because they are woodland glens, and some are white like frosted cakes because they are lands of ice and snow. And some are blue because they are caves beneath the ocean, where mermaids with sea-green tails live on coral reefs, and anemones grow in the sea. And they all gleam with purple and gold, and shine in the sun like visions from fairy isles of childhood dreams. On all the floats are "throw boxes" filled with Mardi Gras favors.

In front of City Hall, Rex brings his glittering parade to a stop, while he receives the keys to the city from a little girl who sits in the mayor's grandstand. She was chosen from among the orphans in the city. Rex sent her a new dress to wear on Mardi Gras, for Rex is the most generous monarch in the world and he wants everyone in his kingdom, especially orphans, to be happy on Mardi Gras. He toasts the child as if she were a Queen. When the parade is over, many people in the grandstand give her their favors to take to the other orphans, and the mayor sends her home in the city's shiniest limousine, with ice cream and cake for the children's supper.

Following Rex's parade is the Parade of Orleaneans. The Krewe of Orleaneans does not use mules, because all the mules in town are busy working for Rex. On other days the mules collect the city garbage, but on Mardi Gras the garbage waits and the mules get bathed and dressed in white. The mules work two shifts on Mardi Gras, in the afternoon for Rex and at night for Comus. During Carnival there are about a dozen elaborate parades with mule-drawn floats. For night parades Negro torchbearers carry flambeaux that cast an exciting, dancing light. The Negroes, torchbearers and muleteers shuffle and strut to the music of the bands. But the mules act very bored.

The Krewe of Orleaneans is composed of fraternal, business and civic groups who mask in picturesque costumes and ride with jazz bands and pretty girls in a hundred spectacularly decorated trucks. The Krewe chooses an orphan boy and crowns him King for a day, gives him a handsome present as souvenir of his brief reign, and guarantees his education. Then the Krewe has a wonderful party and the young King plays host for the children of his orphanage. All day long the jazz bands play and people dance in the streets. People who are not in costume buy masks and balloons, and the city is a seething mass of color and gaiety. On Mardi Gras thousands of little children wear costumes, and the streets are filled with small girls in hoop skirts and little boy pirates. There are clowns and cowboys and all the comic-strip characters, sheiks and Hottentots, coolies and Indian princes, and animals with dreadful heads and long tails. The shrill shrieks of excited children mingle with the cries of street hawkers and the delighted exclamations of grownups. And over the bedlam drifts the lovely smell of peanuts and hot dogs and humanity, of dust and green grass and popcorn.

20

INTRAMURAL SHENANIGANS

Debutantes could live without Stratford Club cotillions and a symphony orchestra. They could live without hunts, the Country Club pool and the Sugar Bowl game. They could live without the Patio Royal and Antoine's, without gumbo and Sazeracs, and café brûlot in a silver bowl. They could live without magnolias and mockingbirds, and moonlight on the Mississippi. But where is the deb who could live without Carnival?

Carnival is not promoted solely for the debutantes. But they certainly get the most out of it. Any girl in her right mind would rather come out at the New Orleans Country Club than at Buckingham Palace or the White House. For the happiest debs in Dixie are Queens of the Carnival balls—and, oh, the times they have! The things they do, and the gifts they get!

I met a lady—a very beautiful lady—who was an attendant at eight Courts the year she came out, and Queen of Comus. Her mother and grandmother had also been Queens of Comus. The year before she came out this lady was Queen of Apollo, which is a subdebs' ball, and the year after she came out, she was Queen of Mystic. Mystic is the only fashionable ball that does not have an unmarried girl for Queen. Mystic always has a matron, and the beautiful lady was married at the end of her first season. Her father one year was King of Comus, and the next year he was Rex.

When I heard about all the royalty in her family, I told the lady that I was writing a book about New Orleans, and that I should like to ask her some questions.

"Carnival is very beautiful," I said, "but it seems childish to me—particularly the King and Queen business. I can't understand . . ."

"The traditions of Carnival," explained the beautiful lady, "are something a damyankee *couldn't* understand." (And when she called me that, she smiled, like the cowpuncher when he called the Virginian something worse.) "Love of Carnival is something you are born with," she said, "and it's part of you—like loving dogs or horses. You have the feeling, or you haven't. No outsider can understand. I know," she said, "that sounds silly. It's simply incredible to the rest of the world. It seems shallow and absurd, and people laugh at us for taking it so seriously."

Then she tried again. "But it isn't absurd at all. It's . . . it's like being a Catholic," she said. "You don't justify your religion, and you don't try to explain it."

So I let the matter drop, because what else could I do? And then she told me about how her father was King of Comus, and he couldn't let even the family know. Men who are chosen King of a Krewe usually make a great pretense, she said, of having nothing to do with the parade or ball. They tell their families that they have to make a business trip, or that they are going hunting. Then they go to the Den and put on their costumes, and they always go by a back street so that nobody will see them.

On Shrove Tuesday her father, who was a lawyer, announced that he had been called out of town, and he packed a bag and bade the family good-bye. They were desolated at the thought of his missing Mardi Gras, and the children cried to see him go. They watched the parade that night from the Louisiana Club, waiting excitedly as the lights and music drew nearer.

At last the King's float moved slowly by while prancing white-robed Negroes held their flambeaux high, and Comus on his glimmering throne raised his shining goblet in the torchlight. But it was not until she had a call-out at the ball and the King took her in his arms, that she knew Comus was her father.

It is said in New Orleans that every young mother leaning over the bassinet of her baby daughter sees a future Carnival Queen. But the fact is that the sacred rituals of Carnival belong exclusively to les bonnes familles. This happy foresight is reserved, therefore, for daughters whose names are in the Social Register. Although it is true that Mardi Gras is everybody's holiday, there is an aristocratic tradition behind the intramural shenanigans, and it is this tradition that makes Carnival such a mannered and a mad and a lovely business.

The charming folderol begins on Christmas Day, when several score New Orleans girls receive visits from royalty, in the person of young Dukes ringing doorbells like the postman. The girls, who have been eagerly watching from behind the curtains, scamper upstairs like children and wait to be called as each young Duke with a big flower box under his arm steps into the drawing room. The box is open at one end and there protrude the mistakable stems of American beauties. And the girls are more thrilled than if the Dukes had tickets on the fifty-yard line and had come to ask them to the Sugar Bowl game. For every girl knows that buried in the roses is an elaborate parchment scroll inviting her to be a Maid at the Carnival ball of the Duke's Krewe.

To a few girls go scrolls designating them as Queens of various balls. The Queens and Maids are chosen by each Krewe's Governing Board. Parents of the prospective Queen are consulted beforehand, because a Queen is a terrible expense to the family. The Krewe's artist designs the Queen's gown and the Governing Board approves it. Then the Captain presents the sketch to the parents. It is understood that it may be fashioned as elaborately as they wish, or as inexpensively as possible. The gown might, for example, be embroidered in simple sequins—or in costly pearls, or glittering rhinestones. If a Queen wears a simple gown, the Krewe buys her an especially magnificent mantle.

There was one Queen whose father didn't have very much money, and she couldn't bear to have him worried about bills. So she insisted upon a quite plain white satin, embroidered in nothing at all but whirls of silver thread. Then the Krewe ordered a mantle, to make up in splendor what the gown lacked. The mantle was lined with sea-green aquamarines and tiny mirrors, cut and polished like gems. When Cinderella went gliding across the ballroom, she was a blinding beauty—and the money her father saved was enough to send her to college.

Then there was another Queen who had her entire dress embroidered in rhinestones. The bodice was tight, with an off-the-shoulder décolletage and a Medici collar of solid gems. The skirt was very full with a tremendous train which was also a blaze of rhinestones, and everybody knew that it cost $3,500 because it was ordered through a local shop and the salesgirls gossiped.

The Krewe presents the Queen not only with her mantle, but with her scepter and crown. The crown jewels are delivered at her home the day before the ball, and her family insures them or keeps them in a vault. But as time goes on they lose their glamour, and sometimes the Queen sells them and sometimes she gives them to the Cabildo. Although there have been several Monarchs in a number of New Orleans families, the crown jewels have never been handed down, nor has the same set ever been used twice. Both Rex and Comus have their jewels made in Paris by the oldest and most famous paste jeweler in the world, and they are imported duty free because Kings get immunity from customs.

One year a certain girl was Queen of three balls. It had never happened before, and it probably never will happen again. She keeps her three crowns and three scepters in the attic. When things go wrong she tries them on, and then she feels better.

One Queen rented her mantle of cloth of gold to an organization in Texas, and someone spilled whisky on it. It came back with a check and a note:

Whiskey is whiskey any way you mix it,
Texas is Texas any way you fix it;
When other good people have gone to bed,
The Devil keeps a-workin' in a Texan's head.

The note was unsigned, but the check was good. So the Queen bought herself a little brace of sables, and she gets more good out of them than she could from a cloth of gold manteau.

Krewes seek to outdo one another in the splendor of their pageants. When Comus, socially impeccable and enormously wealthy, observed its Golden Jubilee, the Queen wore a mantle of golden brocade that trailed the ground for twenty-four feet. Down the center, running lengthwise, was an insert of gold net embroidered in Strasbourg rhinestones, to simulate a trellis. The border of the mantle was weighted with huge grapes of pearls, relieved by leaves of silver. And all the silver leaves glittered with tiny rhinestones that sparkled like dew. The Queen's long gloves and little slippers were dipped in fourteen-carat gold. And the King toasted her from a goblet encrusted with solid white rhinestones that had "Comus" spelled out in jewels of topaz.

The Queen of Comus wears a tiara and scepter of rhinestones in a lily-of-the-valley design, so bejeweled that not one bit of the metal shows. Other Krewes dream up a different crown, I think, for every Queen. The jewels of several Carnival organizations are displayed in Canal Street windows for several days before Mardi Gras.

If you want to see the golden mantle that the Queen of Comus wore, you will find it in the Cabildo. When the Queen was married, she used it for an altarcloth and it was so beautiful that even the Pope would have been thrilled to say Mass on it. But right after the wedding her mother sent it to the Cabildo.

At Momus's ball there is less pomp than at Comus's. But you could cut the excitement with a knife, because the Knights didn't make Christmas calls like the Dukes did, and nobody knows until the night of the ball who is to be Queen or Maids. The debutantes wear the white dresses in which they came out. The Queen can depend for her glory upon the mantle that the Knights will give her (which will certainly save her father a pretty penny), and the Maids will need only armfuls of roses.

Breathless with delight, the Queen is escorted from the call-out section to her throne. Seamstresses, wearing dominoes to hide their faces, scurry from the wings and curtsy to her Majesty. They stoop to adjust her mantle and spread its radiance about her, and scurry back to the wings. Then the Maids, who have been presented with parchment scrolls, take their places about the throne. The throne is built within a great pink rose, and the Queen is "Queen rose of the rosebud garden of girls."

To play the hoped-for role of Queen, girls are trained in grace from babyhood. As children they play-act for the beautiful night when dreams may come true, and instead of playing "house" or "school," they play "Carnival."

There was a Carnival Queen whose twins were born during the war. Before they were nine months old, though their father was missing in action, she had them costumed for Mardi Gras—Pierrot and Pierrette, in their baby carriage on the gallery.

There are Carnival balls in dancing schools with Kings and Queens, where little girls learn to curtsy, and small boys to act like Kings. The little girls are taught to smile as Queen Elizabeth does, with their eyes and not with their teeth—and to glide when they walk. For subdebs there are special Carnival balls, Harlequin and Apollo.

Queens chosen at Christmastime go back to dancing school to brush up on curtsies and posture, for a girl must walk gracefully while supporting the incredible weight of her headdress and trailing mantle. Sometimes the mantles are so heavy they are supported by a little padded harness. But though her shoulders bleed, a girl must raise her scepter with royal unconcern. Though her ermine be hotter than mink, she must look as cool as a goddess on an iceberg.

There are smart shops in New Orleans, Town and Country among them, that have special Queen's Rooms where fittings are accomplished in secrecy, and Queens dress for the balls. On that day, rain or shine, a marquee is erected from the door of the shop to the street, so that if there should be a sudden shower a Queen would have nothing to worry about. It takes Town and Country about three months to create a Queen's gown, and the Queen stands for fittings until she almost dies.

I knew a Mardi Gras Queen who had her gown made at the Liberty Shop, and it was so heavy with rhinestones that it took three people to lift it over her head. On the night of the ball three women from the shop helped her dress, and she had a man from Hollywood to make her up. When she was ready she looked like a young Queen on her wedding day and her mother cried, she was so beautiful. She carried a bouquet of white orchids. Her mantle was cloth of gold with bowknots of silver lamé crested in rhinestones, with a Medici collar of gold lace peppered with rhinestones, and it was bordered with ermine.

The Krewe sends a limousine to take the Queen to the Auditorium and the chief of police sends a motorcycle escort, and the Queen and her mother go whirling off to the ball. Her mother of course has a very elegant gown too, and like all New Orleans ladies she wears twenty-button white kid gloves. There are more long kid gloves at Carnival balls than in the Golden Horseshoe at the Metropolitan Opera, or at the Court of St. James's on a big night.

* * *

In Creole society it was proverbial that ladies should dress to the teeth and always to please the men, and the tradition has persisted. In the daytime they wear fluffy clothes with ruffles and dirndls, and they almost always wear candy-box hats. All but the mayor's wife, and she buys hers from Walter Florell. Mrs. deLesseps Story Morrison is the youngest and prettiest First Lady the city ever had.

In her Florell hats and Mainbocher gowns, she stands out among
the ladies of New Orleans like Hedy Lamarr in the Convent of the
Ursulines.

Even the debutantes would rather look pretty than smart. Given
their choice of Clare Potter or Tina Leser they will pick a Tina
Leser any day.

In New Orleans nice girls don't talk about sex. But they spell it
with a capital S. They don't wear clothes to hide their figures but to
show them, in a nice refined way, of course. Dixie girls will be
pretty, sweet maid, and let who will be chic. By contrast with fashionable New Yorkers, they appear very much dressed. It is a conviction in the South that men dislike smart, functional styles and
prefer simple pretty things, swirls and curls, and rose-petaled ruffles
and soft-drifting tulles.

New York newspaperwomen covering Mardi Gras were entertained at luncheon in the 1840 Room at Antoine's. It was a fashionable luncheon to which the ladies wore their prettiest dresses
with orchids on their shoulders. They chattered and twittered over
poulet en cocotte like pretty redbirds in the cedars, and it was all
very charming but not very clever.

"I haven't heard anything discussed at luncheon," remarked one
of the newspaperwomen to their hostess, "that sounds as if anybody read the *New York Times.*"

"Oh, dear, no," said the hostess. "We read the *Times Picuyane*
and the *Item,* honey."

Cultivated society avoids controversial subjects but has made
small talk an art. It isn't what the girls say that men find delightful
but the darlin' way they say it, and when the ghost of lil old Scar-
lett O'Hara sits down at the table, the New Yorkers might as well
pick up their dolls and go home.

* * *

A priest told me of visiting an old Creole lady who was about to

*Creole beds, "wide as a battlefield, deep as a haymow," were made
by Seignouret and Mallard.*

die. She lay in her big Seignouret bed awaiting the end. The girandoles tinkled in a little breeze that crept through the curtains, and the old lady roused herself and smiled at the pretty sound. Life had been pleasant and now she was ready to go.

"Le bon Dieu has been very good. I have had all," she said, "that a woman could ask." Emotion overcame her as she recalled the goodness of God. "Twice, mon père," she said, "I was Queen of Carnival."

Raising herself in the dimness of her vast bed, she lifted her hand and gravely beat a measure on the air. Her face lighted and her little blue-veined hand moved gently to and fro.

"I think," the priest said, "she could hear the angels singing, 'May the fish get legs and the cows lay eggs.' She could hear them twanging on their golden harps, and she was keeping time to the music. She knew that St. Peter was peering through the pearly gates waiting to welcome another Carnival Queen, and that little old thing could hardly wait."

Index